Celebrity Culture and the American Dream

Using examples from the first celebrity fan magazines of 1911 to the present, *Celebrity Culture and the American Dream* considers how major economic and historical factors shaped the nature of celebrity culture as we know it today. Equally important, the book explains how and why the story of Hollywood celebrities matters, sociologically speaking, to an understanding of American society, to the changing nature of the American Dream, and to the relation between class and culture.

Karen Sternheimer is a sociologist at the University of Southern California, where she is a faculty fellow at the USC Center for Excellence in Teaching. She is also the author of *Connecting Popular Culture and Social Problems: Why Media is not the Answer* (2009), *Kids These Days: Facts and Fictions About Today's Youth* (2006), *It's Not the Media: The Truth About Pop Culture's Influence on Children* (2003), and is the editor and lead writer for everydaysociologyblog.com. She has provided commentary for CNN, MSNBC, The History Channel, and Fox News.

Celebrity Culture and the American Dream

Stardom and Social Mobility

Karen Sternheimer
University of Southern California

Routledge
Taylor & Francis Group

NEW YORK AND LONDON

First published 2011
by Routledge
270 Madison Avenue, New York, NY 10016

Simultaneously published in the UK
by Routledge
2 Park Square, Milton Park, Abingdon, Oxon OX14 4RN

Routledge is an imprint of the Taylor & Francis Group, an informa business

© 2011 Taylor & Francis

The right of Karen Sternheimer to be identified as author of this work has
been asserted by her in accordance with sections 77 and 78 of the Copyright,
Designs and Patents Act 1988.

Typeset in Adobe Caslon, Trade Gothic and Copperplate Gothic
by Florence Production Ltd, Stoodleigh, Devon
Printed and bound in the United States of America on acid-free paper
by Walsworth Publishing Company, Marceline, MO

Library of Congress Cataloging-in-Publication Data
Sternheimer, Karen.
    Celebrity culture and the American dream: stardom and social mobility/
    Karen Sternheimer.
        p. cm.
    1. Social mobility—United States.   2. Social classes—United States.
    3. Celebrities—United States.   4. American Dream.   5. Fame—Social
    aspects—United States.   I. Title.
    HN57.S774 2011   305.5'1309730904—dc22
    2010032719

ISBN13: 978-0-415-88678-9 (hbk)
ISBN13: 978-0-415-88679-6 (pbk)
ISBN13: 978-0-203-83149-6 (ebk)

For my parents,
who did everything to ensure that I would make it big.

CONTENTS

FIGURES

PREFACE

CELEBRITY CULTURE AND THE AMERICAN DREAM

Stardom and Social Mobility

Love it, hate it, or love to hate it, celebrity culture is one of the hallmarks of twenty-first century America. Never before has it been so easy to know so much about so many people, even people we might not *want* to know about. We seem to be on a first name basis with them, give them nicknames, and sometimes even feel as if we know all about them. We hear about their romances, their escapades, and, of course, their failures. Entering this fishbowl does not require any unique skill or talent; in fact, many people join the celebrity realm by just allowing the public into their lives (or their bedrooms), such as Paris Hilton, Jon and Kate Gosselin, and the cast of *Jersey Shore*.

What Does Celebrity Culture Tell Us about American Society?

Rather than simply superficial distractions, celebrity and fame are unique manifestations of our sense of American social mobility: they provide the illusion that material wealth is possible for anyone. More than simply changes in taste or style, the fluctuating nature of celebrity culture reflects and reveals the so-called American Dream itself, a dream that continues to evolve and change along with our expectations about what it means to achieve success in America.

Using examples from the first celebrity fan magazines of 1911 to those of the present, *Celebrity Culture and the American Dream* considers how major economic and historical factors shaped the nature of celebrity culture as we know it today. Rather than simply hypothesize about the "effect" celebrity behavior might have on the rest of us, this book uses a sociological lens to examine how celebrity stories serve to reinforce the prevailing notion of success. Celebrities seem to provide proof that the American Dream of going from rags to riches is real and attainable.

The goal of this book is to use a sociological imagination to take an in-depth look at our culture of celebrity—something familiar to all readers —and understand its broader sociological importance. While I primarily focus on the connections between celebrity culture and concepts of social mobility, this book also provides an opportunity to examine issues such as consumption, social change, and social structure. Celebrity culture also reflects shifts in gender, marriage, families, relationships, and race relations in addition to political and economic changes, and this book can be used in a wide variety of courses about American society.

Books by and about celebrities dominate the trade market today, and dozens of academic titles about celebrity culture have been published over the past two decades. Most of these books are written primarily for a scholarly audience, offering comprehensive theoretical discussions that would be difficult for lay readers and undergraduate audiences to connect with. This book aims to avoid academic jargon in order to provide a straightforward discussion about the role celebrity culture plays in American life.

Key features—*Celebrity Culture and the American Dream*:

- explores the relationship between celebrity culture, consumption, class, and social mobility;
- discusses social changes pertaining to class, gender, marriage and divorce, and race;
- includes numerous pictures from fan magazine articles and ads;
- examines the connections between celebrity culture and economic, political, and social changes;
- considers the importance of the structure of the entertainment industry in order to understand how celebrity culture is manufactured;
- includes questions at the beginning of each chapter to help readers focus on central issues within each time period.

ACKNOWLEDGMENTS

This book might have one author, but many people made vital contributions to this project along the way. I am especially appreciative of my editor, Steve Rutter, for his unbridled enthusiasm for the book, and to Leah Babb-Rosenfeld for her assistance with the entire publishing process. Many thanks to the reviewers, Kerry Ferris of Northern Illinois University; Denise Bielby of University of California, Santa Barbara; David Grazian of the University of Pennsylvania; Josh Gamson of University of San Francisco; Laura Robinson of Santa Clara University; Sally Raskoff of Los Angeles Valley College; Steve Sherwood of University of California, Los Angeles; and Carl Boggs of National University for providing ample and useful feedback, which without a doubt made this book much better than it would have been. Alex Masulis, Karl Bakeman, and Betsy Amster took time out of their busy schedules to provide valuable feedback on many chapters of this book.

My first introduction to old fan magazines took place at the Academy of Motion Picture Arts and Sciences' Margaret Herrick Library in Beverly Hills. The helpful staff pulled magazines for me to read and enthusiastically suggested other materials that might be useful in my research. It was a pleasure just to sit among the historical documents in their reading room. My research and this book would not have been possible without the dedication of Ned Comstock of the University of Southern California's Cinematic Arts Library. Ned went out of his way to help keep my student research assistants busy sifting through and copying pages from hundreds of magazines. His continued enthusiasm for the project made its completion possible. Thanks also to John Brockman of the Cinematic Arts Library, who along with Ned scanned images from the magazines that appear in this book. I am also grateful for Steve Bingo's help at USC's Von KleinSmid Center, assisting students in viewing reels and reels of microfilm.

From 2006–2010 I was blessed with help from numerous undergraduate students, who spent hours examining magazines at the library for this project. Thanks, in chronological order, to Laila Eisner, Vanessa Van Munster, Ashley Kalimada, Lisa Siragusa, Hala Mohammed, Sheri Leung, Inna Inger, Brigitte Khoury, Janet Baum, Kathleen Mendoza, Jessica Sackman, Maxine Pezim, Brandon Estrada, Alana Chatfield, and Victoria Wood. Your hard work and ideas made this book possible.

I could not have written this book without years of academic nurturing at USC, and I am especially grateful for the years of enthusiastic support in the department of sociology. Thanks especially to Mike Messner, Barry Glassner, Elaine Bell Kaplan, and Tim Biblarz. A special thanks to the department's staff, Melissa Hernandez, Stachelle Overland, Lisa Rayburn-Parks, and Amber Thomas for your help. Other colleagues and friends provided invaluable support as sounding boards, especially Sally Raskoff and Molly Ranney.

I am grateful for the support of my sisters, Laura and Linda, brother-in-law Jacob, and nephew Eli. My parents, Lee and Toby, nurtured my earliest interest in Hollywood growing up and supported my decision to major in drama in college and my subsequent move to California. This book would not have been possible without their continued confidence and support.

1

THE AMERICAN DREAM

CELEBRITY, CLASS, AND SOCIAL MOBILITY

If you are like me, you are probably not immune to the occasional lure of celebrity stories. There is something tempting about tuning in to celebrity gossip and the ongoing personal sagas of famous people. The car wreck cliché works well here—it can be hard to look away, even if what we see also disgusts us. Bad celebrity behavior seems to be ubiquitous today, or at least *news* of bad behavior follows us everywhere and is a regular feature in mainstream news outlets.

As a sociologist who has written about popular culture and kids, it is not unusual for a reporter to ask me whether celebrity excesses have negative effects on children, or why kids seem to look up to celebrities. Critics parse their life choices and wonder what effect they might have on the rest of us. Do they make us hate our bodies? More self-centered? Materialistic? Disdain marriage? More likely to abuse drugs or alcohol? My answer, typically, is that it's not so much that we simply see celebrities as role models—often we love judging and condemning them as much as, if not more than, aspiring to be like them—but their importance serves as a useful window into better understanding American society.

Rather than just having personal influence over individual behavior, talk about celebrities reveals central sociological issues within American society, one of the most central being the promise to allow its members to rise from obscurity to fame and fortune. The American Dream, which shifts and mutates with changes in the economy and the political and

1

social backdrop, seems very real when we see the plethora of people who have entered the realm of celebrity.

The meaning of celebrity seems to be stretched thin; it does not now (nor has it ever) only apply to people with measureable talent or skill. Opportunities to be part of this world have never been greater with the advent of reality television, YouTube, MySpace, and the internet in general. For the purpose of this book, I define a celebrity as anyone who is watched, noticed, and known by a critical mass of strangers. We can think about celebrity culture as the atmosphere swirling around celebrities, the public and private conversations we have about them, the lifestyles celebrities unwittingly promote through coverage of their private lives, and the products that become part of this lifestyle. Ultimately, celebrity culture is amorphous and means different things to different people. Much like perfume that takes on a slightly different scent with each wearer, consumers make different meanings of celebrity culture, as sociologist Joshua Gamson found in his study of celebrity audiences.[1]

When I started this project, I set out to explore how and why celebrities' personal lives have become so public and to trace what I first suspected was a progression from little to enormous coverage of celebrities' personal lives over the last several decades. Fan magazines seemed like the best way to get a good historical picture of any changes over time. I have the good fortune of being on the faculty at the University of Southern California with access to its Cinematic Arts Library, which boasts a large collection of old movie fan magazines, as does the nearby Academy of Motion Picture Arts and Sciences' Margaret Herrick Library. While celebrities come in many varieties well beyond Hollywood (athletes, musicians, writers, and politicians, to name a few), most of this book will focus on movie stars covered in fan magazines. The last three chapters provide more discussion of athletes, musicians, politicians, and business executives, as traditional movie magazines broadened their coverage in the 1960s and eventually went out of print and the magazines that replaced them included more than movie stars. The last two chapters rely on analysis of *People* magazine, which rose in popularity as the old fan magazines' circulations waned and which offers broad coverage beyond movie and television actors.

The first movie fan magazine, *Motion Picture Story Magazine*, began publication in 1911, with several others starting in the decade following that. As I discuss in Chapter 2, these magazines began with the explicit intention of promoting the industry and featured stories often written by studio publicists, or at least with the studios' significant cooperation. Film historian Anthony Slide describes this practice as "an incestuous relationship built on trust and mutual necessity."[2] Rather than independent journalists covering a growing industry, fan magazines served as advertising copy, first for the movies and eventually for their stars. The earliest magazines focused mainly on describing the plots of "photoplays" to generate interest in seeing more movies. The magazines resembled literary journals of today, with lots of copy, few photos, and practically no gossip. At least not at first. Movie stars' private lives intrigued audiences as much then as now, at least based on letters sent to the magazines. The names have mostly faded into obscurity, but the fans' interests were remarkably similar to ours today: Is she married? Does he have children? Where is she from? What does she like to do in her free time? By reading just a few issues of fan magazines, it became clear that interest in celebrities' personal lives is nothing new, only that the information now travels quicker and through many more channels compared to a century ago.

That was the end of my initial hypothesis. But I didn't want to stop reading the old magazines. There was something alluring about them, and I couldn't quite figure out what kept drawing me in. It took many months of reading, reflecting, and writing to realize that, among other things, the old fan magazines offered the promise of a better life. The stories about the movies and their new stars not only attempted to sell the industry, but sold the idea of the American Dream itself. What the dream looked like at any given time changed—from hopes of a middle-class life, the promise of wealth, and hope during dark times to the promise of suburbia and affluence. All of these dreams are reflected in a century of fan magazines, which provide glimpses into what the American Dream looks like when realized. Celebrity culture seems to provide a continual reaffirmation that upward mobility is possible in America and reinforces the belief that inequality is the result of personal failure rather than systematic social conditions.

The Sociology of Celebrity

Media coverage of celebrities may seem meaningless, shallow, and without substance. But examining celebrity culture more closely provides a window through which we can better understand American society. This book uses celebrity coverage as a tool in order to illuminate sociological phenomena within American life. So while I use many examples of celebrity stories in fan magazine articles as examples, at the core my purpose is to use the familiar concept of celebrity culture to explore issues central in sociology, such as class and social mobility, social change, gender, race, marriage, and relationships.

Gender, Race, and Upward Mobility

We cannot really understand American social mobility over the last century without looking at the unique opportunities for female mobility, particularly with the invention of Hollywood. Women appeared on movie fan magazine covers far more often than men, and women were more likely to be the subject of magazine features. The industry not only provided women with careers and the chance to make lots of money, but women are the primary consumers of celebrity culture sold through fan magazines. Female writers could find steady work writing for fan magazines during a time when journalism offered women few opportunities. From the 1910s, fan magazines offered examples of women who had become independent and financially successful. And yet failed relationships comprise a major focus of celebrity morality tales. The centrality of the family in America's agrarian history and the historical suspicion of people—especially women—who live outside the family's confines reverberate throughout American history in celebrity coverage.

These stories of female mobility came with many warnings and were far from feminist texts. Women who seemed greedy, who appeared to manipulate men, or who otherwise failed to conform to conventional notions of gender served as morality tales for female readers. Since the publication of the earliest fan magazines, stories scrutinized female celebrities' romantic relationships as if taking a continual pulse on whether their financial success would be tempered by relationship failure. Rather than providing a singular message about women's mobility, celebrity stories reflect conflicting ideas about women: at some times promoting their independence—particularly during World War II—and at other times emphasizing more traditional roles, as many stories did after the war ended.

Just as the magazines focused on predominantly female readers, until the 1960s celebrity stories all but ignored performers of color and seemed to presume a white audience. In the 1910s and 1920s especially, fan magazine ads and articles might reference exotic beauty products of the Orient, clearly defining nonwhite, nonwestern people as "other," sometimes looked upon with enchantment and sometimes with fear. References to Africans or Native Americans as savages were not unusual, and African Americans were all but ignored until the 1940s, when any coverage tended to rely on stock racist caricatures. Latino performers often changed their names to pass as white, or if not would serve as "fiery" Latin lovers from exotic locales south of the border in fan magazine coverage. The American Dream characterized in movie fan magazines was an explicitly Anglo dream for the better part of the twentieth century, reinforcing the idea that nonwhites were outsiders in this fantasy until the mid-1960s. Whiteness became conflated with normality within these texts, and tales of upward mobility predominantly emphasized opportunities for whites. Those characterized as "other" were largely regarded with amusement at best and disdain at worst in the pre-civil rights era magazines.

Thinking Sociologically about Celebrity

Just as gender and race are ever present in fan magazine texts, sociology's central paradigms can also help us understand the nature of celebrity culture. Celebrity stories can help us make sense of our identities—not simply by telling us how we should look, feel, think, or act, but through a social process of negotiation. Symbolic interactionists view identity construction as not just an individual experience, but one based on our interactions with others. Talking about celebrities, whether we express admiration, sympathy, or condemnation for them, offers us a framework through which to construct our social selves. For instance, criticizing a celebrity's behavior offers the critic a chance to position themselves as holding superior morals or values. We might take cues from these discussions about how best to manage the impressions we give off in public as well in both our "front stage" and "back stage" performances of self.[3]

Celebrity culture also provides a window into broader, macro-level social processes. Applying the concept of functionalism, we can interpret celebrity stories as providing common ground for interactions within a diverse society. Functionalists view social cohesion and stability as central for maintaining a healthy society, noting that various parts of society have a purpose, or function. Celebrities create a shared set of characters for us to talk about and often give us the chance to reinforce shared values when a celebrity is involved in scandalous behavior. Just as sociologists Daniel Dayan and Elihu Katz wrote that media events like inaugurations, royal weddings, and state funerals create social integration and shared rituals, celebrity stories might do that as well, albeit on a much smaller scale.[4] I would argue that one of celebrity culture's central functions is to provide continual examples that the American Dream of rising from the bottom of the economic ladder is real for those willing to work hard. Functionalists would view this message as one that promotes common values, productivity, and, ultimately, social stability.

However, conflict theorists could read this same message as profoundly troubling, even providing a sense of false consciousness and encouraging people to ignore the barriers to wealth many people face. Rather than view celebrity stories of working hard to attain stardom as promoting the smooth functioning of American society, conflict theorists would challenge that this message enables inequality to continue. Drawing on the conflict approach, critical theorists such as Herbert Marcuse, Max Horkheimer, and Theodor W. Adorno (known collectively as the Frankfurt School) even viewed popular culture as a form of propaganda, distracting the masses from their economic interests and ultimately duping a susceptible public into ignoring the domination of the elite.

Likewise, Italian sociologist Francesco Alberoni referred to celebrities as the "powerless elite" in a 1962 essay.[5] While present-day commentators wonder whether celebrities wield undue influence on the public (and especially young people), Alberoni contends that although stars might have significant wealth and fame, in the grand scheme of things Hollywood celebrities tend to have little real power. Yes, they might lend their stardom to a political cause and have more power than the average citizen, but they are not the true power brokers in American life. Alberoni describes celebrity as:

> . . . a cultural product of the economic power elite, having as its object to supply the masses with an escape into fantasy and an illusion of mobility, in such a way as to prevent their taking stock of their real condition as exploited masses.[6]

From the perspective of the media conglomerates that produce and sell celebrity-based content, their primary intent is to make a large profit rather than brainwash the public. Many of these companies, like traditional news outlets, are struggling to remain afloat. Their sole focus is to stay in business—and for executives, the focus is to keep their jobs—rather than a desire to control the masses with lots of superficial celebrity content. So while political economic explanations can help us understand celebrity culture, there is no unidirectional power enforcing this relationship. We are complicit in our desire to be amused rather than informed, to be able to peer into the fishbowl of celebrity and see what it is like on the inside.

I would modify Alberoni's point to instead suggest that the American public in particular is not manipulated by a conspiring cabal as much as we *collude* with this fantasy. Italian philosopher Antonio Gramsci's discussion of hegemony might better help us understand one of the roles that celebrity culture plays in American life. Rather than only a top-down relationship, the concept of hegemony refers to a public that actively embraces the prevailing social system, as it appears to be common sense. Notions such as the American Dream are so pervasive because, as a central defining principle, the myth of mobility makes Americans feel good about ourselves and is woven into our sense of nationalism. We are not bound by ethnicity as much as other nations are, but instead by principles such as the idea that success is possible for anyone willing to work for it. Thus we are complicit in our desire to believe that the idea of the American Dream is real, and celebrity stories help us enjoy the dream vicariously.

Economic arrangements can by no means completely explain the phenomenon of celebrity culture in the United States, but they are a central facet in a multidimensional process. Celebrities have existed throughout human history in a variety of types of social systems, as author Leo Braudy demonstrates in his book, *Frenzy of Renown: Fame and Its History*. In drawing connections between celebrity culture and American social mobility, I am not suggesting that celebrity culture is unique to the United States, nor is it limited to capitalist systems rooted in mass consumption either. Instead, our current mode of *experiencing* celebrity culture has an affinity with the economic, political, and social realities of a given time. German sociologist Max Weber observed that capitalism had an affinity with Protestantism in seventeenth century America; likewise, capitalism and celebrity culture enjoy an important synergy today. Weber also noted how people derive status through their positions within organizations; likewise, celebrity content has historically been produced in the context of large organizations. At one point in history, a handful of movie studios were the primary organizations that created celebrities; today the process is much more decentralized, with the internet and social networking tools playing an important role in constructing celebrities. Understanding celebrity culture requires us to consider the mechanisms by which people become celebrities.

This book draws from all of these sociological perspectives, taking a mostly structural perspective to understand how fan magazine articles and ads shift in form to reflect the economic, political, and social realities of their time. Conflicting and shifting notions of social mobility are a central theme in the decades of fan magazines I analyzed for this book, just as this theme is of central debate in American life. Casting a sociological lens onto celebrity culture creates the opportunity to explore numerous issues; while this book primarily focuses on the issue of social mobility, it is certainly not the only sociological phenomenon that celebrity culture reflects.

The American Dream: Horatio Alger and Morality Tales

The deep-seated American belief that both hard work and luck can lead anyone to rise above their beginnings makes celebrities' life stories particularly meaningful. The term "American Dream" became popular during the 1930s, but its roots are far deeper. In the mythology of the American Dream, opportunities abound and are rewarded to those most deserving: the hardest workers, the brightest, and the most talented. This dream supports the notion of individualism, so central in American political doctrines that it dates back to the Declaration of Independence. Freedom from European-style monarchy meant the freedom to achieve economic success without having a title. The American frontier promised practically endless amounts of land and opportunity for homesteaders to make of it what they could. Thus, throughout American history the notion of individualism and celebration of the "self-made man" served to justify inequality. If you were poor, you obviously just didn't try hard enough.[7]

Author Horatio Alger wrote a series of short stories at the end of the nineteenth century that came to embody the American Dream of moving from rags to riches. His stories typically feature a young orphaned boy born into poverty who not only works hard, but is of solid moral character. The boy rises above his origins after someone takes note of his worthiness and rewards him with an opportunity to become wealthy through hard work. Many celebrities seem to personify the so-called Horatio Alger myth: rising from nothing to achieve great wealth through hard work and determination. Because celebrities are so visible, they can serve as continual reminders that success is rooted in the individual's uniqueness and determination while ignoring the roles power and privilege play in achieving wealth in American society.

Contemporary celebrity stories often serve as modern-day morality tales, especially if the main character does not seem to work hard or possess a strong moral core—yet the fates still reward them with riches. This is a constant theme in celebrity gossip: the chosen one is not really worthy after all. The public flogging that so often follows not only serves to reinforce certain moral precepts (about industry, sobriety, and chastity), but also reflects an attempt to cling to Alger's notion of worthiness. While these celebrity tales might remind us that in reality wealth is not necessarily bestowed fairly, the focus on celebrities' moral failings reveals an attempt to cling to the ideals of the Alger myth and the belief that we live in a meritocracy.

Just as the Alger myth possesses a moral component, the lingering impact of Calvinism surfaces in the way celebrities are conceptualized in America. Early American Calvinists believed that economic success was a sign of God's blessing, and thus wealth and abundance could be explained in individual terms, not systematically. Celebrity culture has a similar function to the lottery: people seemingly plucked from obscurity, possibly ordinary in some ways yet special in others, get noticed and become materially blessed.[8] The famous appear to prove that anyone can be successful in American life, even if they have no real skills. Their "specialness" is enough. Similarly, we often view famous people as having magical qualities, or at least presume that they must lead magical lives because they have been blessed with fame. People anointed celebrities might possess some rare quality; that quality might be talent, but it doesn't have to be. In the past and in the present, fame might also be bestowed upon the infamous, those whose behavior is uniquely outrageous and whose personal boundaries are limited enough to enable the public to see what is normally regarded as private behavior. While part of their fame emerges from public judgment or even character assassination, as lightening rods they can sometimes cash in, or at the very least command continued attention as stars of their own morality tales.

Hollywood has historically produced the dreams that fuel the continuing belief that America is a place where true social mobility exists, providing that you are one of the elect. Part of the fascination with the private lives of celebrities—their relationships, their backgrounds, their challenges—involves learning what it is really like to be one of the chosen. And just as quickly as someone can be celebrated, any false move and the public will revel in their moral condemnation.

Celebrity, Class, and Consumption

These mixed emotions we have about celebrities' lifestyles also reveal a central contradiction within American culture: the coinciding desire for plenty and the lingering value placed on self-restraint. The Puritan ethic of self-denial, thrift, and austerity surfaces now and then, made visible by examples of outrageous celebrity excesses and failure to maintain self-control. Rather than resolve these tensions, celebrity stories tend to heighten the contradictions between thrift and consumption.

We have a contradictory relationship with excess in our society, exemplified by our growing rates of obesity and years of piling up consumer debt. Celebrities and others can be used as vessels both to celebrate consumption and warn of its dangers. We can condemn celebrities for their pleasure-seeking behavior and at the same time ignore our own.

In some ways, celebrities comprise what sociologist Max Weber called a "status community": people at similar economic levels who have similar cultural and social interests and consumption patterns. Likewise, in *Distinction: A Social Critique of the Judgment of Taste*, French sociologist Pierre Bourdieu describes how notions of taste and style are linked to social position. Celebrities' consumption habits become associated with high status and an aspirational lifestyle, and celebrities receive many free high-end goods in the hope that they will make an item trendy. You might be wondering how celebrities can sell a lifestyle when so many of their personal choices are criticized and celebrities are held up as examples of excess, narcissism, and immorality. Even if we feel disdain for an individual celebrity, as members of this elite status community they serve as examples of what wealth and status might bring. We can hate them and still love the stuff they own.

Celebrities have served as representatives of the link between status and consumption throughout at least the last century. The earliest movie stars appeared in ads for beauty products, much as today. But stars don't need to be paid spokespeople to promote products. Paparazzi shots of celebrities' private lives promote a consumption-based lifestyle, highlighting their expensive clothes, cars, and vacations. Many contemporary fan magazines filled with pictures of celebrities on the red carpet or paparazzi shots of their daily lives are little more than catalogues of advertised goods that we might buy to feel like we are joining their status community.

In part, the intense coverage of celebrities' personal lives has to do with a consumer-driven economy. Consumer purchases comprise more than two-thirds of economic growth in the United States today; without continual encouragement to consume, the engine threatens to stall. Not only does a celebrity lifestyle promote consuming high-end goods, but trying to achieve celebrity-like physical perfection sells billions of dollars worth of diet products, cosmetics, and cosmetic surgery.

Celebrities are both commodities themselves and provide cheap content for struggling magazine and television industries, and gossip websites on shoestring budgets. The idealized lifestyle of the American Dream constantly changes, in part due to changes in standards of living, but also because a consumption-based economy requires that we continually aspire to have new material goods. Each of the chapters of this book highlights the ways in which celebrity culture is intertwined with the consumer marketplace, from the promise of self-employment and freedom from physical labor sold in the 1910s to the self-as-brand style of celebrity in the twenty-first century.

And though we might not have their wealth or fame, we might feel that through consuming goods celebrities might favor, and living a lifestyle we see as similar to theirs, that we are achieving some degree of upward mobility by joining an elite status community. We might not be wealthy, but we can feel special because of the things we have, just like celebrity status is often conferred based on lifestyle rather than talent. Specialness in a consumer-based economy is marked and established by the attention we pay to how we, those around us, and celebrities consume goods. So often we justify buying things that we cannot quite afford because we tell ourselves we deserve it—that it is a gift we give ourselves because we are special. It is ultimately an empty measure, but a common yardstick nonetheless, one that can obscure the systematic nature of economic inequality.

Class Unconsciousness

Just as celebrity stories reveal competing narratives about consumption, they also highlight contradictory notions about class, status, and upward mobility. As representations of those who have made it in America, celebrities come to represent the wealthy to the public. They might not seem worthy of the riches bestowed upon them, and how they spend their money is a central facet of their notoriety: How generous are they? Do they make absurd demands in their contracts? Are they pampered crybabies? Ultimately, celebrities' lifestyles reveal the material blessings of wealth, and those that go broke spending reaffirm the Horatio Alger notion that poverty is the result of poor individual choices, rather than systematic inequalities.

Celebrities seem to provide a visible example that we have an open class system, not based on family lineage but rather on one's own talent, skill, and specialness. Despite the belief that success is primarily the result of our own actions, being born into the right family can make it easier to become a celebrity, a part of the American caste system that we seldom recognize. How many celebrities can you name who have rich or famous family members and a name that likely aided in their pursuit of fame? Paris Hilton (great-granddaughter of the Hilton Hotel founder), Angelina Jolie (daughter of actor Jon Voight), George Clooney (nephew of singer Rosemary Clooney and son of news anchor Nick Clooney), Nicole Richie (daughter of singer Lionel Richie), and Jennifer Aniston (daughter of actor John Aniston) immediately come to mind. Not that they are (all) without talent, but celebrity helps maintain the illusion of total social mobility and individualism. With the exception of Hilton and Richie, we tend to view the others as talented in their own right, rather than beneficiaries of inherited status.

Of course there are many examples of celebrities who do come from modest, non-celebrity backgrounds. They serve to reinforce the belief that anyone can make it to the top and enjoy the material rewards of success.

Witness the thousands upon thousands who turn up for *American Idol* auditions. Surely many of them know that they can't sing (and are soon told as much), but the urge to be known and the hope of a lucky break is enough to make them willing to be humiliated in a ritual separating the elect from everybody else. By staying focused on individual talent, we can believe that we live in a meritocracy rather than a stratified society based on one's social position at birth. The continued popularity of this show allows us to engage in a seemingly democratic selection of new celebrities. However, while *Idol* winners and other celebrities might have talent, others leverage infamy into celebrity status, challenging the notion of fairness embedded in the credo that hard work and talent yields success.

Americans of the twenty-first century, unlike our predecessors a century ago, are notoriously class-blind. To some degree we are aware of issues such as race and gender inequities, thanks in part to the civil rights movement and the visibility of race and gender. But class is another story. There are a number of reasons why we have trouble seeing class. For one, a majority of Americans identify themselves as middle class, regardless of their income, and have since the 1920s.[9] The absence of a strong labor movement in American politics, along with declines in union membership, also helps to explain why awareness about class stratification is low. When politicians do occasionally bring up economic stratification, pundits from the right accuse them of sparking "class warfare," which has become akin to complaints that civil rights leaders "play the race card" when they bring up inequality.

Celebrities provide visible representations of our often invisible upper class. While we might not know much about those at the top of the economic ladder until a major scandal breaks, celebrities are always visible representations of the wealthy. Their wealth—if it exists at all—might be paltry in comparison to corporate CEOs and other captains of industry, but celebrities embody the lifestyle of excess and moral failure and serve as ready-made whipping boys for class-based animosity. While those on the right may resist general critiques of the wealthy, they can easily join people across the political spectrum in calling out the moral failures of Hollywood celebrities. Celebrities are the embodiment of the contradictions between conspicuous consumption and thrift, and serve to reinforce so-called middle-class values of self-restraint, both personally and economically.

Celebrities and their stories occasionally make class lines particularly visible. Take Paris Hilton's brief time in jail in June 2007. After she was initially released early, public outcry was intense; CNN even broke into its coverage of a major political development to cover Hilton's arrival in court. Suddenly the public saw an example of how privilege can provide advantages in the legal system. In reality, this goes on every day and takes a particularly onerous toll on people at the lowest end of the economic spectrum. But Hilton's celebrity status illuminated this inequality, if only briefly, until she was sent back to jail.

Inside Edition reported that Hilton's health could be at serious risk if, while in jail, she were infected with MRSA, a staph infection several inmates had contracted. Of course, any inmate could catch this, and the many low-income people who do go to jail are also unlikely to have adequate (if any) access to health care. But in this case, this became a public problem because someone we thought we knew could have gotten sick. Once Hilton left jail, the justice system's inequities went back into the shadows, at least until the next celebrity was in trouble with the law.

Hilton's story reminds us of how conflicted America is about class. We celebrate those at the top and are eager to know more about them—presumably so we can figure out how to get there ourselves. On some level we even take vicarious delight in the riches others have, never mind that many CEOs' wealth comes at shareholders' and consumers' expense, or that the money we plunk down to see a mediocre movie—and tons of commercials—helps pay huge movie star salaries. But when they seem to get away with murder (sometimes literally) their privilege and the fault lines of class become clearer. It is far too simple to suggest that celebrities are worshipped, but rather, they can become vessels into which we load otherwise displaced class aspirations and resentments.

Rather than a serious challenge to economic stratification, celebrity critiques help us to focus on individual character traits instead of systematic inequality. One way we do this is by seeing ourselves as consumers first, workers second. Our salaries and wages might be stagnant, but if we can consume like we are wealthy—and are given enough credit—we are more likely to overlook our own economic interests in favor of the newest gadget or cute handbag. At the very same time when remaining middle class in America is increasingly difficult, we have immeasurable opportunity to peer in on the lives of celebrities and others, such as the women of the *Real Housewives* series, whose excess is at once regaled and disdained. Likewise, the presentation of celebrity lifestyles over the past century reflects the contradictions and economic realities of their times.

Meanwhile, the real power brokers—corporate leaders and government officials—slip out of our view. They are usually less visible and we seldom know who they are; even if we do, they tend not to be as interesting to watch, and their societal roles are more complex than celebrities', who tend to be attention seekers. Our judgments, critiques, anger, and sometimes even hatred of celebrities reflects a distorted sense of class consciousness. While Americans seldom speak openly of class stratification, celebrities appear to represent the powerful elite and become the recipients of both admiration and scorn.

Studying Celebrity Culture

Celebrity is by nature ephemeral; anyone who has walked along Hollywood Boulevard's Walk of Fame has likely seen many stars whose names they had never heard before. Today's big star can easily become a has-been pretty quickly. Because celebrity culture is fleeting—what is big gossip news today is likely to be forgotten or become trivia in weeks—it is difficult to gauge fully, and these memories can shift and change with time. This makes studying celebrity culture in both the present and the past a challenge.

Fan magazines provide us with rich artifacts to help us better understand how celebrity has shifted and changed along with American society over the past century, akin to catalogues of what the American Dream might promise at that particular moment. These magazines provide snapshots in time and tell us about celebrity culture and the commodities that surround fame at any given time. This book focuses on the way in which celebrities are publicly manufactured in these magazines: how they are promoted in fan magazines, how their purported lifestyles are reported on, and how products are sold along with celebrity news and gossip. Advertisements represent the remnants of past consumption; it is possible that nobody ever bought some of the products for sale in the back pages of fan magazines, but their marketing reveals significant aspects of how the "good life" was sold at any given time. Many of these ads likely appeared in other magazines at the time, and it would be a mistake to suggest that the products sold *only* applied to the study of celebrity culture. In fact, as Roland Marchand details in *Advertising the American Dream*, advertisements have their own unique contexts and meanings that go well beyond the subject matter of the publications in which they appear.[10] Nonetheless, advertisements, along with fan magazine stories, provide examples of representations of success, which form the basis of the analysis throughout this book.

While fan magazines provide a great deal of information, they are of course only limited representations of both celebrities and society. Especially in our internet age, magazines represent only a tiny fraction of celebrity-based content. They do not enable us to presume how audiences made meaning of their content, nor are fan magazines the only texts that present meanings of the American Dream to audiences. Marketed primarily to white women throughout their history, fan magazines speak to a limited audience. Representations of the American Dream could have certainly been different if the texts I studied were meant primarily for men or people of color. So this analysis in no way provides the final word on the meanings of the American Dream, but instead provides snapshots of how the notions of individual success emerged in manufactured celebrity stories.

As I noted earlier, the old fan magazines colluded directly with the old studios for their content, and as film scholar Anthony Slide notes in *Inside the Hollywood Fan Magazine*, writers fabricated many of the stories. So rather than journalistic accounts of how celebrities really lived, the articles in the old fan magazines served as fantasies for readers. Whether readers themselves found these fantasies inviting, we can't know, but the themes within the tales the writers spun provide the basis for this book.

Unfortunately, my analysis could not possibly include every fan magazine published since their first publication in 1911. Slide estimates that nearly three hundred different publications were in print over the last century, and so analyzing more than a small cross-section would be difficult, particularly because many titles are now hard to find. On the surface, fan magazines appear trivial and their one-time ubiquity meant that few libraries would take the time and use their resources to archive them.[11] And just like old fan magazines, most libraries do not now subscribe to *Star*, *OK*, *Life & Style*, *In Touch*, or the like, making it difficult to access old issues of many tabloid-style magazines either.

My analysis is based on a convenience sample of approximately 600 issues of eight fan magazines I could readily access. Along with fifteen research assistants, for four years I scoured the magazines for thematic patterns, looking for shifts in the content of both the articles and advertisements. Rather than conducting content analysis, which would have involved counting the occurrence of specific phenomenon and creating quantitative results, my intention was to focus on qualitative descriptions of the thematic shifts we observed.

Therefore, this book is not intended to provide a generalizable sample of historical fan magazines, since my access was limited to the collection at the University of Southern California's Cinematic Arts Library. The library has partial collections of *Picture Play* (1915–1941), *Motion Picture Classic* (1915–1931), *Motion Picture* (1911–1977), *Photoplay* (1911–1980), *Modern Screen* (1930–1985), *Movieland* (1943–1974), and *Screenland* (1920–1952). While the library's collection of *Picture Play*, *Motion Picture Classic*, *Motion Picture*, and *Screenland* are rather limited, mostly ending in the 1950s, its collection of *Photoplay* and *Modern Screen* is much more substantial, and therefore the book contains many more examples from these two magazines—among the best-selling ones over time—than from the others. Most movie fan magazines from the early days of Hollywood faded away by 1980, replaced by *People* in 1974 and *US Weekly* in 1977.

The last two chapters of this book are based on an analysis of *People* (1974–present); not only does the magazine offer access to its entire archive at people.com, but its reputation as being celebrity (and publicist) friendly provides some thematic continuity with the traditional fan magazines. And while fan magazines comprise only a small piece of celebrity culture—and arguably an increasingly less important piece today—I have decided to use them as the core of my analysis as long-running sources of what fans often view as "official" celebrity stories.[12] Using more gossip-centered sources such as the *National Enquirer*, *Star*, or the myriad of websites and blogs devoted to unflattering stories would lead to a fascinating future study of discourses that seek to expose and humiliate celebrities, particularly in comparison with mainstream publications that garner celebrity cooperation.

Celebrity Culture and the Shifting American Dream

Through my analysis of celebrity stories, I identified eight major shifts in the magazines' construction of the American Dream fantasy. This is not to say that there were *only* eight versions, that these versions are mutually exclusive, or that the stories and advertisements presented a uniform view of success in America. For clarity, each chapter emphasizes a dominant central theme, but it is important to note that debates existed even within these narratives. Likewise, we cannot infer from the magazines how readers interpreted and made meaning of these themes, however repetitive they might have been. And while each chapter focuses on a specific chronological period, sometimes a chapter's central theme actually has roots in a previous era. For that reason, some chapters reference developments that took place earlier, such as early rumblings of a Red Scare during the Depression that exploded in Hollywood after World War II.

Each upcoming chapter explores how celebrity tales constructed the American Dream, with special attention to the economic, political, and social context to better understand how and why the promises of upward mobility changed over time. Following these shifts chronologically, the book is organized around the predominant themes in both the magazines' articles and ads, starting with a discussion of the historical relevance of each theme. As you can see from the descriptions below, six of the themes reflect core principles of the American Dream. Two of the shifts represent brief but significant departures from this myth—during World War II and then again during the 1960s and early 1970s, when the dominant themes in fan magazines challenged individualism and materialism, before rebounding to tell stories of rising from rags to riches once again.

Theme #1: Beyond Subsistence

In the first two decades of the twentieth century, fantasies of upward mobility had less to do with becoming fabulously wealthy and were more about being self-sufficient and enjoying a life beyond subsistence and mindless labor. Most of the working population held unskilled labor positions, and the possibility of owning one's own business or using one's mind instead of body for work held great promise in the shadows of the Industrial Revolution. Not coincidentally, the birth of the film industry and the rise of creative professions beckoned fan magazine readers to dream of new careers that previously did not exist. The new movie industry also offered employment opportunities to women, just as the first wave of feminism sought new social roles for women. Both the movie industry and its mostly working-class patrons would seek entry into middle-class society during the early decades of the twentieth century. Fan magazines provided etiquette advice for a large immigrant population, and ads promised to help them look more like native-born, middle-class Americans.

Theme #2: Prosperity and Wealth Arrive

After victory in World War I, boom times arrived in the 1920s. Immigrants and members of the working class increasingly joined the ranks of the middle class, which seemed to provide evidence that prosperity would be available for all willing to work for it. And while celebrity tales of the Roaring Twenties describe abundance, these stories also warn of immorality, especially in the case of young women whose virtue could be ruined by greed. As women gained the right to vote with the passage of the Nineteenth Amendment in 1920, they also experienced upward mobility and became more financially independent. It was women who were most likely to grace the covers of fan magazines; they could find careers of their own in the new movie industry, either in front of the camera, or writing "scenarios", or increasingly as writers for the new movie magazines. Along with these new careers came new anxieties about gender roles and a backlash in many articles about scheming, heartless women. Articles and ads promoted "reducing" at the very same time that women's opportunities began to expand, reflecting both the abundance of prosperity and reaffirming the importance of self-control for women, a vestige of the Puritan ethic at a time when women had new opportunities outside of the family.

Theme #3: Pull Yourself Up by Your Bootstraps

Just as the promise of wealth and abundance seemed within reach in the 1920s, the realities of the Depression challenged the notion of the Horatio Alger mythology that success comes to those who work hard and possess strong moral character. It is probably not an accident that the term "American Dream" was coined in 1931 by historian James Truslow Adams just as the Great Depression might have caused many to doubt whether it really was possible to make it in America. Like many Americans who went from riches to rags—or at least comfort to poverty—during the

Depression, many celebrities experienced downward mobility after the silent era ended, which coincided with the onset of the Depression. Rather than victims of circumstance, stories about these former stars often highlighted their personal failings and profligate lifestyles as the central cause of their plight. Anxieties about personal failure—relationships, divorce, and even hygiene—emphasized that failure was still an individual's responsibility, rather than due to the collapse of the economy. Celebrity fan magazines did nothing to dispel the Alger myth; in fact, like many lavish movies of the era, celebrity tales heightened attention on the great wealth of celebrities.

Theme #4: We're All in This Together

While the notion of individualism is usually central to the American Dream mythology, American entry into World War II changed the kind of celebrity stories the magazines told. Much like the days following the attacks of September 11, 2001, World War II brought a resurgence of nationalism and a departure from the pursuit of personal gains. The American Dream took a backseat to collective sacrifice. Fan magazines no longer highlighted personal extravagances during a time of national sacrifice. In fact, the magazines emphasized how celebrities suffered like everyone else, with a spouse on active duty, rationing, or by serving in the armed forces themselves. While stories of the girl or boy next door rising from nowhere to become America's next big star continued, wealth meant donating and volunteering to the war effort, not consuming with excess. In fact, celebrity profiles and magazine ads frequently reminded readers to use their products slowly, not to buy things on the black market, and not to ask for a raise at work. Stars who refused pay cuts were branded unpatriotic at a time when patriotism and the greater good were considered central.

Theme #5: Suburban Utopia

Victory in Europe and the Pacific meant the end of rationing in America, and the end of the emphasis on the collective good. And yet despite the tremendous amount of economic growth that took place in the years following World War II, postwar celebrity stories emphasized the middle-class lifestyles stars allegedly led during the late 1940s and 1950s. Celebrities were often pictured in modest suburban homes, spoke of how they were careful with their money, and described their families as the center of their lives—not glamorous Hollywood night spots. These baby boom years meant emphasis on children and the joys of parenting and marriage—female celebrities seemed to go out of their way to tell fans that their careers were far less important than being wives and mothers. As divorce rates rose, celebrity stories appeared to have an explanation: women didn't know their place, and threatened the American Dream of having a family and living comfortably in the suburbs. A bigger threat seemed to emerge as well: communists among us. At the very same time that economic prosperity was available to a greater number of Americans than ever before, vocal and strident members of Congress feared the core of the economic structure itself was at risk. Refuting the collectivism of the war years, the postwar Red Scare emphasized individual effort and material success as not only American, but as morally superior as the Cold War began.

Theme #6: Is That All There Is?

The Hollywood celebrity machine experienced a major shift just as the country entered into an era known for social unrest in the 1960s and 1970s. Just as the meaning of the American Dream was itself in flux, and the concept of the dream itself challenged, celebrity stories focused more on rebellious behavior and celebrities as anti-heroes who challenged social conventions. The major studios' power had collapsed after antitrust rulings forced them to sell their theater chains, as well as following the deaths or displacement of celebrity movie moguls, known for the autocratic rule of their companies and the stars within them. The structure of celebrity production changed as performers increasingly became independent contractors, no longer beholden to long-term studio contracts with carefully crafted images. Studio morality clauses no longer bound celebrities to control their behavior, nor would studios necessarily wield their authority to kill an embarrassing story since the star was no longer their property. Consequently, stories about celebrities focused more on questioning conventional norms about marriage, family, and relationships, particularly as societal shifts about sexuality and relationships were taking place. Celebrity coverage also increasingly questioned whether fame and wealth could bring happiness, focusing on the loneliness and emptiness stars sometimes felt after reaching the top.

Theme #7: Massive Wealth as Moral Reward

The ambiguity over the meaning of success—heightened by new age seekers and the growth of the self-help industry—led to a crisis in what the American Dream itself meant. This dilemma was presumably solved by America's first Hollywood president. With Ronald Reagan's 1980 election there was a decisive return to a clear notion of the American Dream, and this time the dream was big. Perhaps as an answer to the malaise of the 1970s, which brought inflation, unemployment, energy crises, and defeat in Vietnam, the new version of the dream promised a fantasy of wealth and riches. Embodied by dramas such as *Dallas* and *Dynasty*, *People* magazine sold real-life stories of stars with similar lifestyles, highlighting their modest origins and newfound riches. The wealthy became celebrities themselves in features that emphasized their ingenuity, hard work, and the lavish lifestyles that came as a reward. Wealth could have a dark side, if it meant taking shortcuts around hard work, but by and large the wealthy had earned their place (and their tax cuts). In the meantime, the gap between the wealthiest and the poorest grew with relatively little complaint as the fantasy of plenty—and the credit to have pieces of the dream—became more and more ubiquitous.

Theme #8: Success Just for Being You

With the internet and so-called reality TV beginning in the 1990s, the notion that fame has never been more accessible to so many people now provides the illusion of opportunity. While your YouTube video could go viral and you might become famous just for being you, the wealth gap continued to widen to levels not seen since the 1920s—that is, until the economy collapsed in 2008. Just as seemingly anyone could be famous for being famous, today celebrities no longer simply sell lifestyles, in many ways their own lives are for sale. Neal Gabler, author of *Life the Movie: How Entertainment Conquered Reality*, describes celebrities' lives as "lifies," semi-public reality shows that might in fact be more compelling than being a traditional entertainer. Those famous for being famous might parlay their status into getting cast in commercials or their very own reality show, thus enhancing their fame and providing a living just for being them. As we will see, "lifies" are not a completely new phenomenon, but are a gradual outgrowth of changes in both technology and consumption taking place amidst a backdrop of serious economic downturn, making celebrity seem like a viable career choice for those struggling economically. As wages remain stagnant and unemployment high, it may be tempting to put your private life up for sale and become a brand yourself. While this form of entertainment has grown far more common, for most people the financial opportunities are actually minimal, at best. The primary beneficiaries of "lifies" are producers and shareholders, who can run cheap content while still collecting advertising revenues.

Unmasking Celebrity Culture

Although I spent four years reading and analyzing fan magazines for this book, I have been a student of celebrity most of my life. I moved to Hollywood in July of 1990, just weeks after earning a degree in drama from New York University. For as long as I could remember, I wanted to be there; in my young mind I thought that if I could be part of the world of Hollywood, I would really matter. I thought of it as a magical place, where all things were possible—the center of my and America's collective fantasy. California uniquely embodies notions of the American Dream, with its seemingly endless sunshine and the promise of opportunities beyond what the industrial Midwest of my childhood could offer. As millions of others have done as young adults, I made my pilgrimage to California in search of success. I had a fond affection for old movies, mostly those of the pre-1970s variety, and my drama degree was a first concrete step towards being a part of them in some capacity. I had met filmmakers, casting directors, actors, and writers at NYU and struggled to figure out exactly where I would fit into this fantasy. But once I spent some time in the physical place called Hollywood, my fantasy started to unravel fast.

I quickly learned that in 1990, sundown on Sunset Boulevard meant hookers and drug dealers, not premieres and limos. Hollywood Boulevard had not yet undergone its revitalization, which came with the Kodak Theater and the shopping complex Hollywood and Highland. It was then a frightening mix of runaways, addicts, and homeless people. The boulevard's grandeur was gone, replaced by souvenir shops selling lewd t-shirts. It seemed as though memories were all that remained.

The notion of Hollywood as a state of mind rather than a physical place is not new, nor is it the subject of this book. My personal quest to attain the Hollywood version of the American Dream led me first to Los

Angeles and, ultimately, to write this book. At the very least, I arrived a generation too late to find the Hollywood of my imagination, although I found vestiges of the fantasy in the old fan magazines I read for this book. Hollywood had changed, along with other economic, social, and political changes of the previous decades. Perhaps my own discovery peering behind the curtain of Hollywood led me to want to understand how and why Hollywood's main byproduct, celebrity culture, has shifted and mutated over the course of the last century.

In short, celebrity culture is about more than just bad role models, more than our culture of consumption. Celebrity culture reflects and reinforces the ever changing notion of what it means to achieve the American Dream. More than simply changes in taste or style, the shifting nature of the Hollywood fantasy reflects and reveals a dream that continues to evolve and change along with our expectations about what it means to achieve success in America. Celebrity culture offers a window into the changes in how we define this success and becomes our vehicle for dealing with issues of social class in a society we like to think of as classless. This book explores the lessons we can take from celebrity culture about the shifting nature of social mobility in the United States.

2

BEYOND SUBSISTENCE

THE RISE OF THE MIDDLE CLASS IN THE TWENTIETH CENTURY

Can you imagine a time before movie stars? This chapter delves into the period in history when movies got their start, and its celebrities were first created. As we will see by examining the historical context of the early twentieth century, for most Americans life was a difficult struggle for survival, and the promise of upward mobility meant becoming economically stable, not necessarily rich. Just as Max Weber wrote of an elective affinity between capitalism and Protestantism in his book *The Protestant Ethic and the Spirit of Capitalism*, the rise of the movies and its celebrity culture coincides with the expansion of the middle class in the early twentieth century. Both the movies and their city-dwelling working-class patrons attempted to upgrade their image in order to appeal to middle-class, native-born Americans. To that end, fan magazines and the advertisements within them both promote the notion of rising beyond subsistence, through becoming part of the industry or through buying products promising to help consumers become (or look and feel) middle class. Genuine opportunities did exist for modest levels of upward mobility as the economy became more automated between 1900 and 1920.

This chapter seeks to answer three central questions. First, how did stories about the earliest movie actors reflect the Horatio Alger myth of rising from nowhere to achieve the American Dream, and why were both the movies and its performers considered socially undesirable in the early twentieth century? Second, how did the industry go about changing its

25

image as well as that of its patrons, and what role did World War I play in this process? And lastly, how did the growth of the movies and its celebrities create more opportunities for women's upward mobility?

Life at the Start of the Twentieth Century

Certainly celebrities existed in the theater and literary worlds, and William Randolph Hearst and Joseph Pulitzer's battles for readers at the end of the nineteenth century commonly featured the notorious in their newspapers. Fame existed long before movies, but photography and film helped audiences feel as though they knew celebrities, particularly with the invention of Thomas Edison's kinescope in 1893. Not only could audiences know what someone looked like, but through seeing their expressions and mannerisms a new form of imagined intimacy developed.[1]

Just as the first nickelodeon opened to customers in 1905, a shift was beginning to take place in American life. The growth of the movie industry in the first decades of the twentieth century coincided with changes in where people lived and how they lived, from survival-level subsistence to increasing stability. As we will see in this chapter, both the movies and a large portion of their audience would experience upward mobility into the middle classes during the early years of the twentieth century. And fan magazines would illustrate the promise of this version of the American Dream through its stories of newly minted celebrities and ads for products that promised to provide entrée into middle-class life. During the early decades of the century, the American Dream was about stability. The new movie industry and its fan magazines reflected this reality.

Life at the turn of the twentieth century was difficult for most Americans. While data on poverty is not as accurate for this period as it would be after World War II, economists estimate that more than half of the U.S. population lived in poverty, and few homes had electricity or the convenience of electrical appliances.[2] In 1910, nearly 24 percent of adults aged 25-and-over had five years of formal education or less; just under 14 percent had graduated from high school, and less than 3 percent attended four or more years of college.[3] More than a third of workers were considered unskilled, and more than half of the population over 10 worked for wages.[4] With no such thing as unemployment insurance, disability pay, food stamps, or public assistance, many families relied on extra income from their children to survive—especially if a parent became ill, was injured, or had died. A study assessing unemployment in 1910 suggested that work was often sporadic; a third of construction workers and 29 percent of textile workers were unemployed that year.[5] For the majority of the American public, subsistence, not affluence, was the primary goal.

Food scarcity was a serious concern, reflected in a 1919 ad for Quaker Oats, boasting of the low cost and high health-value of oatmeal. "The 32-cent package of Quaker Oats contains 6,221 calories of energy," the ad begins, noting that a consumer would have to buy 53 cans of tomatoes, 21 cans of peas, 50 large potatoes, 750 oysters or 9 pounds of veal cutlets to get the same number of calories. "Ten people can be fed on Quaker Oats at the cost of feeding one on meats."[6] In contrast to the plentiful calories of food today, at this time consuming enough was still a major concern for those at the bottom of the economic ladder. Infant mortality rates were high; in 1915 about one in ten infants died before their first birthday, and in some cities the rate was as high as three in ten.[7] Until the mid-1910s, one of the leading causes of infant death, particularly among the poor, was spoiled milk.[8] In 1910, only 18 percent of American homes had refrigeration in the form of iceboxes; electric refrigeration would not become widespread until 1940.[9]

Modern medicine was still in its infancy, and most of the lower-income moviegoers likely had little regular contact with doctors. In 1910, there were approximately 1,293 doctors per million Americans, compared with 2,207 per million by 1987.[10] When working-class Americans did see a doctor, it was most likely for a major illness or injury rather than minor aches and pains. In the first two decades of the twentieth century, before the advent of antibiotics, the market for promoting good health was still wide open for hucksters and questionable claims. Americans were on their own when it came to their health and overall well-being.

Despite the hardships, America offered a beacon of opportunity for European immigrants. Between 1890 and 1910 nearly 13 million new immigrants arrived and settled in America's rapidly growing cities.[11] Although most Americans still lived in rural areas and more than one in ten residents still worked on farms in 1910, the country was rapidly urbanizing.[12] Never before had so many people lived in such close proximity in the United States as they did in cities like New York, nor was the gap between rich and poor ever so apparent. Just following the

Figure 2.1 Unlike today, when products boast of low calorie content, cheap foods providing high
calorie counts would appeal to struggling families.

Source: Image from March 1919 issue of *Motion Picture Classic* courtesy of University of Southern California
Cinematic Arts Library.

so-called Gilded Age—where a select few were able to earn massive wealth
from shipping, steel, oil, and real estate before the days of a federal income
tax—turn-of-the-century Americans were much more aware of the
boundaries of class than we are today. Nineteenth-century beliefs that
poverty resulted from immorality were bolstered by the popularity of social

Darwinism, which saw the poor as weak links in the survival chain. These beliefs would spawn the eugenics movement, a so-called science that attempted to quantify the intellectual capabilities of people based on country of origin and mapped the hierarchies of white races (and which would provide inspiration to Adolph Hitler later in the century). This created significant animosity towards working-class immigrants during a time already rife with labor strikes and violent reprisals. It might be hard for us to imagine now, but at the turn of the twentieth century, European ethnic distinctions created significant barriers to social mobility, particularly for those of southern and eastern European descent.

In spite of these lingering ethnic and class-based tensions, the second decade of the twentieth century was a time of optimism about upward mobility. While most workers might have had few assets—less than half of Americans owned their own homes in 1915—as real wages rose the dream of reaching the middle class grew more obtainable.[13] The mass marketing of personal products meant that people could begin to invest more in *looking* middle class, if nothing else. By 1916, the personal savings rate had reached double digits for non-farm workers, and an increasing use of credit meant that purchasing power could expand further.[14]

Extending credit could serve to provide modest upward mobility and quell any labor unrest. Just a generation earlier, buying on installment would have been a source of embarrassment. As sociologist Robert D. Manning describes in *Credit Card Nation: The Consequences of America's Addiction to Credit*, Horatio Alger's mid-nineteenth century stories of social mobility involved thrift, hard work, and self-denial, not reliance on credit. In fact, debtor's prisons loomed as a deterrent for those unable to pay their creditors. Religious leaders promoted thrift itself as a moral virtue, and riches as one of Satan's temptations.[15]

Notions of self-restraint were not just about salvation. Manning notes, "Puritan thrift . . . encouraged workers to tolerate the harsh labor discipline of the new industrial order." Likewise, the expanding availability of credit at the end of the nineteenth century—and arguably in the twenty-first as well—enabled workers to accept relatively low wages at a time when those at the highest end of the economic spectrum profited tremendously.[16] Gradually installment purchases lost their bad reputation; in 1914 retailers offered credit to its wealthiest customers to buy high-ticket items, which took on an aura of prestige.[17] Two years later, most states had passed the Uniform Small Loan Law, which made it easier for some lenders to circumvent usury laws and charge higher interest rates for small loans.[18] As Americans gradually had more money to spend, ideas about consumption shifted from self-indulgence to a means of self-improvement and even a path to upward mobility. By the time movies and fan magazines became widely available, audiences were primed to imagine a life free from poverty and hard labor. The expansion of the movie industry itself offered hope of new opportunities to live in comfort.

Enter the Movies: Humble Beginnings

The first movies debuted among this backdrop of the growing promise of upward mobility into a middle-class life. The growing popularity of movies made several burgeoning moguls—often of immigrant, working-class origins themselves—into wealthy men who capitalized on their success by building their businesses into large studios that controlled the production, distribution, and exhibition of movies. The film industry began on the east coast, with most production taking place in New York and New Jersey. Inventor Thomas Edison held the patent on his 1893 invention, the kinescope, and he tried to maintain dominance in a growing industry, charging expensive fees that made it difficult for independent producers to enter the industry. Fledgling movie producers migrated to California gradually in the 1910s, in part because the mild climate made year-round filming easier, but Hollywood's inception was mostly the result of trying to escape paying Edison's trust and to avoid paying union wages. After World War I, film production expanded in the west, particularly after the 1915 Supreme Court decision *United States v. Motion Picture Patents Company* ruled that Edison's actions violated antitrust laws and studios no longer faced the ongoing threat of litigation. By the early 1920s the mythic "Hollywood" was born, a distinctly American fantasy, one that could be invented out of whole cloth in a region that was still largely undeveloped. In contrast to the industrial northeast, Hollywood could become a fantasy land of celebrity and upward mobility, where the American Dream could be realized.[19] It is not an accident that the industry that would shape images of the American Dream for years to come would do so in the west, which symbolized the idea of manifest destiny of the previous century. And as the studios grew more powerful and wealthy, they themselves seemed to prove that the Horatio Alger myth was real.

The industry would have a significant stake in maintaining this illusion as its corporate power grew—selling the dream to an eager public would be a very profitable enterprise for years to come.

The proliferation of movies during the first decades of the twentieth century bore a special bond with the American Dream of upward mobility. For one, movies can only be a viable source of entertainment when enough people have the time and the money to see them. The growth of the movie industry and the invention of Hollywood coincided with a growing sense that upward mobility was likely, as workers gained traction economically. Cheap nickelodeons offered entertainment to those with little money and a little bit of leisure time. Watching movies in the 1910s, the industry's boosters promised, opened the door to adventure, particularly for the working-class city dweller. Labor strikes helped shrink the work week during the early years of the twentieth century, from twelve hours a day, six days a week in the mid-nineteenth century and towards a five-day work week. In addition to time, working-class Americans began to have more discretionary income as real wages increased in the first two decades of the twentieth century, and they increasingly spent both at the movies. Aided by a steady stream of immigrants into cities, the first silent movies relied on gestures and exaggerated facial expressions that were easy for people with limited English skills to understand. Activists attempted to clamp down on nickelodeons, arguing that both drinking and movies could be dangerous influences on the masses. Both the movies and the anonymous performers within them were considered morally suspect.

Initially, films were mostly private peep shows that often featured nudity and sexual themes.[20] The "nickelodeon," so-named for the nickel price of admission, was nearly always located in an urban storefront in the early years of the twentieth century, often in seedier parts of town. Movies began in cities as a decidedly lower status, urban pastime, and reflected the chasm of class division; clearly this form of entertainment was not for the well-heeled. Being in one of these films was not a badge of honor either. It was no accident that the earliest movies had no movie stars. The first films had no credits, and performers were barred from generating any personal publicity.[21] Edison did not want any single person to become more famous than his invention and made sure the earliest films had no credits. At first this was not a problem for performers, as stage actors who appeared in the movies certainly did not want to sully their theater reputations by being known as "picture players." Rather than creating idols or celebrities, the middle classes viewed the earliest movies with suspicion. Far from idols, for the most part people in show business were not considered respectable, nor was appearing in movies initially a stepping stone to wealth.

While nickelodeon revenues were healthy, the reputation of the industry needed improvement to avoid widespread regulation of movies as tools of the "dangerous classes." The elite viewed nickelodeons as on par with bawdy burlesque shows and carnivals; not the sort of place a self-respecting middle-class person would visit. As cultural historian Robert Sklar notes, nickelodeons "belonged in the same class as brothels, gambling dens, and hangouts of criminal gangs."[22] In 1908, the mayor of New York ordered that nickelodeons be shut down as places of iniquity that would threaten the morality of women and children. This concern about movies had less to do with the new medium than the social changes taking place at the time. As the nation began to urbanize, reformers considered cities themselves a threat to the morality of their inhabitants.

Not only were working-class immigrants the first movie patrons, but early films frequently featured pro-labor themes that pitted the underdog against the stuffy elite, and included themes frequently sympathetic to the plight of workers. Rather than concerns about sex and violence (which were certainly prevalent in early filmmaking), the threat of regulation was about class conflict during a time when labor strikes threatened to create social unrest.[23] To avoid government interference with the industry, movie makers had to gain loyalty from more than just the working classes.

Making Movies Middle Class

In order to draw a more respectable audience and get politicians and reformers off of the industry's back, movie content had to change. Peep shows gave way to increasingly more technical storytelling, the most famous (or infamous) of the era being D.W. Griffith's *The Birth of a Nation* (1915). Its racist tale of the Ku Klux Klan was not a problem for many white, rural audience members—the same people who would otherwise be most critical of a medium that attracted urbanites and immigrants. Movies began to move away from working-class themes as well. Quelling mainstream criticism also meant steering clear of themes that dealt with the economic divisions in the United States. The changes in content also helped to eliminate criticism that movies were the milieu of the "dangerous classes" as movie producers sought to upgrade their audience.

Beyond simply appealing to more native-born middle-class patrons, the industry also sought to transform its existing working-class audience by promoting more refined behavior in newly created fan magazines. Beginning with *Motion Picture Story Magazine* in 1911, newsstands and movie theaters sold fan magazines in an attempt to create a more refined image of both the movies and their players. When the 1915 Supreme Court decision *United States v. Motion Picture Patents Company* ruled that Edison's trust violated antitrust laws, studios could freely publicize the performers, something Edison frowned upon. By the mid-1910s it became evident to industry heads that the players could help sell movies to more mainstream audiences. The movie studios heavily subsidized the magazines, which tended to print only favorable stories about its players to promote the industry and generate public interest in going to the movies. By the end of the 1910s, at least half a dozen movie magazines were on sale, mostly in theater lobbies. The magazines became a central ancillary to the film industry. By 1918 five different magazines could boast of a circulation over 100,000; two had more than 200,000 readers each month.[24]

The earliest issues included little information about players and instead provided summaries of movie plots. In an age before movies created celebrities, the magazines focused on moviemaking itself to educate readers in the basics of filmmaking. Beyond just promoting movie patronage, the magazines actively sought to link movies with propriety. The magazines also stressed the educational value of movies. A 1915 issue of *Picture Play* told of the great books that came to life in movies, and the opportunity to see far away places at a time when only the wealthy could afford leisurely travel.[25] *Motion Picture Classic* contained an ongoing feature called "Better Pictures for the Children," based on the premise that if movies were okay for children, they were indeed wholesome entertainment that would appeal to average Americans.[26]

Several early fan magazine stories suggested that movies had become a pastime of the elite. And if those of "higher breeding" accepted movies, then presumably middle-class audiences would as well. A 1912 *Photoplay* story quotes a "wealthy philanthropist" who argued that, "moving pictures

... give easily comprehended instruction on hygiene and proper living to the people of the tenements."[27] That same year, *Photoplay* promised that, "plans are being formulated for the active acquirement of moving picture houses of the better class,"[28] and that movies were "the highest type of entertainment in the history of the world."[29] By 1915 "society folk" had apparently become interested in movies and were filming their own important events, such as weddings. To industry boosters, movies were now on par with the theater. "For an industry like ours to have redeemed itself within such a short space of time sufficiently to attract the whole-hearted attention of the elite is an accomplishment to be proud of," *Motion Picture Classic* told its readers.[30]

It is questionable whether the wealthy really accepted movies "whole-heartedly" by mid-decade. A 1910 survey found that 72 percent of moviegoers were working class, and only 3 percent were described as members of the "leisure class."[31] As late as 1924, estimates suggested that the majority of moviegoers were only "moderately well off."[32] But clearly the industry needed the approval of the elite and the middle classes in order for its stature to rise. To do this, the movie industry aligned itself with mainstream notions of class and status in America. It also sought to train its audience in the customs familiar to the native-born middle classes. A 1915 issue of *Motion Picture Classic* contained an article instructing audience members about "moving picture etiquette," to ensure proper behavior when seeing a movie, such as telling moviegoers to remove their hats. The article also assured readers that what they saw on screen was not real.[33]

Middle-Class Legitimacy through War

The timing of World War I was fortuitous for improving the film industry's standing by portraying its players as patriots. Further, because Europe was increasingly consumed by war in the mid-1910s, American films grew to dominate the industry. Prior to the war, French, Italian, German, and English films enjoyed larger audiences than American movies did.[34]

Photoplay directly addressed the link between the movies and patriotism in a series of editorials. A *Chicago Tribune* statement was reprinted in the magazine's February 1918 issue. Titled "Patriotism at the Movies," the brief comment notes that "The moving picture theaters are becoming community centers of patriotism ... In communities largely made up of persons of foreign birth or extraction the work of the movie theaters . . . has been of special value."[35] Silent films also erased one of the most salient indicators of region, ethnicity, and immigration status: the accent. Movies could identify its players as uniformly American, and despite the diversity of their origins, performers seemed to be of one people. The war thus served as an opportunity for new immigrants to become Americans and imbibe in the flowing patriotism that the movies helped supply. *Photoplay* was not shy about proclaiming that movies helped foster democracy. A June 1918 editorial claimed that "The Moving Picture is the Fifth Estate because it is Democracy's own child."[36] An October 1917 editorial similarly concluded that "the photoplay is the most democratic of diversions."[37] In January 1919 the magazine went as far as to detail "How the Motion Picture Saved the World," in an article that described how films of American troops preparing to deploy to Europe let French soldiers know that the Yanks really were coming to support them.[38]

The movies, and their first newly emerging movie stars, proved to be central in promoting the industry's patriotism and legitimacy. Charlie Chaplin and Mary Pickford, along with her second husband Douglas Fairbanks, actively campaigned for citizens to purchase Liberty Bonds to fund the war. Movies and movie stars aligned themselves with the great cause, trumpeted their patriotism, and helped generate widespread approval for both movies and movie stars. A March 1918 *Photoplay* article told of actors who became soldiers, including a posed-looking photo spread of the men digging trenches, attending "revolver practice," and standing guard.[39] And citing a practice that would run well into this century, a July 1918 story in *Motion Picture* told of how movies entertain troops and keep morale high.[40] In so doing, both magazines could gain legitimacy and highlight how the film industry was quintessentially American, insisting that the fates of the two would be bound together.

Picture Players: From Humble Origins to Middle-Class Legitimacy

In addition to promoting support for the war, the profiles of the picture players stressed their wholesome, small town American roots (real or imagined). The players thus provided an unexpected shortcut to legitimacy for the industry. Fan magazine readers wanted to know more about the people who populated this new industry, and the public wrote letters to the magazines' publishers, asking to know more about them. What are their names? Are they married? What are their hobbies? How does she keep her skin so lovely? As picture players became famous, they served as useful vehicles for projecting ideas about class, the status of the movie industry, and the promise of upward mobility into middle-class respectability.

As noted earlier, many people found movie actors and other performers to be morally suspect. Early promoters first needed to assure the public that the people in pictures were respectable and as virtuous as they were. While contemporary gossip magazines feature celebrities out and about under the heading "they're just like us," today the implication is that everyday snapshots make them seen less superior than and more like everyday people. By contrast, the earliest stories often attempted to show that the players were respectable and not socially *inferior* to the public.

Movie magazines provided benign back-stories for players to create the impression that movie players were reputable, though not necessarily glamorous icons or heroes. The earliest featured players were cast as wholesome, average Americans who were like readers, only luckier. When the magazines featured players' homes, they detailed simple, middle-class dwellings. A January 1919 issue of *Photoplay* describes player Geraldine Farrar's home as a place of "comfort and simplicity" and states that Farrar "loathes over-decoration at home."[41] Family backgrounds and hobbies filled the brief gossip sections of magazines, mirroring society pages in order to give the appearance of lineage and proper upbringing. A 1915 issue of *Picture Play* notes in its "Stories of the Studio People" that "Rhea Mitchell learned to ride a horse."[42] Other hobbies the magazines mention include knitting, playing piano, decorating, and other "respectable" pastimes.

In a two-page spread, *Motion Picture* features players doing household chores, under the headline "Who Says the Stars Dont [*sic*] Work?"[43] The five actresses all supposedly enjoy scrubbing floors, doing laundry, cooking, and washing the car, implying that they are clean and hardworking. Perhaps as a precursor to the Paris Hilton–Nicole Richie series, in September 1918 *Motion Picture Classic* featured a photo layout titled "Gloria Swanson Tries the Simple Life," in which the star is shown fishing, hunting, tending to a bull, and horseback riding.[44] Unlike Paris and Nicole, Gloria appears to take to the pastoral setting and appreciate the value of hard work. Also unlike the present, where actors stress how

Here's a star who doesn't allow any one to take the joy out of her young life. Lila Lee hasn't balked at anything yet, not even at going down on her knees before a floor pail, so we think she'll be versatile

Figure 2.2 Staged publicity photos such as this one emphasized the wholesomeness of early movie performers.

Source: Image from November 1918 *Motion Picture Magazine*, courtesy of University of Southern California Cinematic Arts Library.

hard they work and try to dispel beliefs that their lives are glamorous, in the 1910s acting clearly *was* play compared with the labor-intensive nature of much of work.

Part of the fantasy the industry cast was an escape from work. It is no accident that movie magazines initially called performers "players." Unlike today, when the word player connotes someone manipulative and even predatory, there is the connection to the more legitimate and respectable plays of the theater, and using the term "players" evokes the image of movies as fun. The players were part of the promotion of movies as part of an exciting adventure, available to all who are part of the illusion, including audiences.

Movie Stars' Upward Mobility

While the majority of American laborers still worked in fields or factories by the late 1910s, movie magazines sold the promise of upward mobility into middle-class comfort. The growth of the industry created the chance to dream of becoming a part of it. Rather than only a pipe dream aimed at the gullible masses, these stories coincide with the growth of real wages and automation, so the appeal of work without physical labor was more than just a dream. The magazines' articles featured many rags-to-riches stories, and the movie industry became a central site of the Horatio Alger fable that a poor, downtrodden person could rise out of poverty through luck and hard work.

Charlie Chaplin became one of the first true movie stars with the success of his famous character, "The Little Tramp," who championed the plight of those with little social status and encouraged sympathy for the mythical everyman. Chaplin's real life also reflected the rags-to-riches ethos of the American Dream; Chaplin was born in England to an alcoholic father and a mentally ill mother, moved around quite a bit, and enjoyed international fame after emigrating to the United States. Chaplin's lifestyle was portrayed as both hardworking and luxurious. A March 1918 issue of *Motion Picture* that features several articles on the war includes photos of Chaplin golfing in Hawaii, described as "the game that kings have quarreled over."[45] But his success is the result of hard work; a May 1918 *Motion Picture* story called "Daily Program" details his grueling studio schedule. Chaplin "works like lightening until 3 am, when everyone is used up" but he is also chauffeured around town to a country club, to fancy locations, and to restaurants.[46]

Most silent movie star stories focused on women's upward social mobility. Women appeared on the vast majority of magazine covers, helping to create a fantasy of upward mobility during a time when the suffrage movement was in full swing. According to census data, women's participation in the paid labor force more than doubled between 1890 and 1910.[47] Many women worked as sales clerks, telephone operators, stenographers, typists, and in other relatively new occupations. The movie industry contributed by offering women careers and independence they rarely had before. Not only did girls and women have onscreen roles, but in its early days, the low status of moviemaking meant that women could get jobs behind the scenes too, writing scenarios and then later writing for movie magazines. The industry seemed to provide special opportunities for women to rise from poverty.

A February 1918 story in *Photoplay* about Virginia Valli tells such a tale. The story describes how Ms. Valli, a young woman working as a stenographer in Chicago, had to walk past rotting food and animals to get to work each day. "She would climb a long pair of dingy half-lighted stairs, go into a dingy, half-lighted office" doing tedious tasks. Her journey also placed her in peril, as she passed by the "voluble sons of Italy" and most of all "she couldn't keep herself neat and dainty, and she had to endure being ogled by express drivers and roustabouts."[48] Virginia struggled to help support her mother and sister, like many other young people during this time, and felt she had no choice but to endure the dangers of the city.

She found work as a dancer, but her mother disapproved, particularly because she had to work late at night and grew thinner and thinner. Then Virginia visited a local movie studio, applied for a position, and went back three times until the director would see her. Now it's the "limousine life" for her, and she no longer has to endure the indecency of city life, clearly unfit for young womanhood. This story may or may not have been true, but helped bolster the notion that movies provided a clear path for upward mobility.

A 1919 article in *Photoplay* tells of a similar tale, of an orphaned girl named Ruth Clifford living with her aunts near the Edison Studios in New Jersey. She watched movies being filmed through a knothole in the fence until someone invited her to come in and watch. Then, of course, she was asked to be in movies herself.[49] The same issue included an article titled "The Rise of Elsie Ferguson: From Chorus Girl to Star of Stage and Screen; but First Elsie Rose, and Rose," which told of how luck, determination, and hard work led to Elsie's stardom. Elsie had a dream as a girl—though by the author's description she was then "not very pretty" but had practiced "dancing and singing like mad" and moved up from chorus girl to star.[50] This theme, of a young woman lifted from obscurity, saved from the depravity of modern times as a result of her own effort, continued for the better part of the twentieth century.

Women's lives suddenly became a topic of interest, particularly for female moviegoers. *Picture Play* regularly featured one article per issue supposedly written by a player about what being part of this exciting new industry was really like. Player Violet Mersereau wrote:

> I really commenced this story by promising to tell you how I spend my time. I should like to take an entire week, as everyday is a new era—yes, not only the conviction that the sun has risen and gone again, but it means, in our world, a brand-new era.[51]

Mersereau (or the publicist who likely wrote this passage) had a point, especially for women. The new industry offered employment opportunities that in many ways upheld traditional views of women. At the same time, the growing industry provided an increasingly respectable outlet for "ambitious girls," as Kathlyn Williams noted in a 1915 *Picture Play* article she allegedly wrote.[52] Williams, known then as the "Jungle Actress," described the bravery needed to work with animals in movies. A 1916 article in the same magazine told of "Girls Who Play with Death," through the risky stunts they performed.[53] A 1915 article in *Motion Picture Classic* remarked on "Women's Conquest in Filmdom."[54]

That women had actually *conquered* the film world is probably a stretch, since men were (and mostly still are) in charge of funding and directing most movies, but the industry did offer women the opportunity to lead very different lives than their Victorian mothers. "The fair sex is represented as in no other calling to which women have harkened in the early years of the twentieth century," *Motion Picture Classic* declared in 1915.[55] The fan magazines characterized movie women as strong and independent, rather than lacking in morality, as was often presumed of the burlesque showgirls of that era and many young stars of our own time.

Perhaps no woman benefited more from the growth of this industry than Mary Pickford, who arguably became the first bona fide movie star upon signing the industry's first million-dollar deal in June 1916.[56] It is likely that her salary did not merely reflect her celebrity, but helped in its manufacture at a time when the median household income was well below a thousand dollars a year. Using the ever-pure Pickford as a symbol that the industry did not taint the innocence of modern-day womanhood, the movies were thus not only construed as safe for women to watch, but also to work in. Not coincidentally, it was middle-class white women who were most likely to challenge the morality of movies, and campaign for their restriction. By luring these same women into the filmmaking fantasy, the threat of government regulation could be contained.

It is no accident that Pickford was the first "anointed one." Her popularity rose throughout the 1910s, and when *Motion Picture Classic* asked readers to send in a ballot with the name of their favorite picture player, Pickford's name consistently topped the list. In 1916 she told *Picture Play* that being a player had become less risky with the advancement of movie-making technology.[57] Pickford appeared at once to embody Victorian womanhood, with long flowing hair and pale skin, while at the same time playing parts that demonstrated pluck, independence, and strength. As such she represented the shift in the construction of femininity at the start of the twentieth century. She was also arguably the first movie star to live her personal life in public. Although her first marriage could have threatened her onscreen image as a child, the magazines did not hide the fact that she was married to picture player Owen Moore. Referred to as "Little Mary," she played the part of a child in most of her films, well into her thirties—and so her strength was never truly threatening to the notion of women as the weaker sex. To reinforce her revered and yet fragile image, news of the most minor illness she suffered made the magazines' gossip pages.

Just as with whites from ethnic backgrounds, who gradually benefited from greater inclusion during this time, women also saw a rise in opportunity during the war. Although women's entry into traditionally male occupations during World War II has been well documented, some of these shifts can be traced back to World War I. In February 1918, *Motion Picture* profiled silent movie actress Gladys Brockwell, who is pictured behind a movie camera, climbing a telephone pole, and driving a horse-drawn cart. "It is a far cry from the simpering, languishing lady of Victoria's day," states the (female) reporter of Brockwell, who goes on to call her an "energetic little feminist" and "an intrepid little star." In describing how well women performed "men's" work during World War I, the title of the article, "Gladys Brockwell Does 'His' Bit," reflects some discomfort with this shift. Nonetheless, the author concludes that: "It is the present crisis that inspired Miss Brockwell to discover just how many of the purely masculine jobs a woman could perform if it became absolutely necessary for men to leave for duty 'somewhere in France.'"[58]

Movie player profiles highlight the unease with changes in women's status. A February 1918 *Photoplay* story about player Olive Tell states bluntly that "some women are beautiful, and some are suffragists." But the article goes on to say that "Olive Tell stands a living, breathing, pink and white refutation of these words." Throughout the piece, Tell's views on women's rights are punctuated with descriptions of her as little, pretty, and pink.[59] She might have had a career, but features like this emphasized actresses' conformity to gendered expectations. Women's social mobility could be problematic otherwise, and so these stories reinforced the idea that picture players had the values and virtues of regular, middle-class folks.

Selling Upward Mobility

Unlike today, when celebrity culture and movies sell the dream of affluence, middle-class stability and respectability formed the hallmark of the American Dream in the 1910s. Movie magazines sold the fantasy of becoming middle class in their advertisements.[60] Not incidentally, the expansion of both cities and the middle classes meant more creative jobs

Figure 2.3 Ads regularly invited fan magazine readers to try to join the new movie industry.

Source: Image from February 1916 issue of *Motion Picture Classic* courtesy of University of Southern California Cinematic Arts Library.

in the growing entertainment industry and in fields such as advertising, so the opportunities to shift from manual work to mental work were real. Above all else, magazine features suggested to readers that they too could be part of this exciting new industry. Rather than promoting fame, ads promised that both male and female readers could use their ideas to make money. Articles gave advice on how to become an onscreen performer, as at the same time ads for pamphlets and books on motion picture acting ran regularly in the magazines' back pages.

The magazines did more than promote their own industry—they sold the fantasy of joining the middle class through work that required little or no physical labor. Although there were few (if any) ads for actual jobs advertised in the magazines, notices for countless booklets from correspondence schools offered the promise of financial security. *Picture Play* included a feature called "Hints for Scenario Writers" in its issues, and ads offered to teach readers "How to Write Photoplays." Contests regularly offered cash for "Motion Picture Plots." A full-page ad in a 1915 issue of *Picture Play* beckoned readers to "Own this Oliver Typewriter for 17¢ a day" for writers of "photo plots, short stories, songs and verse."[61] Ads for typewriters, paid for in installments, regularly appeared in full-page offers. The ubiquity of these ads implies that the new movie industry was desperate for "scenario writers" and that all you needed was a typewriter to improve your circumstances.

Writing is just one creative field that movie magazine advertisements offered readers in search of a better life. Many ads focused on self-improvement and developing talents. Ads promising to teach creative skills such as ventriloquism, sign painting, pitching, magic tricks, and song writing suggest that readers could use skills previously considered hobbies for employment and movement into the middle classes. These products promised consumers they could educate themselves through correspondence courses and encyclopedias, reinforcing a central facet in the American notion of mobility, that success is a function of one's own individual work and effort. All of this was possible in the privacy of your own home, no less.

Ads for skilled labor positions reflect the shifts in the labor market during the first decades of the century, when a sizeable proportion worked in positions classified as unskilled, where no prior training was needed. One ad offered the chance to earn a high school diploma at home; at this

"You Get the Job"

That's what the trained man, the expert in his line, hears today from the man that hires.

Worth-while jobs are not given out haphazard. Training lands the job—training that means high-grade work and a short cut to results. And training wins quick advancement to still better jobs.

The day of the "Jack-of-all-trades" is passed. This is the time of the specialist. No concern can afford to place a high-grade equipment in the hands of low-grade men. Competition forces employers to meet skill with skill.

The business of the International Correspondence Schools is to supply training; to give job-getting and job-bettering ability; to raise salaries.

Every month upward of 300 I. C. S. students write to Scranton to tell of positions secured or bettered—of earnings increased and prospects brightened—through study of I. C. S. Courses. Last month the number was 416. The letters came from every section and from all sorts and conditions of men.

If you wish to make sure of the job you want—there is an I. C. S. way for you. To find out all about it, mark and mail the coupon. Doing so will commit you to nothing, place you under no obligation, and may prove the turning point in your career.

Don't wait.

Mail the Coupon NOW.

- -

International Correspondence Schools
Box 1049, SCRANTON, PA.

Please explain, without further obligation on my part, how I can qualify for a larger salary and advancement to the position, trade, or profession before which I have marked **X**.

Bookkeeper	Concrete Construction
Stenographer	Electrical Engineer
Advertising Man	Electric Lighting
Show-Card Writer	Mechanical Engineer
Window Trimming	Civil Engineer
Mechanical Draftsman	Surveyor
Industrial Designing	Stationary Engineer
Commercial Illustrating	Building Contractor
Civil Service	Architectural Draftsman
Chemist	Architect
Textile Manufacturing	Structural Engineer
English Branches	Plumb. & Steam Fitting
Automobile Running	Mining Engineer

Name_____

St. and No._____

City_____ State_____

Figure 2.4

Fan magazine ads regularly promised readers they could help them get jobs and move into the middle class.

Source: Image from May 1911 issue of *Motion Picture Story* Magazine courtesy of University of Southern California Cinematic Arts Library.

time, less than one in five American adults had completed high school.[62] Patterson Civil Service Schools promised that they could get men "lifetime positions. No strikes, no 'layoffs,' no 'straw bosses'."[63] An ad in the October 1915 issue of *Motion Picture Classic* tells of "Men and women wanted for U.S. Government Jobs: $65–$150 per month, vacations with full pay. No layoffs. Short hours. Common education sufficient. 'Pull' unnecessary." Jobs in sales, metals prospecting, electrical lighting, stenography, telegraphy, nursing, and other skilled trades suggested that steady work and middle-class status were possible for a small fee.

Correspondence courses claimed to give participants the inside edge to lucrative sounding middle-class positions. Apparently, middle-class status was just around the corner for those willing to make a small investment and teach themselves the requisite skills. Drawings that accompanied the ads for booklets and correspondence courses show men in jackets and ties, and occasionally distinguished portraits of men suggested the potential to join the so-called leisure classes. Entrepreneurial opportunities could be yours just by subscribing to the right course, according to the ad copy. "Let us Start You in Business," one ad offered.[64] Other ads claimed to give readers the chance to "Be a Banker" and even be part of a "$250,000 Partnership if You 'Know How'."[65] These ads probably promised more than most readers would ever receive from booklets or correspondence courses, just as scenario writing was not going to become most would-be writers' source of income. But the ads sold the fantasy of social mobility.

While the relatively short involvement of the United States in World War I did not provide quite as many economic opportunities for women as World War II would decades later, it would be a precursor for what was to come later in the century for women and reflect the growing number of women in the labor force. An ad for a sales position inquired, "Do You Need More Money to Help Your Husband; to Help Your Children; to Help Yourself?"[66] Fan magazine ads also promised wartime opportunities for women. "Wanted: Traveling Saleswomen," a January 1919 *Photoplay* ad beckoned. "The war has caused a tremendous shortage of salesmen—*Women must be trained to take their places*" (emphasis in original).[67]

The increase in discretionary spending meant more money to spend on cosmetics and more jobs in the beauty industry. "We Need Women!

$12–$25 per week beauty specialists," another ad beckoned—a potentially lucrative position considering the median annual income was $687 in 1915, or about $13 a week.[68] The Woman's Institute of Domestic Arts and Sciences, Inc., offered a correspondence course in dressmaking and millinery for women to learn at "home in [their] spare time."[69] The institute offered a Fifth Avenue mailing address in New York City, providing the appearance of legitimacy.

Upward Mobility through Self-Improvement: Appearing Middle Class

Attaining middle-class status would require work and determination, and increased scrutiny of one's appearance (down to your eyelashes, nose, and even nose pores). Just as ads for learning a craft at home implied that people could rise through their own effort, ads suggested that beauty products were vital tools in the self-improvement kit to become middle class. Along with an emphasis on actresses' attractiveness, ads and articles promised that attractive women could ensure their own financial success.

Beauty products long predated the introduction of movies and movie magazines. But the movies helped to create a single standard of beauty seen by millions of audience members. Estimates suggest that nearly one-third of the American population went to movies weekly in 1910, and nearly one-half by 1920.[70] Never before did so many people from geographically and ethnically diverse backgrounds see the same images with as much frequency. Magazine ads offered photographs of their favorite players, perhaps among the few photos people would own, reinforcing a growing uniformity in beauty standards. Additionally, per capita expenditures for personal care grew between 1910 and 1920, and nearly doubled between 1910 and 1929.[71]

During the first decades of the twentieth century—as with today—how you looked provided specific social cues about your class status. An important tool for monitoring one's appearance became commonplace in the 1880s—the household mirror. A clear complexion took on special significance at the beginning of the twentieth century as the primary indicator of social status. Weathered skin implied outdoor labor; a dry, chapped complexion also meant that one was continually exposed to the elements. A dark complexion revealed an ancestry outside of northern or western Europe, which were still favored in terms of social status.

But most centrally, having a clear and youthful complexion denoted cleanliness. And cleanliness revealed high status, particularly in cities where infrastructure struggled to keep pace with population growth. New immigrants, who often lived in crowded, dirty tenements, could fight stereotypes of poor hygiene by paying special attention to their faces. Movie fan magazines offered products for their readers to look more refined, or at least more like the middle class supposedly did. Appearing middle class meant freedom from the soot of cities and the sights and smells of toiling outdoors or in a factory. The focus on complexion as a sign of cleanliness also relates to the science of germs, relatively new in the early days of the twentieth century. Scientists who at one time believed that disease was caused by dirty air now blamed bacteria. A blemished complexion allegedly revealed an unclean home, one that allowed germs to flourish.[72] Soap ads were ubiquitous, and along with perfume encouraged female readers to smell more genteel. Ads also appeared for vacuum cleaners, bathtubs, and hot and cold running water.

For women, beauty became one of the central ways of conveying (and improving) status. The ad copy for soaps and lotions said as much. "It is a well-established fact that many refined and beautiful women" use Hinds Honey and Almond Cream, according to its makers.[73] An ad for Ponds notes that members of a "fashionable (New York) skating club" regularly use their product to prevent chapping."[74] Ingram's Milkwood Cream makes the rewards for proper skin care very apparent. A drawing of couples in formal attire, apparently at a ball, features a tuxedoed man kneeling before a young woman, possibly proposing marriage. "Kneel to the prettiest," the ad exclaims.[75]

In the 1910s, women of privilege were pampered, shielded from work or concern. "Powdered Saxolite" promised to do that for working-class women, or at least their complexions, as its ad claimed it would "remove traces of age, illness, or worry."[76] "Beneath the soiled, discolored, faded or aged complexion is one fair to look upon," once consumers used "Mercolized Wax."[77] These ads insisted that consumers' histories should not interfere with their potential for looking like their more refined, affluent counterparts.

As status was particularly linked to ethnicity at the start of the twentieth century, ads promised to help consumers achieve the "right" facial features. Products supposedly would give users a "dainty white"

Figure 2.5 Ads emphasized that women's upward mobility was tied to their appearance.

Source: Image from August 1916 issue of *Motion Picture Classic* courtesy of University of Southern California Cinematic Arts Library.

complexion, a reference not only to refinement but also the lighter toned, native-born Americans of western and northern European ancestry. Even before the age of plastic surgery, advertisers encouraged women to make their noses straighter, perhaps to hide an eastern European background. "You Have a Beautiful Face—But Your Nose?" chided an ad for a nose shaper.[78] Changing the appearance of an "ill-shaped" nose, the ad insisted, would bring prosperity and acceptance. "In this day and age," the copy reads, "attention to your appearance is absolutely necessary to make the most out of life."[79] Failure to attend to such an important detail would "injure your welfare," and would have a serious impact on the "failure or success of your life."

Depilatory creams and powders promised consumers they could literally remove working-class roots. "GOOD TASTE demands the instant removal of all superfluous hair from the face, neck, and arms," instructs an ad for Bellin's Wonderstoen hair-removing tablet (emphasis in original).[80] By removing unwanted hair, the makers of X-Bazin depilatory powder told working-class women that they could appear more like the "beauties from Paris and New York" who had used their product "for 75 years."[81] Ostensibly using products like this would not just improve the way a woman looked, but would help her pass into middle-class propriety.

The movies and the middle classes expanded together in the first decades of the twentieth century. Just as the movie industry redefined itself as a pastime for respectable Americans, a large proportion of its core audience experienced upward mobility. The promise of the American Dream of middle-class comfort seemed realistic, and just as the population moved from subsistence wages to growing leisure time and discretionary income, celebrity culture would shift. No longer would fan magazines need to prove that picture players were good enough for the population to go to movies, but instead movie stars came to represent the staggering wealth some Americans earned during the boom years of the 1920s. Much like the 2000s, credit became even easier for more people to obtain and helped fuel the economic boom that eventually went bust. In the next chapter we will see how celebrity culture both shaped and reflected the American Dream of 1920s-style affluence, suggesting that prosperity and wealth could be yours for the asking.

3

PROSPERITY AND WEALTH ARRIVE

BOOM TIMES AND WOMEN'S SUFFRAGE IN THE 1920S

If the teen years of the twentieth century held the promise of a life beyond industrial labor, the twenties seem to deliver on the promise. And celebrity culture shifted along with the era's economic growth (which I will describe in the upcoming section). Publicity stories no longer constructed celebrities as living simple lives, having risen from subsistence to middle-class comfort. Instead, celebrity stories of the 1920s stressed the possibility of riches and fame, along with some of the moral hazards it brought, particularly for young women. Celebrity tales reflected the tension between attaining massive wealth and maintaining self-control in times of plenty, particularly as women had greater opportunities. Reflecting the Horatio Alger myth of rising from poverty to wealth and the Puritan ethic of self-restraint, stories both celebrated the blessings of wealth while warning of the dangers of plenty.

As the economy became more automated and jobs in offices and department stores opened to women, upward mobility afforded many young women more independence than their Victorian mothers were likely to have experienced, especially as the film industry grew. Just as women's opportunities expanded—both in Hollywood and with women's suffrage following the passage of Nineteenth Amendment in 1920—fan magazines warned of what could happen without enough self-regulation: you might never find a husband. Women's upward mobility seemed real but threatening; those who became wealthy celebrities appeared to be a threat both to men's moral grounding and their bank accounts in celebrity stories. Not coincidentally, ads and articles encouraged women to exert greater self-control over their bodies through "reducing" with diet, exercise, and numerous advertised products. Thus, this shift in the gender order appears to have produced something of a backlash—perhaps a response to anomie, the lack of clarity about changing social norms. This backlash could also have been an attempt to fight against the threat women's mobility seemed to pose to patriarchy.

This chapter explores how celebrity tales of the 1920s boom years suggest that wealth is readily attainable to all Americans—even women— and that failure to achieve or maintain wealth is a product of personal failure rather than the result of structural conditions. It addresses the following questions: How did representations of the American Dream shift from the 1910s to the boom years of the 1920s? Why did concerns about morality rise during the 1920s? How was this concern linked with shifts in the gender order?

Boom Times

For many Americans, the lifestyle of hard labor and struggle for basic survival began to change at the end of the 1910s. By the mid-1920s many in the working classes experienced modest upward mobility. In the first decades of the twentieth century, real wages rose, and the percentage of workers in white collar positions increased from 17.6 percent in 1900 to 29.4 percent by 1930.[1] Likewise, the proportion of unskilled workers steadily declined from 36 percent of the workforce in 1910 to 26 percent by 1940.[2] Discretionary spending rose from 20 percent of household earnings to 35 percent between 1900 and 1930, making it easier for workers to afford frequent visits to the movies, among other non-essential goods and services.[3]

While in 1910, 52 percent of the population aged 10-and-over were employed; gradually, children and teens would exit the non-farm paid labor force. In 1900, 31 percent of fourteen- and fifteen-year-olds were employed; by 1920 that percentage had dropped to 18 percent and continued to fall throughout the century, creating more leisure time for young people.[4] Leisure time for people of all ages expanded throughout the decade, as the eight-hour workday became more common, and fan magazine ads and articles were more likely to feature people on vacation than in the previous decade.[5] Creams promising to whiten skin gradually gave way to tanning products, as browned skin transitioned from a mark of the laboring class to one of the leisure class.

After World War I, many goods previously only available for cash became available for credit. This happened in part because a brief recession from 1920–1921 created a surplus of goods merchants needed to sell. This increase in credit fueled the economic boom of the 1920s; more borrowing led to more consumption. This includes borrowing money to buy stocks on margin; brokers required only 10 percent of the purchase price to make a sale before the market crashed in 1929. The Dow Jones Industrial Average nearly quadrupled between 1920 and 1929, from nearly 110 points in 1920 to over 380 in 1929 (before crashing to a low of 41 points in 1932).[6]

The years preceding the crash seemed to prove that the American Dream of prosperity was real and that it was reaching a larger and larger proportion of the population. Economist Martha Olney argues that Americans viewed purchasing durable goods as another way of saving and investing in the 1920s, particularly for products meant to last and improve the quality of life.[7] This is especially true for items such as cars and appliances, which were likely first-time purchases for many families during the decade. Olney notes that the personal savings rate fell from an average of 5.5 percent in the 1898–1916 period to just 3.9 percent between 1922 and 1929.[8]

While the working classes slowly made economic gains and transitioned into a more stable existence, movies gradually gained the interest of the more well-to-do, and movie magazines likewise spoke to a broader, more affluent (or aspirationally affluent) audience. Newly built movie theaters appeared in more prosperous areas and attracted people who would have never entered a nickelodeon in a working-class neighborhood. The most elaborate "picture palace" of its time, The Roxy, first opened in 1927 in New York City, featuring ornate designs, a full orchestra, comfortable seating, and high admission prices that all but assured that the well-to-do would not be offended by too many of the "wrong" kinds of people. Entrepreneurs realized that more than the actual movie content, it was the audiences associated with early movies who really deterred the elite from seeing movies. In contrast with the early days of the movies, the movies now became synonymous with prosperity.

Increasingly, stories of celebrity wealth told of the servants stars employed, the exclusive clubs being built in Hollywood, and even line-by-line itemizations of how stars spent their money. The facetiously titled "Struggling Along on $50,000 a Year" (the equivalent of more than $637,000 in 2010 dollars) catalogued the $10,000 a year one star spent on clothes (the equivalent of more than $127,000 in 2010 dollars) and what the servants and even the house payments cost, while noting that performers had to supply their own wardrobes for films. The article did add that $5,000 went to church and charitable donations (the equivalent of more than $63,000 today), describing the "unfailing generosity . . . which most players of the stage and screen" possess.[9]

A 1924 *Screenland* article describes the sorts of demands stars made of their cooks, maids, and chauffeurs—quite a shift from pictures of actresses scrubbing their own floors in the 1910s.[10] In one such household, "you will find a cook, a nurse, and a chauffeur" as well as "a gardener to take care of the grounds" at one star's Beverly Hills home. Another family has an "Italian cook . . . a Chinese servant, house boy and gardener combined, and a chauffeur." Other households claim "six big cars," homes that "look like a country club" and special, themed rooms for entertaining.[11] Pictures of elaborate homes became a regular feature in celebrity fan magazines, as did photos of stars lounging by pools and other symbols of leisure. *Photoplay* featured a two-page photo spread of a "new and ultra-exclusive" country club that boasted $2.5 million (the equivalent of more than $30 million in 2010 dollars) in improvements to the massive estate.[12] If celebrity life of the 1910s was part of an exciting new industry that promised freedom from want, the 1920s celebrity was clearly enjoying the good life, practically on permanent vacation in the endless sunshine of southern California. Hollywood came to embody the boom time of the 1920s, where anyone with talent and luck could presumably get rich.

Movie stars increasingly appeared in photographs wearing furs and jewelry, walking advertisements for the material rewards of success. Actresses frequently promoted clothes and jewelry, but men were also part of the increasingly opulent lifestyle. Actor Adolphe Menjou, described as "the screen's most sophisticated gentleman," wore a French linen handkerchief, jade and diamond buttons on his waistcoat, and carried a gold cigarette case, according to a *Photoplay* article titled "Why Women Like Sophisticated Men." The author concludes that women "cannot afford to be seen with a man who appears ordinary."[13]

Monetary value came to define performers' worth. A 1925 *Photoplay* article describes the insurance policies protecting the actors' (or, more likely, the studios') assets. According to the story, Louise Lazenda's hair was insured for $100,000. Kathleen Key's neck was worth $25,000, while Edmund Lowe's nose had a value of $35,000. Blanche Sweet's face had a hefty price tag: $150,000 should something happen to it. Others had their legs, eyes, and weight covered by such policies.[14] As early as 1920, a star's bankability was a common topic, enumerating the celebrity-as-brand's earning potential from other marketing ventures and investments.[15]

With the growing attention paid to affluence, fan magazines encouraged readers to join in. Although by the 1920s the bulk of movie magazine ads were for beauty products, Ford ran a series of ads of a family looking out the window, spying a neighbor on their middle-class suburban street with a new car. "How did he get the money to buy a car?" the copy asks, noting that weekly payment plans make it possible for those with "even the most modest income" to own a car.[16] By 1927, more than three-quarters of all car purchases were made on credit, a development encouraged not only to increase sales, but to ensure a steady stream of revenue year round for the once seasonal auto industry.[17]

By this time the movies had all but abandoned working-class themes, and fan magazines reflected the economic growth of the 1920s and the dream of prosperity. For the most part, the ads for working-class jobs so common in the 1910s disappeared, but ads promoting upward mobility did not; calls for young women to enter contests to be in the movies remained, as did products for men to take charge of their careers.

These ads reflected the growing opportunities to shift from working-class to middle-class status, reflecting other advice literature of the time for self-made success during an era of economic expansion. As historian Charles R. Hearn describes in his analysis of this advice literature, independent, powerful businessmen were highly revered during these boom years, much as they would be again by the 1980s.[18] Success was increasingly considered the result of individual will, and entrepreneurship became practically a religion. A 1928 *Motion Picture Classic* ad for the book *Instantaneous Personal Magnetism* promised to teach readers —particularly salesmen and businessmen—how to "feel a new surge of power" and "lose all fear." "You *can* sway and control others. You *can*

Figure 3.1 Ads such as this one emphasized the possibility of middle-class status through consumption.

Source: Image from June 1925 issue of *Motion Picture* courtesy of University of Southern California Cinematic Arts Library.

command success. You *can* influence people to do the things you want them to do," the ad pledged (emphasis in original).[19] An ad for another book, *How to Work Wonders with Words*, promised to teach readers how to "dominate others almost overnight" by learning public speaking skills. "It is the power of forceful, convincing speech that causes one man to jump from obscurity to the presidency of a great corporation," and possibly even "a post of national importance."[20] Upward mobility seemed just around the corner for anyone willing to get in the game and work on themselves. The abundance the American Dream had always promised seemed to have arrived, and fan magazine articles and ads let readers know that success was rooted in hard work and personal achievement.

The Sin of Plenty

The indulgences of this new age of prosperity brought with it a serious moral backlash. With remnants of the Puritan ethic of self-denial still strong in the fibers of American culture, it is no surprise that morality tales of the evils of too much continually emerge in celebrity culture. Fan magazines described Hollywood as an almost Eden-like paradise where dreams came true. But much like in the biblical tale, with Eden comes a fall from grace. These morality tales centered around failures of self-control; just as Eve couldn't resist temptation, neither could some in Hollywood.

Hollywood's first major sex scandal erupted in 1921. Roscoe "Fatty" Arbuckle and friends allegedly spent a lost weekend of debauchery in a San Francisco hotel. When it was all over, actress Virginia Rappe was dead, and Arbuckle was believed to be the last one alone with Rappe in his hotel room. Her clothes torn, the presumption was that she was crushed under his great weight when he attempted to rape her, and Arbuckle was charged with manslaughter.[21]

Although medical evidence suggested that Rappe had died of a ruptured bladder and Arbuckle was acquitted (after three highly publicized trials), Hollywood's reputation as a den of iniquity remained. Scandals such as Arbuckle's reflected the view that in this place of plenty, women's virtue was fragile and easily corrupted if not protected by men and powerful social institutions. Consider that at this time in the Jim Crow South, lynching African-American men after alleged threats to white women's virtue was still common. Echoing initial concerns about the immorality of nickelodeons decades earlier, reformers took Hollywood to task, complaining that movies had the potential to corrupt the morals of the nation. One crusader, Canon Chase, general secretary of the Federal Motion Picture Council, called for censorship to ensure wholesome films and to rein in Hollywood's "pandering to the sensational."[22]

Not surprisingly, industry boosters were on the defense. Movie magazine articles focused on the virtue of movies—a 1920 *Photoplay* article titled "If Christ Went to the Movies" claimed that Jesus would approve since movies provide people with relaxation and enjoyment. Others argued that the censors themselves were the problem, "able to see filth that is invisible to the ordinary human eye," and that claims of immorality of movie people were highly exaggerated.[23] Leonard Hall wrote a satirical essay for *Photoplay* titled "Exposing the Hollywood Orgy," describing a Hollywood party that involved no debauchery but was instead heavy with shop talk. "Hollywood works too hard to monkey around all night over a bottle. The boys and girls are on the set bright and early, especially bright, or else!" Hall concludes, "Mother, keep the kiddies away from Hollywood. First, they may be talked to death. Second, they'll get to bed so early they won't be able to sleep past noon."[24]

Several other *Photoplay* articles insisted that Hollywood should not be singled out for the immorality of a few. "Matrimonial infelicity is not peculiar to any class of people these days," one story in the magazine concludes.[25] "The governor of a great state is sued for seduction . . . a leading banker is accused by his wife of illicit love affairs . . . But does the world conclude that governors, or bankers, or ministers, or lawyers—as a *class*—are therefore rotten . . .?" (emphasis in original). Rather than Hollywood being the problem, the author suggests it is instead its high profile, as "The most talked-of city of America . . . a small community populated by famous people who exist in the white glare of the merciless spotlight . . . [with] as much privacy . . . as a Broadway traffic policeman."[26] Speaking of Broadway, *Photoplay* reminded readers in a July 1920 article that stage performers were more likely to be at the mercy of a director—and perhaps his casting couch—than screen actors due to the greater complexity of studio operations.[27]

Still, the movie industry wanted to avoid any government regulation and to continue to enlarge its middle-class audience. The solution was to install a decency czar, Will Hays, in 1922. Hays devised a set of standards that studios had to follow beginning in 1927. Most of these restrictions involved sexuality, eliminating images of prostitution, obscenity, and "excessive or lustful kissing." Adultery could only be alluded to if the perpetrators were duly punished. Additionally, interracial relationships (that is, between African Americans and whites) were strictly forbidden.[28]

All of this happened in a backdrop of what might be called the true sexual revolution of the twentieth century, and concerns about shifts in the gender order brought about by an increase in opportunities for women. While the advent of the birth control pill came later in the century, diaphragms and condoms became widely available during the 1920s. With prosperity, the growth of cities, and greater opportunities for women within them, young women entered universities in larger numbers. In 1900, women comprised about 27 percent of college students. By 1928, almost 39 percent of college students were female.[29] That same year *Motion Picture Classic* advertised a new magazine, *College Humor*, featuring stories of "young women who have made their mark in college circles, in society, in careers . . . the Junior League, sororities, glimpses of women in business, the woman in the professional world, her ambitions, her resourcefulness and her accomplishments."[30]

Increasing college enrollments brought new opportunities for privacy away from parents. While we tend to look back on the past as a time of modesty compared with the present, concerns about young women's increasing openness to sexual experimentation grew during the 1920s as well. Growing prosperity increased leisure time for adolescents; more middle-class teens went to high school than ever before and were less responsible for contributing to the household income than their parents were during adolescence. With this growing independence came the opportunity to spend more time alone in automobiles or in darkened movie theaters, away from the watchful eye of family.

What played on the screens of the 1920s also concerned moral reformers. Perhaps because few silent films (or silent moviegoers) survive, many people are not aware of the sometimes risqué content of early films. While contemporary audiences may have seen a clip from *The Kiss* (1896)—a supposedly scandalous film very tame by contemporary standards, featuring a Victorian couple locked in an embrace kissing—most of us have not seen the silent films with nudity and explicit sexual themes. Likewise, movie magazines frequently featured risqué photos and ads for books that promised racy content. One book contained the "imagined love making" of historical figures, or so claimed its ad. Ads for the books *Primordial* and *Sinful Peck* detail how the "instincts of the race" surface when a boy and girl are shipwrecked on a deserted island.[31] Other books offered instructional manuals on sex, although only for married customers.

Fan magazines joined the debate about the amount of sex in movies. "I've been hearing on every side that the flappers were going to the dogs and the whole country was sex crazy . . . and look at the things people talk about that were never mentioned in public before," magazine writer Ivan St. Johns wrote in a 1926 issue of *Photoplay*.[32] At the same time, magazines reflected the increased openness about sexuality. A March 1926 advice column in *Photoplay* titled "To Pet or not to Pet" is one such example. A reader, presumably a young woman, writes, "Petting is my biggest problem . . . I get a kick out of petting and I think all girls do no matter how much they deny it . . . The boys all like it and I can't seem to make myself dislike it." Columnist Carolyn Van Wyck responds by saying that petting is okay, as long as it leads to marriage. Girls who are "husband hunting," Van Wyck warns, need to be especially careful not to go too far and lose the man's respect. Despite changes in sexual behavior and growing opportunities, articles such as this, as well as ads, reminded women that finding a husband was still the only respectable goal in the long run.[33]

Women's Virtue and Social Mobility

At their core, concerns about Hollywood morality were tied to fears about women's mobility. Opportunities in Hollywood and the increasingly automated labor force in America's growing cities increasingly drew young women, often beyond the traditional supervision of family members. The industry's critics might have been upset by movie content, but the changes in the status of women likely underscored calls for a more wholesome Hollywood. As with today, the hostility towards some women is quite palpable in the 1920s celebrity stories, especially if they are viewed as shallow, but most often this is the case if they refuse to conform to traditional gender arrangements by becoming a dutiful wife. As such, ads of this time play on the fear that being too independent will leave young women husbandless and alone.

It's no wonder that Hollywood seemed on the leading edge of this shift, where women had careers, not just jobs, and could sometimes make more money than men did. Concerns about the state of marriage grew in the 1920s, and much as today, Hollywood was blamed for its family-unfriendly culture. But as a 1925 *Photoplay* article commented that when an Iowa farmer abandons his wife and child, nobody outside the town knows about it, whereas a Hollywood divorce was national news.[34]

The meaning of marriage was clearly changing. Divorce rates nearly doubled from 84 divorces per thousand in 1906 to 166 per thousand in

1928.[35] Following World War I, when women took on some traditionally male jobs for the war effort, gender dynamics began to shift. Sex outside of marriage, while not new and certainly not discussed openly, became more frequent, particularly as more young women entered colleges and universities and lived independently.[36] Historian Stephanie Coontz recounts in *Marriage, a History: From Obedience to Intimacy, or How Love Conquered Marriage* that marriage's transition from a primarily economic arrangement to one based on romantic love and personal fulfillment took place throughout the last century. She notes that as love gradually became the ideal foundation for marriage, marriage itself became less stable. Concerns about marriage may seem like a contemporary issue, but as Coontz notes, worries about the future of marriage date back more than a century.[37] These concerns are clearly linked with women's upward mobility, as seen in fan magazine articles and ads.

One 1929 article claimed that men could one day become little more than "excess baggage" on a woman's quest for fame, especially if they were not also part of the movie business or did not earn more money than their rising star wives.[38] This decrease in economic interdependence, not widely experienced by most in the general population for another half-century, meant that marriage became more about fun and romance in celebrity culture than ever before. Gossip items told of players marrying after three-week courtships, and of multiple marriages and divorces before a star's twenty-fifth birthday. Marriage, in the gossip pages at least, seemed to be very volatile. A 1926 *Photoplay* article, "Why Women Like Sophisticated Men," reflected on this trend, noting that love and romance don't really last very long. "You hear of so many engagements that never reach the altar," a 1925 article called "Languishing Romances" lamented.[39]

While most American households still required the full-time labor of at least two adults, those who could afford to hire domestic help during the boom years of the 1920s could live well outside of marriage. An article about bachelor's homes viewed this trend as dangerous; writer Katherine Albert calls those who live comfortably outside of marriage "an attack upon the time honored custom."[40] Presumably, living uncomfortably in cramped, dirty quarters without home cooking serves as a prime motivation for men to get married. The movie bachelors who could hire decorators, cooks, and maids might have no need for wives, the author feared.

Figure 3.2 Despite more professional opportunities for women, ads warned that failure to monitor one's body continually would lead to loneliness.

Source: Image from July 1925 issue of *Photoplay* courtesy of University of Southern California Cinematic Arts Library.

While many ads used fears of social rejection to sell products starting in the 1920s, one of the biggest anxieties ads addressed was that the reader might never marry, or if they did, that they would not stay married for long.[41] The ads in movie magazines suggested that halitosis and body odor would prevent these busy (and clueless) women from getting married if they didn't stay focused on their appearance.

Movie magazines became one site of debate about women's mobility, and articles about movie stars contributed to concerns about the "new woman." A March 1922 *Photoplay* article written by legendary ladies' man

Rudolph Valentino gives readers decidedly mixed messages about women. "I do not like women who know too much," Valentino writes, but also complains that "A love affair with a stupid woman is like a cold cup of coffee."[42] The same year that Valentino's article ran, Gloria Swanson told *Photoplay* her ideas about "modern women," which she arguably was herself. Nonetheless, Swanson states that "No woman in the world is ever happy with a man unless that man is her master."[43]

Perhaps as women began to enter the workforce in slightly larger numbers and gain some financial independence—particularly in Hollywood— men were unsure of their place in this new society. A May 1927 article in *Motion Picture Classic* titled "Where *Men* are Men," (emphasis in original) makes very clear that the boundaries between men and women can be maintained, or at least that they were not as blurred in Hollywood as they might otherwise seem.[44] Notably, articles such as this were penned by men, who perhaps felt threatened by women's growing success as magazine writers. While most traditional journalism remained male-dominated, the new vocation of celebrity journalism offered many opportunities for women.

Throughout the 1920s, ads chided men for being weaklings, embarrassments to their gender, and disappointments to their wives. The solution that ads offer are books that promise to teach the reader how to broaden his shoulders, widen his neck, and develop "live, red-blooded, he-man muscle."[45] While in the ads targeting women all men seemed handsome and doting, the ads directed at men suggest that they are not any less flawed than their female counterparts. "Don't commit a crime against the woman you love," an ad for an exercise book warned men, claiming that many men are "UNFIT to assume the duties and responsibilities of a husband and father" if they were out of shape (emphasis in original).[46] "Could she love him were he bald?" another ad asks (the answer in the ad, as you might imagine, is no).[47] Love is too fragile, the ads indicate; to be anything but perfect means risking abandonment. While women could work on their complexions, smiles, and smells, men could improve their chances at love by bulking up, keeping their hair, or by taking dance lessons at an Arthur Murray dance studio.[48]

Fan magazine articles suggest that the new women could be dangerous. Not unlike our contemporary view of young female celebrities, the 1920s

Figure 3.3 Men were also warned by advertisers to monitor their bodies, and that they would be to blame for lack of success if they failed to do so.

Source: Image from June 1922 issue of *Picture Play* courtesy of University of Southern California Cinematic Arts Library.

Figure 3.4 Women's burgeoning independence was often described as threatening in articles such as this one from the December 1927 issue of *Motion Picture Classic*.

Source: Image courtesy of University of Southern California Cinematic Arts Library.

era starlets were characterized as shallow, good-time-girl flappers. Some girls, apparently, were born this way. A 1927 *Motion Picture Classic* article, "The Seven Ages of a Gold-Digger," portrays women as materialistic from birth to old age. "At six months our little gold-digger has learned to cry loud enough to make a gentleman fork over his new platinum watch," warns the author.[49]

A 1929 article in *Photoplay* fought suggestions that Hollywood is a "manless town" by describing Hollywood "girls" as materialistic schemers; worse than just gold-diggers, only platinum would do for these soulless she-devils. If men had lost ground, these articles suggest, it was taken away by 1920s-era bad girls.[50] Rather than the stock market crash that year, the real threat to manhood was cast as the dreaded new woman. And a 1929 article quotes a psychologist who lends his expertise to reaffirming that the new women were shallow and simple. "Women are child's play," the article states, while including "analysis" of women's temperaments based on their hair color (blondes are exhibitionists, brunettes "experience love emotions most keenly," and, of course, red-heads are fiery).[51]

Women had to be careful not to alienate men completely; fan magazine articles warned of the dangers of being too independent, and ads seemed to provide a remedy to win over men. Marriage remained the primary vehicle of social mobility for most women of this era, despite legal and social changes that enabled women to take a more active role in public life. *Photoplay* promised new wives that its ads "would help her to become the capable, wise housewife she wants so much to be."[52]

"How can a man keep his wife a sweetheart? Can a shopworn girl happily marry?" an ad for an advice book asked. Elinor Glyn, author of *This Passion Called Love* and *The Philosophy of Love*, promised that these books could offer the "Solution to all the perplexing problems of love and marriage, about which most of us know so little."[53] Another book, *What Made Him Propose*, also promised to help readers unlock the mysteries of marriage.[54] These and other ads in the 1920s suggested that love and marriage were in trouble, but for the price of a book consumers could obtain the secrets to getting the love they wanted.

Ads for beauty products suggested that through increased self-improvement efforts, women could eventually marry. Rather than the changing social and economic environment putting strains on marriage,

Figure 3.5 Ads admonished women that ignoring domestic chores could lead to loneliness.

Source: Image from the February 1928 issue of *Motion Picture* courtesy of University of Southern California Cinematic Arts Library.

personal hygiene ads suggested the cause was personal failure. "Often a *Bridesmaid*, but never a *Bride*," chided an ad for Listerine, warning that the dreaded halitosis could easily mean being single at "that tragic thirty mark" (emphasis in original).[55] Body odor would also mean men would turn away, warned an ad for Odorono.[56] A bad complexion would also scare the men away, but clear skin, courtesy of Ivory soap, could mean an abundance of dates. "Goodness! *Another* suitor?" exclaims the woman who uses Ivory (emphasis in original).[57] Poor housekeeping would also mean a lifetime of loneliness. "Which girl would you marry?" a cleanser ad asks, showing a dirty sink next to a clean one.[58] For women with jobs—or those even interested in a career—ads such as this reminded them that while they might be able to earn money on their own, ignoring domestic skills would derail their future. Despite modest opportunities for women in the workforce, the wage gap between men and women did not begin to erode significantly until 1980. Hollywood stars aside, most women still depended on men's earnings for economic survival, and marriage was still vital for women financially.[59]

While during the 1910s movie magazines stressed that women could be successful by appearing less working class, increasingly thinness became equated with social mobility, hard work, and self-control. The 1920s were a perfect storm of sorts for encouraging restriction from plenty. As social mobility became more of a reality and starvation seemed less likely for many Americans during the boom years of the 1920s after World War I, slimming and reducing took off. When the United States entered the Great War in 1917, leaders stressed the importance of food conservation. During the 1920s, food preparation times fell because more households had refrigerators and canned goods and frozen foods became more available.[60] During times of want, the focus on weight loss typically takes a back seat to maintaining strength.[61] In the 1920s, however, starvation was no longer seen as the biggest threat to health, and thinness came to symbolize success rather than economic failure. Movie magazine articles detailed how movie stars such as Clara Bow became successful only after losing weight. Described as "a fat little schoolgirl" who exercised her way to fame, Bow "was fatter than most of her chums" but through hard work and determination lost weight and became a star.[62]

As the war years gave way to prosperity, there was a heightened focus on slimming, particularly in celebrity magazines, which advertised a variety

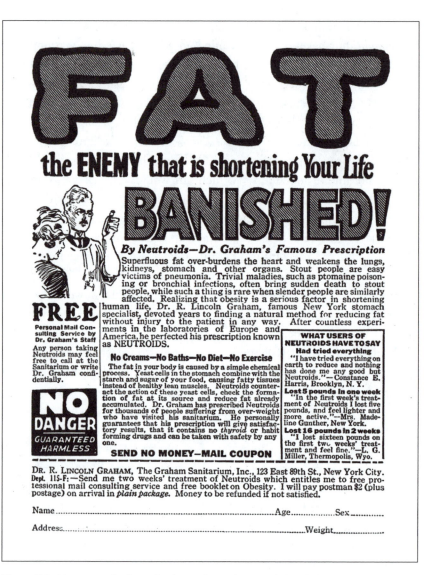

Figure 3.6 As women gained new freedom and wore less restrictive clothing, ads such as these emphasized the importance of being thin.

Source: Image from the June 1925 issue of *Photoplay* courtesy of University of Southern California Cinematic Arts Library.

of new products that were geared towards thin women. The passing of the Nineteenth Amendment in 1920 was a watershed moment in the women's movement, and many suffragists had engaged in hunger strikes to draw attention to their cause in the years prior to its passing. Suffragettes also perceived corsets as patriarchal prisons, but once removed they needed to regulate their own bodies. Having a less-rounded or matronly figure also represented freedom in that women would be taking control of their own bodies by reducing. In contrast to Victorian ideals of frail, fainting women, by the 1920s more active notions of womanhood became acceptable for those in the middle and upper classes.[63] At the same time, too much attention to one's appearance seemed to suggest the sin of vanity and arouse moral suspicion.

On the other hand, much as today, fan magazines criticized women who became too thin for *losing* control of their bodies. Following the 1926 death of actress Barbara La Marr from tuberculosis, *Photoplay* ran a three-part series on how "Reduceomania" caused "Wholesale Murder and Suicide." Apparently, Ms. La Marr "fell victim to fashion's demand" and was reducing at the time of her death. The article quotes doctors, warning of the danger for women in particular, in their "desire to emulate the corsetless, pliant, bob-haired flapper." Dieting itself, the article claims, has become a disease. "Women are courting tuberculosis, grave stomach disorders, Bright's disease, glandular ailments, disastrous nervous troubles and even death" by reducing, the second of the series warned.[64] In the nineteenth and early twentieth century it was not uncommon for doctors to attribute death to tuberculosis rather than dieting, as the disease also created the emaciated appearance of starvation and was significantly more common. Historian Joan Jacobs Brumberg argues that the shift towards self-regulation and internal control coincided with less female supervision, especially for those living in cities. Girls and women in the early twentieth century saw self-control as not just a way to lose weight, but a sign of moral fortitude.[65]

As Brumberg details in *Fasting Girls: The History of Anorexia Nervosa*, from medieval times through to the nineteenth century "fasting girls" claimed to have abstained from eating for weeks, months, or even years. Rather than being seen as vain or mentally ill, these girls were thought to embody spiritual purity and holiness. Some claimed to eat nothing but the holy Eucharist wafer, leading many at the time to think that their lack of consumption was a bona fide miracle. Most of these claims were later debunked and found to be fraudulent, but historically there has been a long-standing connection between declining food and sanctity.[66] And the growth of celebrity culture helped promote the promise that self-control through dieting could bring success.

From Boom to Bust

Throughout the silent movie era, the Hollywood fantasy of joining an exciting new industry promising the good life seemed limitless. Looking right, working hard, and being lucky was supposed to guarantee upward mobility. Those who made careers in the movies might not have all been super-rich, but they had seemed to achieve the early-twentieth-century dream of prosperity and freedom from punishing physical labor. The feel-good days of early Hollywood suggested that the only direction a successful performer could go was up. That these careers could come to an abrupt end with the advent of the talkies at the end of the 1920s would have been unimaginable just a few years prior, as movie audiences grew and theaters became larger and fancier. Just as the American Dream suggested hard work only led to success, downward mobility in the film industry had not seemed possible.

From the time the first movie with sound was released (*The Jazz Singer* in 1927) to the end of the decade, silent films gradually faded away. Many silent stars would not make the transition; the fan magazines of the 1910s and 1920s reflect the limited staying power of many silent performers, whose names are mostly unknown to all but the most ardent film buffs today. For many who seemed to have achieved the American Dream in the silent movie industry, the introduction of sound put a rapid end to their careers. In 1929, fan magazine articles detailed the plight of those who lost roles with the introduction of "the microphone era." Performers became secretaries, sales clerks, taxi drivers, and waitresses. One story details a conversation the writer had at a "shabby little restaurant on the beach" with a waitress who only recently had been in movies. "Please, for God's sake, don't tell anybody you saw me here . . . I'm just tiding myself over until people get sick of these stupid talkies."[67]

Language became a problem for many actors, particularly those with accents considered undesirable. Foreign performers were no longer part of the visual melting pot of whiteness, and even American-born actors with regional accents could be banished from the industry. As film scholar Robert Sklar noted, critics worried that working-class accents could "corrupt the idiom" of American English.[68] Dialect coaches worked with actors to make sure they could make the transition to speaking roles and to create an air of sophistication that would also reflect notions of the upper class, which would become so central in the films and celebrity culture of the 1930s.

Perhaps it is a coincidence that the crash of many movie actors' careers would foreshadow an even bigger jolt of downward mobility felt not just in Hollywood, but worldwide. The stock market's crash in 1929 and the Depression that followed posed serious challenges to the notion of the American Dream. During the roaring twenties, success appeared to be a reward based on personal effort and an individual's personality, both in Hollywood and in business. But no longer would having the right look, weight, or wardrobe mean a job in movies; neither would simply having the ability to "dominate others" in conversation—as so many ads suggested—mean success in the business world.

The prosperity of the 1920s came largely on credit, based on the assumption that the economic improvements of the first two decades of the century would continue unabated, and that saving was less necessary than in the past. If any of this sounds like the crash of 2008, there are certainly similarities. Both eras featured the illusion of prosperity based on easier access to credit. And some people did become very wealthy during these two decades: as in the 2000s, during the 1920s the wealthiest 1 percent of the population controlled more than 20 percent of the nation's wealth. By contrast, between 1945 and 1985, the wealthiest percent's share hovered at around 10 percent.[69] Despite the fan magazines' suggestion that massive wealth was just a diet, correspondence class, or starring role away, only a minority of Americans enjoyed the riches associated with the Roaring Twenties.

As this chapter details, the Puritan ethic of hard work, self restraint, and delayed gratification might have become less central to the American Dream during the boom years of the 1920s, but moral suspicion about celebrity culture revealed lingering vestiges. The crash at the end of the decade called many of these beliefs into question: if people worked hard, saved their money in a bank, and yet still became unemployed and lost everything when their bank failed, what does this imply about the American Dream? The next chapter answers this question, as well as how celebrity culture shifted in the wake of the dream's biggest challenge. Celebrity culture became an important vehicle in maintaining the fantasy of upward mobility when most people were headed in the other direction.

4

PULL YOURSELF UP BY YOUR BOOTSTRAPS

PERSONAL FAILURE AND THE GREAT DEPRESSION

The American Dream and capitalism itself would be tested during the Depression. Unemployment shot up from an average of 3 percent during the 1920s to nearly 25 percent in 1933, and did not return to single-digit levels until the United States entered World War II.[1] With no social safety net (no unemployment insurance, and no Federal Deposit Insurance when thousands of banks failed and people lost their savings), Americans had every reason to doubt the notion that hard work would yield success. Millions had worked hard and had seen their circumstances improve, only to lose everything through no fault of their own.

The Depression challenged the notion that anyone with drive and determination could improve themselves enough to become middle class. Additionally, the degree of inequality between richest and poorest was at its highest point during the Depression; some economists have estimated that nearly three-quarters of the U.S. population lived in poverty during the mid-thirties.[2] The dramatic economic downturn created a challenge for the movie industry and celebrity culture, which previously had served as a champion of the American Dream of success through hard work. Even the fantasy industry was not immune to the economic downturn—box office revenues slumped and nearly one in three movie theaters had closed by 1933.[3] While about 65 percent of the American public went to the movies at least once a week in 1930, in 1933 only 40 percent did.[4]

However, if your only source of American history was a movie fan magazine, you might think the Great Depression never happened. Rather than confront the discrepancy between the dream and the nightmare so many people experienced during this decade, celebrity fan magazines (and many of the decade's movies) focused even more on a fantasy of romance, wealth, and privilege. While this could have easily alienated many fans, celebrity culture was perhaps a main mechanism for keeping the American Dream alive during this time, amplifying the notion that becoming fabulously wealthy was possible even during the Depression.

Besides publishing tales of massive wealth, fan magazine articles and advertisements came with warnings about personal failure. Hollywood has-beens appeared to be to blame for their downward mobility, and articles warned women that family problems were likely their fault if they were too independent. Desperate advertisers warned consumers that a failure to use their products would lead to loneliness and divorce. Rather than the economic circumstances, these stories suggested that individuals brought problems associated with the Depression on themselves. The fan magazines' fantasies served both as a distraction from the faltering economic system as well as a salve that might act to maintain social stability during a time ripe with potential for unrest. Rather than simply a top-down imposition, it is likely that readers could take solace in the notion that it was still possible to become rich in America, even during the Depression.

This chapter examines three central questions. First, why did celebrity stories emphasize massive personal wealth during the Depression when so many people lived in poverty? Second, how are concerns about independent women and divorce related to the economic downturn? And third, how did both fan magazine articles and ads support the notion of individualism in the face of a structural collapse of the economy?

Celebrities in Fantasyland

As historian Charles R. Hearn details in his book *The American Dream in the Great Depression*, the "gap between myth and reality" widened during the Depression, venturing into the realm of fairytale.[5] During the Depression years, Americans were likely to "cling to their expectations even if this meant ignoring or distorting objective reality," Hearn concludes.[6] Not only did the American Dream provide a source of hope for those struggling during the Depression, images of wealthy celebrities served as a useful diversion during a time when many people did begin to question the future of American capitalism.

Fan magazines mostly presented a portrait of lives of wealth, opulence, and leisure. The stars of the day certainly did not seem to be strapped for the most part, nor did they appear to scale back lavish lifestyles. If anything, the celebrity culture of the 1930s suggested that movie stars were part of an American aristocracy and populated a fantasy life of abundance. This might seem counterintuitive; one might predict people suffering for basic survival would at the very least feel resentful of, if not downright hostile towards, increasingly fabulous displays of celebrities' wealth. As Mrs. A. Fessia of New York City wrote to *Photoplay* in March 1933:

> In these hard times it has been those pictures of sophistication and glamour and grand people that have made us more dissatisfied. They have helped to magnify our trouble, until we have forgotten how to smile.[7]

Some fans, however, seemed to appreciate the diversion from the grind of the Depression, as this March 1933 letter to *Photoplay* from J.L. Thomson, of Lynchburg, Virginia, indicates:

> Temporarily unemployed, dejected and dog-tired, I wandered into the theater today. I was so "down in the dumps," I hardly knew what was showing, and cared still less, suspecting I'd sleep through most of it anyway . . . What a tonic it turned out to be! And what a buoyant spirited fellow emerged two hours later! Faith restored in my country, myself and my fellow citizens!"[8]

Helen Payne of Chattanooga, Tennessee seems to concur that movies should provide a "tonic" in a letter to *Photoplay* in May 1932:

> The other night I was feeling very downhearted, having just lost my job. I spent my last money for a movie, hoping it would cheer me up. But it didn't, for in five minutes I was weeping right out loud in public, for the whole picture was about the troubles of a

heroine whose husband had been killed. Now I ask you, is attending movies like that a way to forget your troubles? Everyone is blue these days. I thought movies were for pleasure. Why do we want to see suffering on the screen? I think it is the duty of every motion picture studio to cut out the heavy drama and give us light, wholesome comedies.[9]

And just as Ms. Payne suggested, movies and celebrity culture during this period provided fodder for dreaming of better days ahead. Despite the economic crisis, Americans had not abandoned the dream en masse.

Instead, stars' lives seemed fun, carefree, and affluent. Gossip pages expanded, including more photos than in previous years. These pictures were clearly staged and intentionally presented numerous images of wealth. Stars on exotic vacations, wearing opulent evening attire at movie premieres or at famous nightspots became commonplace, as were photos of celebrities frolicking on the beach. Child star Shirley Temple might not have been photographed at nightclubs, but *Photoplay* featured the bungalow specially built for her to play and take her meals while on the set. She had her own miniature dinette for mealtime, a reception room and a radio, all scaled down to a child's size—certainly a luxury at a time when many parents struggled to maintain roofs over children's heads.[10]

No expense was spared for the children of stars either. Marlene Dietrich's baby had a bodyguard, according to a 1932 *Photoplay* story. In the wake of the Lindbergh kidnapping for ransom that same year, other wealthy celebrities took no chances. The article, "How Movie Babies are Guarded," tells of the bodyguards and rudimentary security systems set up to protect against ransom kidnappings. In describing the lengths to which stars would go in order to maintain security, the story also lists the gates, private roads, secret alarms, round-the-clock sentries, and servants employed in order to protect the super-rich from the rest of the world. In this context, living behind gates off of private roads in homes comparable to "a baron's castle," as one article described, does not seem excessive, but necessary.[11] Ransom kidnappings have been and continue to be most likely in societies with vast degrees of economic inequality; it is likely that the threat posed to these children was very real.[12] And yet in all of the discussion of the precautions celebrities took to protect their

Figure 4.1 Fan magazine articles emphasized the glamorous lives of celebrities during the Depression.
Source: Image from the September 1932 issue of *Photoplay* courtesy of University of Southern California Cinematic Arts Library.

families, the stories make no mention of the underlying reasons that they might have been at higher risk for kidnapping.

The Hollywood publicity machine continued to crank out tales of celebrity wealth throughout the Depression. An October 1937 *Motion Picture* magazine spread, "It's the Sporting Thing to Do," features movie stars enjoying lives of leisure, which many Americans could only dream of in a year when unemployment remained high, at 14 percent.[13] Their activities were decidedly upscale: playing golf, tennis, and polo, riding their own horses, and swimming in their own pools.[14] When they weren't in their own pools, the stars attended pool parties and had tennis matches with other famous friends.

Big stars could even afford to buy more friends, referred to as "stooges," similar to entourage members today. A 1934 *Photoplay* article described the many types of stooges, some of whom served as diet monitors, personal assistants, sycophants, or protectors, while others were basically professional partiers. Regardless of responsibility, all were paid to make their star's life easier.[15] In contrast to fan magazine stories about people like Charlie Chaplin from earlier decades, Depression-era tales focused much more on celebrity life as fun rather than hard work. Tales of excess only fed the fantasy.

Gossip pages also revealed the stars' salaries, which seemed to be growing while most Americans' incomes were shrinking. While this could have been a source of resentment, the stories enumerating celebrity wealth seemed to suggest that it was still possible to earn a lot of money in America. According to a March 1937 gossip item, Carole Lombard signed a contract with Paramount that paid $150,000 per movie at three movies per year. Her annual income of $450,000 would be the equivalent of more than $6.8 million in 2010.[16] Actors had so much money they sometimes turned away paychecks, as Roland Young apparently did after receiving an additional $7,000 (equivalent to turning away more than $106,000 today) when shooting for a film ran long. "I stopped work every day at five sharp, so I don't feel entitled to overtime because they had to shoot longer," Young told *Motion Picture* magazine.[17] Despite their large paychecks, actors were not as financially independent as they might have seemed on the surface. With the studio system firmly in place, they had relatively little control over their films, their image, and even their incomes. Stars who overstepped their boundaries could be shelved indefinitely or purposely cast in unflattering projects, while studios reaped the profits.[18]

Nonetheless, the image of freewheeling celebrities persisted in gossip pages. A 1937 gossip column reported that Margaret Sullavan and husband William Wyler bet MGM executive Paul Kohner and his wife $1,000 (more than $15,000 today and close to the median household income at the time) on who would have a baby first.[19] Actor Noah Beery paid off more than $200,000 (the equivalent of more than $3 million in 2010) of Hollywood debt by finding success in British films, according to the gossip column.[20]

For the average household struggling to get by on just over a $1,000 a year, these dollar amounts would have been enormous. In fact, according to the U.S. Census, nearly ten million families had no income at all in 1939.[21]

Despite the reality of hard times for most Americans, ads for stays at luxury hotels such as the Drake in Chicago maintain the fantasy of living a life of opulence, and even ads for everyday products contained elements of glamour and sophistication.[22] A 1933 ad for hand cream featured a woman using a washboard and tub to clean clothes while wearing an

Figure 4.2 Advertisements frequently included people dressed in evening wear, such as this woman doing the laundry.

Source: Image from the March 1933 issue of *Photoplay* courtesy of University of Southern California Cinematic Arts Library.

evening gown.[23] A Noxema skin cream ad included a woman in an evening gown with a tuxedoed man behind her.[24] Others depicted successful women in business; an ad for nail polish notes that "You absolutely can't tell the Girl with a Career from the social butterfly these days. She wears the same elegant clothes, lunches at the same smart restaurants and goes in for the same alluring Variety in nail tints." The ad insists that nail polish makes simple clothes "look like a Paris original."[25]

High society figures also appeared regularly in ads. A 1934 ad for Camel cigarettes featured Mrs. Thomas M. Carnegie, Jr., who, according to the ad copy, winters on "Cumberland Island off the coast of Georgia," summers in Newport, always travels with her dog, and "is a deft and delightful hostess," her special dish being shrimp Newburgh. "Camels are made from finer, <u>more expensive</u> tobaccos than any other popular brand," the ad notes (emphasis in original).[26] It is curious that high society figures such as Mrs. Carnegie and models in evening wear would become common components of advertising during the depths of the Depression. Rather than face a serious challenge to the American Dream and capitalism itself, advertisers cranked the dream machine into high gear when people otherwise had little reason to believe in its promise. But there were subtle hints of the economic crisis in the celebrity magazines, too.

Downward Mobility and Personal Failure

While the magazines rarely mention the Depression directly, occasionally they ran stories about a celebrity's slide from fame. A 1932 article, "Stars Who Have Vanished," details the plight of stars who did not cross over into talkies.[27] The label "box office poison" could derail even the biggest star, as producers became risk averse during the Depression. "Careers hang by the thin thread of fate," noted an article called "Nobody is Safe in Hollywood." "Everyone's value is just as great as the success or failure of the last picture they were in."[28] An ad for malted milk reflected this job-related anxiety. *King Kong* star Fay Wray and co-star Bruce Cabot are pictured at the studio commissary eating sandwiches and drinking milkshakes. "We stay slim . . . or we lose our contracts," the ad copy reads, implying that malted milk is a diet drink.[29]

For the most part, the stories suggested that the celebrity was solely responsibly for their decline, rather than the structural changes in both the industry (from silent movies to talkies) and the broader economy. Take, for example, a 1931 *Photoplay* story about Francis X. Bushman, who apparently went from earning $6 million dollars during his film career in the 1920s to losing it all. "Today he is flat broke—but oh, he had a swell time!" Rather than the victim of economic circumstances, his fortune disappeared because, as he happily admitted, he spent it all living the high life. "I'm not a bit sorry I spent it. I had a whale of a good time . . . I circled the globe thrice, and have visited more than forty countries."[30]

This is no morality tale, no warning about what a reversal of fortune can do, nor is this story in any way a critique of consumer capitalism. Bushman reveals no regret in hiring a chauffeur, a valet, and "five or six secretaries" in his heyday and vows he will never beg for work, confident in his ability to earn a living.[31] Losing a fortune apparently isn't a tragedy, it is a great party. And while millions of Americans lost their savings through no fault of their own when banks failed, Bushman's tale is one of personal responsibility. He brought it on himself, in keeping with the mythology of the American Dream, where we are all solely responsible for our failure or success.

Job insecurity spread beyond onscreen talent. Director D.W. Griffith, director of *Birth of a Nation* and a filmmaker whose techniques helped to shape modern movies during the 1920s, denied allegations that he was out of money in an article called "The Star-Maker Whose Dreams Turned to Dust."[32] Despite making more than 400 movies that grossed more than $60 million, the magazine suggested that he made poor business decisions. "He was never extravagant in the spectacular, superficial way that some others have been," but instead it was his failure to take out patents that cost him millions.[33] His story is another tale of someone at the top of his profession who supposedly lost it all due to personal failure.

In sharp contrast to earlier decades, when articles and ads suggested that Hollywood's dream was available to anyone willing to take a chance, a 1936 *Photoplay* story, "They Aren't All Actresses in Hollywood," details the difficulty many people face getting and keeping non-performing jobs in the movie industry. One woman (with a Columbia University education) had risen from the secretarial pool to translate French scripts and "was able to buy a car, lovely clothes, and live in a charming home," but had to work long hours, which contributed to the collapse of her marriage. "And then one dismal day in 1933, at the very depths of the

Depression, the studio shut down tight and Simonne's beautiful job vanished in the holocaust. There were dozens of girls in the same jobless boat, but that didn't help Simonne's spirits in the least." Despite seven years of industry experience, it took her over a year to find a new job as a stenographer—at less than half of her previous weekly salary.[34]

Hers and other stories serve as a contrast to the pictures and articles that suggested unlimited wealth was still available in Hollywood. "There are two hundred girls waiting for Sally Page's job sewing," a caption under the seamstress's photo noted.[35] While one of the only movie magazine articles to mention the Depression by name, this story is laden with happy endings for the industry's hard-working insiders: they may lose their marriages, but in the end those featured all eventually found jobs. Ironically, stories such as these heighten Hollywood's allure of exclusivity and enhance the Hollywood fantasy. Even if it's only a few who find work, the glamour and excitement seem well worth the risk, especially for people who might have few other options.

Most signs of the Depression were given as hints rather than explicit tales of loss like Simonne's, Bushman's, or Griffith's. A photo in a gossip column features actor Charles Kaley with his hand in his pocket. The caption above quotes Kaley, "Keep one hand free for hand-shaking, and the other on your bank-roll."[36] A photo of three starlets in a pool is called "the most annoying picture of the month" by the magazine, deriding the women for "playing around in a Hollywood pool while the rest of us slave."[37]

While most magazine ads either ignored the Depression, or as noted earlier, seemed to go out of their way to feature images of wealth, some ads recognized that consumers needed to watch their money carefully. Ad copy for Colgate toothpaste reads, "Though it costs only _half_ as much I like it _twice_ as well," a sharp contrast to the majority of ads that mostly ignored value as a selling point at the time (emphasis in original).[38] And unlike in the prosperous 1920s, ads for products promising jobs reappeared in movie magazines during the Depression. "Have You a Boy Friend Who Needs a Job?" asks an ad for _Opportunity_, a magazine for job seekers, which encourages women to purchase a subscription for the man in her life. "You will probably be doing him a great favor at a time when he needs it," suggests the ad.[39] Women increasingly needed to work in the paid labor force, if they were able to find a job in the first place.

Have You
A BOY FRIEND
WHO NEEDS
A JOB?

YOUNG woman, you can help him get one! Strange as it may seem in these times, there is a group of 500 manufacturers seeking bright young men—and women, too.

They can work right in their own home towns, and are offered an amazing variety of quick-selling novelties and high grade merchandise which every home must have.

Go right out today and invest ten cents in a copy of OPPORTUNITY MAGAZINE. It's on all newsstands. Give it to him and say, "Boy, there's your chance. Don't say I never gave you a start in life. Some day you may come to me and thank me for starting you in a real business career."

Even if he has never sold anything —if he has the gumption and any personality at all, he can make a success of direct selling.

OPPORTUNITY tells him how to do it. The positions are there. It's up to him.

Obey your impulse and do it today. You will probably be doing him a great favor at a time when he needs it.

If your newsstand is sold out of OPPORTUNITY MAGAZINE, send us 10 cents, and we will mail a copy to him immediately. Address Dept. B.

OPPORTUNITY

The Magazine That *Finds Jobs* and *Teaches Salesmanship*

919 North Michigan Avenue
CHICAGO

Figure 4.3

Signs of the Depression occasionally seeped into fan magazines, as in this ad asking readers if the man in their life needs a job.

Source: Image from the May 1932 issue of *Photoplay* courtesy of University of Southern California Cinematic Arts Library.

One ad promised women that they could earn $32 a week selling hosiery (and keep free samples for themselves).[40] As many families became dependent on women's wages, the balance of power between men and women continued to shift.

The Threat of Women's Independence

Rather than the collapse of the economy, fan magazines often cast independent women as a central reason for families struggling to get by and remain intact. Women gradually gained ground in the labor force during the Depression: from 23 percent of all women aged 14-and-over working for wages in 1920 to over 25 percent in 1940.[41] This may seem like only a modest increase, but the real change was in the percentage of *married* women who worked: 23 percent in 1920 compared with 36 percent in 1940.[42] Women's labor was cheaper, making their employment prospects better at times, which further shifted the gendered balance of power.

Hollywood once again was on the cusp of these changes, as its female stars provided visible representations of female independence and wealth. A 1932 *Photoplay* article, "Hollywood is a Woman's Town," boasts that "women decide how men shall spend their money and their leisure hours."[43] That same year a *Motion Picture* story, "The Women Who Made them Famous" credits women with the success of stars like Clark Gable and Maurice Chevalier.[44] While this handful of famous women had far more money or power than the vast majority of American women did at the time, they served as symbols of the threat some felt might arise as women gained status.

Clearly actor Douglas Fairbanks, Jr., felt threatened by women's rise in Hollywood. Fairbanks expressed his displeasure about the increasing status of female stars in a 1934 *Photoplay* article. He claimed that he was quitting Hollywood because leading ladies got too much attention.

> The best that any [male star] can look forward to is the ignominy of finding himself cast opposite the woman star who is momentarily in the ascendant. And to submit to that sort of thing is too stultifying for most men.

Perhaps his disdain was related to his 1933 divorce from Joan Crawford, who seemed unlikely to defer to anyone, onscreen or otherwise. Perhaps her star power, and that of her peers, left some bitterness. His last film, he complained, was "all [Katharine] Hepburn from start to finish."[45]

Hepburn's rise to fame during this time was no coincidence. She embodied both independence and aristocracy, and though she was frequently cast as the romantic lead, she had a toughness that many Depression-era audiences could likely draw strength from. That is, until she was deemed "box office poison" by the end of the decade. Her film comeback in 1940's *The Philadelphia Story*, originally a Broadway play written for her, highlights a central struggle of the "new woman": she may be too independent for her own good. Her character's father even blames her independence for his infidelity. She reunites with her ex-husband in the film (played by Cary Grant) only after agreeing to become more like a good yacht: easy to control.

Women who seemed beyond male control were the villains of 1930s celebrity tales. A 1936 *Photoplay* story claims that men and women in Hollywood were truly equal (never mind that all studio bosses and nearly all directors were male), but this was no celebratory piece: equality created the dreaded "predatory female." The men in Hollywood, apparently, were no longer safe but were ruthlessly pursued by these new women, a "reversal of the age-old formula of boy seeks girl."[46]

These women, and others like them, did not just threaten the unsuspecting, innocent men of Hollywood, such as Clark Gable, Gary Cooper, and Robert Taylor, who are named in the article, but America more generally. "She is wearing apron strings," actress Kay Johnson says in an interview with *Motion Picture Classic*, "with the happiness of some struggling, nagged male dangling from the ends." The article, aptly titled "Is the Devil a Woman?" answers yes, citing Eve succumbing to temptation, Helen of Troy causing war, and Salome's seduction of John the Baptist as proof. She warns that we are "on our guard against bad women who are obviously such—the siren with her painted sneer, the flirt with her shallow mind, [and] the parasite with her empty heart." But we really have to be on guard for the seemingly "good" but devious woman—"the Devil's own masquerade."[47]

While strong women might terrorize their hapless husbands, they are also cast as the central cause of divorce. "Are Women Stars the Home Wreckers of Hollywood?" asked *Motion Picture* in 1932 (the answer was yes). Women who were more famous, and especially those who were wealthier than their husbands, allegedly caused significant threats to their marriages. The article offers no solutions, but the message not to make more money than the man of the house is clear. In the depths of the Depression this could indeed be a problem for women able to find work if their mates could not.[48]

Several celebrity interviews supported the notion that changes in the gender order would doom a marriage. "To make a success of marriage, a woman must lead her man's life!" said actor Frank Morgan in an article called "A Private Wife for Me." "I want to be <u>head</u> man at home," he said, noting that a wife's focus should always be on taking care of her husband and supporting his career (emphasis in original). A wife with a career, especially in show business, would distract her from fulfilling her duties to her husband.[49] And while actor Edmund Lowe, married to actress Lilyan Tashman, believed that women should have a career of their own, his rationale is anything but feminist in nature. "Most American wives have too little to interest them and therefore too much idle time on their hands." And these "idle" women, according to Lowe, often fail to get their housework done or provide proper meals for their husbands. His wife, he bragged, never neglected her household duties even though she worked full time.[50]

Hollywood might have been populated with ambitious women, but these women were doomed to fail at marriage, according to many of this era's celebrity profiles. In a 1936 article tellingly titled, "Why Madge Evans Has Never Married," the actress states "career before marriage for me!" She goes on to say that she plans to "finish one job before [she] begin[s] another," implying that women can have one or the other, but not both. The article's author agrees, noting that if she were to try and do both at once, "the chances are ninety to a hundred against her."[51] A *Modern Screen* article focused on young rising star Deanna Durbin, and noted that her success could put her at a disadvantage on the marriage market. "Before she is twenty-one, Deanna will have earned $1,600,000. Will her wealth be a stumbling block to marital bliss?" Clearly, occupational success is viewed as threatening to the traditional gender order and therefore one's prospects for marriage.[52]

Ginger Rogers has "shelved romance," according to an article called "No Time for Love."[53] "Rosalind Russell has had thirty-one years of spinsterhood and thinks maybe enough's enough," according to another story. Rather than defending her single status, Russell's response supports the idea that marriage is the only path to happiness. "I think it's unhealthy to live alone," she agreed.[54] While Cary Grant's single status was also the subject of a 1940 article, it was tellingly titled "Why Cary Grant is Hard to Get."[55] His bachelor status makes him a prize to be won rather than someone to pity.

Other articles instructed readers—mostly female—that women's independence was wholly unnatural. A 1933 *Photoplay* article featuring an interview with famed psychologist John B. Watson assures readers that it is a primal need for men to be in charge. In fact, the expert concludes, some women actually prefer men who beat them. "It's quite possible, of course, that you fit our description of the woman who would desert home and fireside and all the nice, safe things of life after just one good, resounding smack from that hardy fellow," the article mentions, "but clearly you would be in the minority."[56] Rather than the effects of the Depression, any instability in marriage was supposedly the fault of an independent woman unwilling to be dominated by (or beaten, in this case) a strong man. The message was clear: marriage brought security, and those women who failed to maintain a marriage were to blame for their instability.

It is ironic that at a time when the Depression created economic challenges for many families, female ambition came to be defined as the most important threat to romance and marriage. The romantic fantasy serves as a counterweight, a lure towards the traditional and away from changes inevitable during an economic downturn, when women's wages would be vital to many households, and few women could afford the idleness actor Edmund Lowe bitterly complained about. The Depression did more than destabilize families economically; it threatened to destabilize the gender order by challenging the industrial-age notion that men could earn wages to support their families.

Downward Mobility and Divorce

As during times of war, the economic crisis strained many marriages. Financial worries can be a major source of stress in any relationship, and the Depression served as another threat to early-twentieth-century marriages. Divorce was still rare but nearly doubled between 1920 and 1930.[57] The divorce rate gradually crept up during the 1930s, from

1.6 divorces per thousand in 1930 to 2.0 in 1940.[58] This might seem like a minute increase, but economist Tomas Cvrcek suggests that "marriages which broke down under the strains of the Depression ... were only officially divorced a few years later."[59] Many marriages essentially ended through desertion, even though the couple might not have sought a legal divorce right away. In 1932, the marriage rate per thousand dipped to its lowest level since data were first gathered in 1887; less than 8 per thousand Americans married that year.

During the Depression marriage became part of the fantasy of upward mobility in fan magazines. Unlike many other Americans, wealthy celebrities could afford to get married and live on their own. Love was a central topic of many articles, featuring stars sharing details about their love lives in articles like *Photoplay*'s "Folks—that's Romance!"[60] A 1930 issue of *Motion Picture Classic* even offered "Lessons in Love," telling readers that they should marry "as soon as you have enough sense."[61] Celebrities' lives seemed to be glamorous romantic fantasies the public could consume during a time that presented serious challenges to real-life relationships. It's doubtful that these storybook romances happened in the way that the fan magazines suggested. Many of these love stories were spun from whole cloth by studio publicity departments in order to keep their stars in the fan magazines' growing gossip coverage. Speculation about the beginning, middle, and end of relationships became a much bigger part of fan magazines during the Depression years.

While glamorizing love and marriage, movie magazines also suggested that marriage was under siege. Divorce became such a common subject that *Photoplay* satirized it in 1933, in a fictional piece where a couple was embroiled in scandal—for being happily married and *not* divorcing.[62] Rumors of broken engagements and divorce became more common in the gossip pages during the Depression. By 1931, Mary Pickford, once the queen of filmdom, was asked about rumors of trouble in her marriage to Douglas Fairbanks. "I cannot deny that there may be a separation. I can only say there is none now." The couple eventually divorced in 1936.[63] Interestingly, Pickford commented that she had never been a happy person, yet the article failed to explore how someone with so much fame, presumably a sizeable fortune, and a marriage with a handsome leading man could be unhappy. To do so would challenge the notion that celebrity, wealth, and marriage meant happiness.

And yet a 1936 *Photoplay* article, "Freedom is Glorifying Ginger," suggests that divorce can be liberating. Ginger Rogers appears exuberant in the story about her divorce; she apparently struggled with the challenge of balancing marriage with a career (she was unable to get off work in time to have dinner with her husband every night, the article explains).[64] Although Rogers seemed to be coping well, movie star divorces served as a warning to the so-called modern woman not to neglect traditional household duties. It is ironic that during the Great Depression celebrity stories warned women that working too much could derail their personal lives.

Appearance and Opportunity: You Control Your Destiny

Hard times demanded that women be vigilant in scrutinizing their looks; failure to do so could lead to unemployment, or worse yet, perpetual maidenhood. Both fan magazine articles and ads warned readers that their future economic and emotional stability rested on their actions. Too much independence would leave them lonely, as would failure to pay enough attention to their appearance.

Advertisers' approach to marketing personal hygiene products became less subtle, playing on anxieties about remaining married and employed.[65] This demand from advertisers bespoke their own desperation, as ad revenues were in jeopardy as sales of nationally branded products declined. We cannot know for sure from these ads or articles that American women necessarily internalized these appearance anxieties, but the instructions could not have been clearer. Failing to stay "dainty" by using the right soap could have dire consequences.

Desperate for consumers, advertisers turned up the anxiety level in their ad copy. "Lady in danger . . . of LOSING HER MAN!" an ad for Cashmere Bouquet shrieked, warning readers to "avoid offending" (emphasis in original).[66] Forget about even having a man, Lux Toilet Soap advised: "The girl who isn't dainty can't hope to win romance."[67] "Don't let a poor complexion spoil your romance," warned a Noxema ad (emphasis in original).[68] "Men won't call the girl who has a dull, unattractive smile!" according to an ad for Ipana toothpaste.[69] "So often it is the girl's fault," warned an ad for Mum deodorant (emphasis in original).[70] "Bad breath keeps romance away," according to an ad for Colgate toothpaste; in another ad, Colgate warned that bad breath could break

Figure 4.4 Desperate-sounding ad copy reflected advertisers' desperation for consumers during the Depression and relied on concerns about women remaining unmarried.

Source: Image from the October 1937 issue of *Screenland* courtesy of University of Southern California Cinematic Arts Library.

up a marriage, too.[71] Besides smelling right, a complexion could mean a soul mate (Woodbury Powder), being "somebody's dream girl," and could even put a man "in a mood for matrimony."[72] "Close the deal with your complexion," suggested an ad for Ponds cold cream.[73] Even ads for Wrigley's Spearmint Gum ("Get Your Man") and Scotch tape ("How to Keep Your Man Happy") used romantic anxieties to pitch their merchandise.[74]

If a marriage ended, it was likely due to a woman's failure to buy the right products, according to advertisers. As incomes fell and households had less discretionary income, if any, advertisers picked up on cultural currents that swirled around marriage. Women, presumably, could preserve their family stability by simply looking attractive enough to quell any family strife the Depression might bring. "Neglect by the husband is often the result of the wife's neglect of herself," warned an ad for a Lysol feminine hygiene product (emphasis in original).[75] Women, author Elinor Glyn counseled, were often at fault "if a husband stops loving his wife," presumably because she did not try hard enough to look and smell her best by buying the right products.[76]

Just as fan magazine articles and ads for weight loss products promised women that being thin would lead to their success during the boom years of the 1920s, Depression-era ads warned that being too thin was even worse. Weight loss suggestions never completely went away, but these ads served as a warning to women that unless they walked the thin line between being too thin and too fat, men would never find them appealing, they would never marry, and their lives would remain economically and emotionally unstable.

In a time of scarcity, being skinny reflected poverty, not self-control as it had just a few years earlier. For those struggling financially and possibly enduring food shortages, fighting off weight loss became a bigger concern. Even ads for girdles promised to add "graceful curves" and a rounder figure.[77] Curves became a status symbol, in contrast to the boyish thinness of the 1920s boom times. In July 1930, a *Motion Picture* article called "Taking the Die out of Diet," warns of the health risks of being too thin: broken bones, tuberculosis, and death.[78] Extra weight became a small insurance policy against disease during a time of want. "You need a nice little protective pud of fat," a *Photoplay* article suggested in 1936. Just as savings might have softened the blow of unemployment, a little excess

Figure 4.5 While ads in the 1920s warned women that they would be lonely if they were too heavy, many Depression-era ads chided women who were too thin.

Source: Advertisement from the August 1935 issue of *Motion Picture* courtesy of University of Southern California Cinematic Arts Library.

fat can help with feeling tired, "nervous, cross, [and] irritable" according to the article, which notes how Ginger Rogers and Katharine Hepburn constantly struggle to keep weight on.[79]

Several ads promised to help. "Don't Be Skinny," one ad warns. "No Skinny Woman Had an Ounce of Sex Appeal," another cautions. "The Fellows Never Looked at Her . . . until she found a way to add 11 pounds quick!" The last ad also speaks to thin men (so they can become "he men" with "normal good looks"), but the weight gain ads mostly address "Skinny, friendless girls." These ads appeared throughout the 1930s and in larger number in the later years of the decade as the Depression dragged on.[80]

One of the most commonly advertised products, Ironized Yeast, included medical-sounding advice for mostly appearance-oriented anxieties. The secret to enlarging a "flat chest," "skinny limbs" and anemia lay in eating yeast.[81] Other food manufacturers also promised that they could help consumers eat sensibly while losing some, but not too much weight. An ad for All-Bran warned that "unwise dieting may do more harm than good," and that their cereal brought "rounded slimness of glowing health," as well as "iron, which brings color to the cheeks and helps prevent dietary anemia."[82] Anxiety about food symbolized the times, a response to the 1920s promise of "a chicken in every pot."[83] By the late 1930s a federal food stamp plan had started as part of the New Deal, which also included funding for school lunches.

It's probably not an accident that one of the most popular films of the decade—and of all time for that matter—involves an epic tale of downward mobility, albeit caused by the Civil War and not the Great Depression. In *Gone with the Wind* (1939), the O'Hara family and other plantation owners lose everything: their wealth, their way of life, and each other. Heroine Scarlett must leave behind her pampered past and become a scrappy businesswoman, who famously vows: "I'm going to live through this and when it's all over, I'll never be hungry again . . . If I have to lie, steal, cheat or kill. As God is my witness, I'll never be hungry again." Like many of the warnings in celebrity tales, Scarlett's independence contributes to her husband leaving her. But the film's last line, "tomorrow is another day," reflects the ultimate sense of American optimism in the face of defeat.[84]

The agricultural South probably suffered the most direct loss during the Depression, with food prices spiraling downwards and banks foreclosing on land. By setting the film in the distant past, *Gone with the Wind*'s exploration of downward mobility could be historicized rather than directly address the struggles of its time. This film served as evidence of past challenges and triumphs, signaling to audiences that just as the South rose again, so too will Americans. The film's eight Academy Awards not only reflected its artistry, but also its relevance at the decade's end.

Keeping the Dream Alive

The Depression certainly challenged the underpinnings of the American Dream and threatened to dismantle it altogether. Celebrity culture played a significant role in keeping the dream on life support during a time that directly challenged the idea that upward mobility—or even survival—was possible in America. Certainly many novels and movies of the time called the dream into question: John Steinbeck's *The Grapes of Wrath* (1939) and its 1940 film version detail how the dream becomes more of a nightmare for the Joads of Oklahoma as they migrate to California. Frank Capra's films, including *Mr. Smith Goes to Washington* (1939), highlight power inequities and corruption that challenge the idea of equal opportunity.

Yet for the most part, the culture of celebrity—the news, gossip, and profiles of movie stars' lives in magazines—continued to produce what seemed like tangible examples that the dream still existed, even during the Depression. The glamour of movie premiers and nightclubs, the palatial estates and lives of leisure the celebrities supposedly led all helped perpetuate the fantasy of abundance in the face of scarcity and stubbornly high unemployment. Surely this portrayal of celebrity lifestyles partially functioned as escapist entertainment, a diversion from the mundane struggles of daily life, but it also became a living, breathing brochure for the American Dream. Celebrity culture proved the dream lived on, somewhere, just as the national anthem celebrates the survival of the flag after the 1814 assault on Fort McHenry. Our flag was still there, and so was our Dream, despite the assault of the Depression.

It's telling that the American Dream of the 1930s not only survived, but intensified in popular culture. Certainly there were detractors; in addition to critical novels and films, membership in the American communist party grew to historic levels during the Depression. But Hollywood proved to be one of the dream's biggest cheerleaders—no surprise considering its moguls' monopoly on film production and distribution reached new heights. Despite an industry-wide downturn in the early 1930s, by the end of the decade studios had amassed significant power.[85] Executives like Louis B. Mayer, Sam Goldwyn, and Adolph Zukor were themselves immigrants who had experienced dramatic upward mobility in the movie industry. With the Hays Code firmly in place, movies no longer threatened conservative sensibilities, but instead promoted patriotism. The industry that once championed the plight of the working class now had a lot to lose if it were to challenge the status quo.

As studio executives transitioned from outsiders to powerful figures in their own right, both movies and the culture of celebrity that surrounded them became increasingly important in championing and defining the American Dream. This function would expand significantly as the United States was drawn into World War II, when the American Dream of the glories of individualism and personal success would briefly recede from fan magazine stories, replaced by tales of individual sacrifice for collective triumph.

5

WE'RE ALL IN THIS TOGETHER

COLLECTIVISM AND WORLD WAR II

As the Depression lingered and war broke out in Europe, a dark cloud hung over Americans. During these tense times, celebrity culture transitioned from promoting the fantasy of attaining massive wealth to one of shared sacrifice after the bombing of Pearl Harbor in December 1941. The American Dream briefly took a backseat to the emerging sense of collectivism and focus on the greater good during America's involvement in the conflict. Patriotism became far more important than attaining individual wealth in fan magazine coverage; in fact, the fan magazines suggested that consuming more than one's fair share would be unpatriotic. The war effort also meant that women who worked were no longer described as threatening, but patriotic. Their upward mobility would uplift the country, rather than wreck their chances of marriage. But anxieties about marriage lingered in fan magazines, particularly as the war drew millions of men overseas. For women, marriage had been the clearest path to upward mobility. The shifts during the war threatened to change that, and what would come next was not yet clear. Fan magazines along with films promoting the war effort clearly attempted to bolster a sense of solidarity and social cohesion. A national crisis such as war can serve to reinforce a sense of unity, further promoting cohesion in an otherwise diverse society.

This chapter explores how World War II temporarily shifted the focus from individualism and the American Dream of material abundance towards shared sacrifice, and how celebrity culture both reflected and reinforced this change. It addresses these central questions: Why did notions of individualism and personal success recede during the war? How was consumption redefined? And lastly, how and why did the war alter stories about women's independence?

Fantasies and Rumblings of War

An October 1939 Gallup Poll indicated that just 16 percent of Americans thought that the U.S. should enter the European conflict.[1] Nearly as many people felt that war was inevitable, though. While the threat of entering the war loomed, in 1940 unemployment remained high at almost 15 percent.[2] Franklin D. Roosevelt's 1940 campaign for a third term emphasized keeping America out of the war, and just as the United States initially took something of an isolationist stance when World War II began in Europe, fan magazines continued to support a fantasy of carefree abundance and wealth. Perhaps as a desperate attempt to create an alternative to the amount of frightening news, celebrity tales before U.S. involvement in the war clung even tighter to the dream of massive wealth. Stories and gossip items detailed how celebrities spent their leisure time and spent their ample paychecks. Magazines ran pictures of stars in evening wear attending premieres, lounging by the poolside or enjoying a polo match, or betting on horses with other celebrities.[3] "Here they sit in $220 boxes, which they may purchase only after paying a $220 membership fee. They are always dressed to the hilt . . . Slacks are taboo, and men in polo shirts or without ties are given an immediate heave-ho," notes one story, which adds that some stars might bet $2,000 to $3,000 in an afternoon, more than the average annual income of Americans in 1940 (and equivalent of $30,000 to $46,000 in 2010 dollars).[4] Claudette Colbert allegedly spent $250,000 on her new home (more than $3.7 million in 2010 dollars); the median price of a home in 1940 was about $3,000.[5]

In a 1941 article, gossip columnist Hedda Hopper describes Hollywood as a caste system, "one of the most class-conscious places on earth," and "the last lap of free gold."[6] Rather than offer a critique of the vast inequality the Depression produced, stories such as this tended to heighten Hollywood's allure during a time when so many continued to struggle. Hollywood, according to a *Photoplay* article, featured some of the world's "most successful human beings," after all, and might have appeared to be the last financial opportunity when the world seemed to be going crazy.[7] A profile of actress Paulette Goddard, called "If You Want to Get There," provided suggestions on how to be as successful as she was, implying that you, too, could follow her path. Yes, she was also married to movie legend Charlie Chaplin, but as the title of the article suggests, you can get there, too.[8] "You Could do it Too!" proclaimed a story about Rita Hayworth, whom the article describes as "The 1941 brand of Cinderella," unknown five years earlier. She did it on her own, buying "her own glass slipper." Her secret: "You have to spend money to make money," easier said than done when unemployment still hovered near 10 percent in 1941.[9] The same issue of *Photoplay* included a feature of newcomer Ruth Hussey, whose plan to leave her modest Rhode Island roots behind worked—she landed a screen test in Hollywood. "Success is not an accident," the story promises.[10] A few pages later, the story of Jeffrey Lynn, born on a small farm in Massachusetts, details his rise to success as the result of hard work. He started from humble beginnings, walking miles to school and being dazzled by the big city of Worcester as a child before becoming a movie idol in Hollywood.[11] Despite fan magazines' attempts to continue promoting the possibility of carefree abundance, anxiety about the United States entering the war in Europe did surfaced on occasion. Celebrity stories could only serve as a distraction for so long.

The Dream of Patriotism

Hollywood seemed to be gearing up for war, and some critics suggested that studio executives wanted the U.S. to enter the war well before Pearl Harbor, which a November 1941 *Photoplay* article vigorously disputed.[12] Despite stories touting the chance to make it big in Hollywood and live a life of wealth and leisure, such as those noted above, fan magazines began retreating from their promotion of the American Dream and instead promoted sacrifice over abundance and equality above all else. With the threat of fascism looming in Europe, celebrity stories began championing democracy and challenging class hierarchies.

A 1940 *Photoplay* story discussed the questions that likely went on during fan magazine editorial meetings and in studio conference rooms. "Will the public want themes that are close to the headlines?" Should "the industry . . . act as one unit in all charity drives and war benefits," or "should people individually contribute to the war effort?" The article also noted that foreign-born stars might face new dilemmas.[13] Anxiety over the possibility of war loomed, particularly with a peacetime draft in the fall of 1940. Who might be drafted? "Conscription Hits Hollywood" addresses this question, mainly by guessing based on actors' ages, and also speculating on who might be too thin or too heavy to pass a physical.[14] It was by no means clear what total war might do to the Hollywood dream factory, nor how celebrity culture might change to address the impending crisis.

A 1940 *Modern Screen* article describes how the Hollywood set felt a unique connection to the people in war-torn Europe. The story contends that unlike those with "old money" wealth in the East who have experienced privilege for generations, Hollywood represents true democratic ideals with equal opportunity for all. "Family names don't impress. There is no such thing as inherited position . . . We have jobs which we must do well to hold on to . . . Nine out of ten of us have survived bad times ourselves."[15] According to the article, you don't even have to be young, beautiful, or talented to reap the riches of Hollywood—a claim questionable then and now—but the story strives to align both the film industry and celebrities with democratic ideals.

Just as with World War I, the threat of entering another war presented stars with a chance to appeal to audiences' sense of patriotism and cement the importance of the film industry as a distinctly American institution. Stories about swanky Hollywood gatherings gave way to coverage of benefits for war relief at chic night spots. A 1940 *Photoplay* article describes which stars donated to war-related charities, challenging the idea that Hollywood was "shut away" from the problems of the rest of the world.[16] "Hollywood Joins the Navy," written by columnist Walter Winchell (who had joined the naval reserves himself) noted which celebrities had joined the military and left movie star careers behind.[17]

The bombing of Pearl Harbor on December 7, 1941, created a sense of national unity perhaps not experienced again until the terrorist attacks of September 11, 2001. According to a Gallup Poll, 97 percent of Americans supported the declaration of war against Japan.[18] Fan magazines left behind tales of individual wealth to become sites of patriotism: printing the lyrics to the national anthem, running multiple stories picturing stars in uniform and entertaining troops, and advice on coping with a loved

Personal emissary of Mr. Roosevelt to South America was Douglas Fairbanks Jr., now a Lieutenant in the Reserve. Lieutenant Commander Wallace Beery is one of Hollywood's best pilots

Figure 5.1 Fan magazine stories focused on celebrities serving in the military, as with these pictures of actors Douglas Fairbanks, Jr., and Wallace Beery.

Source: Image from November 1941 issue of *Photoplay* courtesy of University of Southern California Cinematic Arts Library.

one overseas. As with the First World War, the conflict presented a marketing opportunity for the industry. "We cannot build combat planes or bombers," an ad from the American Motion Picture Industry notes,

> but we *can* build morale ... we can give America the hours of carefree relaxation which will make its work hours doubly productive, the mental stimulus that will carry us on and on with heads up through dark days and bright, through good news and bad ... to victory."[19]

While decades earlier movie magazines claimed to provide fans with opportunities to relax and enhance their personal success, the needs of the larger collective took priority during the war.

Celebrity stories also became a central source of patriotism. A *Motion Picture* article featured celebrities opining about the meaning of America. "While many Americans are poor, most of them have the money to go into . . . [a market] and buy enough to eat. And for those who haven't the money, you know that there are relief agencies to see that they don't starve," actress Ann Sheridan observed of the "abundant life" she saw in Depression-era America. "The American way of life means the best standard of living in the world," Robert Taylor stated, adding that "No one was afraid . . . of landing in a concentration camp" (although Executive Order 9066 establishing Japanese internment camps was signed into law earlier that year).[20] Celebrities symbolized ideals of opportunity and abundance, reminding readers that the American Dream was part of our unique heritage and worth fighting for overseas.

Along with newsreels and war movies, fan magazines served to bolster the image that Hollywood was quintessentially American, with its stars supposedly leading the charge in the war effort. "Actresses sew, knit, make surgical bandages and raise money," according to one story, which pictures performers busily volunteering, in contrast to glamorous images of celebrity lives of leisure published just months prior. "There are as many two-fisted, red-blooded Americans in the movie capital as there are back in Kankakee," the article concludes.[21] "Call yourself a loyal American only if you have gone through the same stirring experience as these stars," a *Photoplay* article about a Hollywood blood drive challenged, listing all the stars who donated blood.[22]

Movie stars sold war bonds by the millions, the magazines boasted; a 1943 *Modern Screen* story enumerated the dollar amount raised by different celebrities. According to the article, Hollywood's effort raised more than $838 million, enough to purchase "eight battleships for your sons! Or 24 cruisers for your brothers. 670 sub chasers, 120 subs, or tanks, bombers, fighters! Our boys aren't ever going to die for lack of equipment, ever again, and we can thank our 'stars' for much of the good work!"[23]

Woe to the star who appeared less than fully committed. According to a Hedda Hopper gossip column, actress Merle Oberon "took a trip abroad to entertain our soldiers, but can't travel three miles for an

Figure 5.2 Ads during World War II frequently featured images of strong women aiding the war effort.

Source: Image from the July 1942 issue of *Modern Screen* courtesy of University of Southern California Cinematic Arts Library.

appearance at the [Hollywood] Canteen" (a nightclub for armed service members) after allegedly reneging on an agreement to be part of a radio show to be broadcast overseas.[24] Stories such as this one were by far the exception. Actors who served in the military frequently provided accounts of their war experiences in the fan magazines. Actor Farley Granger joined the U.S. Navy and wrote an article about how he felt as he left home for active duty.[25] Stars such as Victor Mature (U.S. Coast Guard), Alan Ladd (U.S. Army), and Tony Martin (U.S. Navy) all discussed their service in *Photoplay* upon their return. The articles imply that celebrities were entertainers second, patriotic Americans first, willing to sacrifice their fame, fortune, and even their lives for the cause.

In contrast to the aspirational lifestyle of affluence that celebrities sold in the past, during the war the dream was about victory, not wealth. Service members could write *Photoplay* and ask to see a picture of their favorite star performing an unglamorous activity that they might have done before going to war. One photo spread features Greer Garson as a cab driver, the wish of Private Sam Bakers, and Claudette Colbert cooking breakfast, as per the request of Private Fred Petrik.[26] It's notable that fans wanted to see celebrities engaged in working-class activities, perhaps to confirm that everyone really was all in this together.

The war became a product sold in place of the celebrity lifestyle of abundance. Ads for war bonds regularly appeared both as standalone ads and as part of product ads. "Greyhound Does Double Duty on America's Highways to Victory," according to an ad for the bus line, which boasted of "carrying workers to more defense projects than are served by any other transportation."[27] Soldiers began appearing in ads more frequently, for cigarettes and even nail polish. "Cutex is Young-American—All American!" reads the ad copy, which included a drawing of two soldiers seeking to dance with a woman apparently wearing the right shade.[28] "Quantico Marines reported a longer lasting peppermint flavor in Beech-Nut Gum," claimed the ad, which pictured a uniformed Marine.[29]

Be a Saver—Not a Buyer!

In contrast to the focus on individual consumption during previous decades, the war years were about shared material sacrifice. Pictorials of stars' homes during the war featured modest houses that suggested middle-class status rather than great wealth. War seemed to be a great equalizer;

just as many Americans eagerly awaited the return of a loved one, celebrity stories of a husband overseas added to the notion that regardless of fame and fortune, movie stars experienced the war much like other Americans. During a time of rationing, it would have been unpatriotic for celebrities to flaunt their wealth or a lifestyle of heavy consumption.

World War II brought a major shift in American consumption. In fact, it practically ground to a halt. With shortages and the need to use raw materials to produce goods for the war effort, ads for products now advised consumers to use them sparingly and conserve whenever possible. Conservation became patriotic and was promoted as a primary means by which the general public could support the war. Ironically, to save the American way of life, citizens were asked to alter dramatically what it meant to be an American consumer. Saving was patriotic, excessive consumption meant taking goods out of the deserving hands of soldiers. In contrast with the wars of the 2000s, when leaders told the public to show patriotism by consuming, rationing and shortages meant that all Americans were implicated in the World War II war effort.

Celebrities were not immune to sacrifice, at least in the stories told by the magazines. President Franklin D. Roosevelt issued an executive order in 1942 that created the Economic Stabilization Board, capping all salaries at $25,000 per year for employees (the equivalent of just under $335,000 in 2010 dollars) and $67,200 for executives (the equivalent of nearly $900,000 in 2010), and preventing salary increases in excess of $5,000 (the median per capita income for Americans was $1,117 in 1944).[30] Incomes in excess of these amounts would be taxed at 100 percent, according to the proposal, which Congress later rejected.[31] As *Motion Picture* reported in 1943, celebrities were reluctant to comment publicly on the wage ceiling for fear of seeming unpatriotic or greedy, but some had threatened to make only one film a year under the cap. "We have a duty to perform," Eddie Cantor told the magazine, criticizing his peers who made such threats.[32]

Americans' median per capita income more than doubled in the five year period between 1939 and 1944, and unemployment rates fell dramatically, from 14.6 percent in 1940 to a low of 1.2 percent in 1944.[33] Savings rates skyrocketed from just under 6 percent in 1940 to 26 percent in 1944.[34] Americans finally had money to spend but were asked not to in order to stave off inflation and keep supplies for wartime goods high. Ads sponsored by the War Advertising Council encouraged people to buy

Figure 5.3 Public service announcements encouraged readers *not* to spend money during the war.

Source: Image from the October 1944 issue of *Motion Picture* courtesy of University of Southern California Cinematic Arts Library.

as little as possible and not to ask for a raise at work in order to prevent inflation.[35] Articles and ads asked readers to buy war stamps and bonds, and little else.[36] Beyond the threat of inflation, many worried that the Depression could easily return if prices got out of control.

"Keep prices down . . . use it up, wear it out, make it do, or do without," a War Advertising Council ad instructed. "Put that money back in your pocket!" another Council ad cautioned, warning that "Rising prices spell inflation. And every inflation has been followed by a cruel and bitter depression . . . we don't want another depression."[37] A World War I veteran appeared in another Council ad. "Think twice before you fight for a wage increase that might force prices up," a man in a rocking chair advises, "Salt away as much as you can out of your present wages. Put money in the bank, pay up your debts . . . Above all, put every extra penny you can lay your hands on into Uncle Sam's War Bonds—and *hold* 'em!"(emphasis in original).[38] Even manufacturers asked consumers to use their products sparingly. "Keep your smile bright . . . but DON'T WASTE PEPSODENT," an ad admonishes, showing readers how to conserve toothpaste (emphasis in original).[39]

Being in show business was no escape from the belt-tightening Americans were asked to do for the cause, or so the movie magazines wanted the public to think. Sacrifice, rather than shopping, was patriotic and the way to show support for American troops overseas. Doing more, not having more, reflected the new patriotism. *Motion Picture* regularly published a "Bulletin from Washington," that detailed the movie industry's cooperation with the war effort. In July 1943, the bulletin noted that to save fabric, female stars and civilians should wear skirts, not long pants. Dark colors were out, thanks to a shortage of dye, and canning was in. "You will also see many pictures of movie stars canning in their kitchens," the bulletin promised. The bulletin also suggested carrying less luggage when traveling since porters would not be available in large numbers. "If you think this is going to be hard . . . think how hard it is going to be on some of the best dressed ladies of Hollywood who will have to get their glamour wardrobes into one small suitcase."[40] Celebrities would thus be sacrificing even more than the average American for the war.

Later that year, another bulletin suggested patching old clothes to avoid further rationing, and suggests making women and children's clothing from men's old suits.[41] *Motion Picture* included a fashion layout in 1944

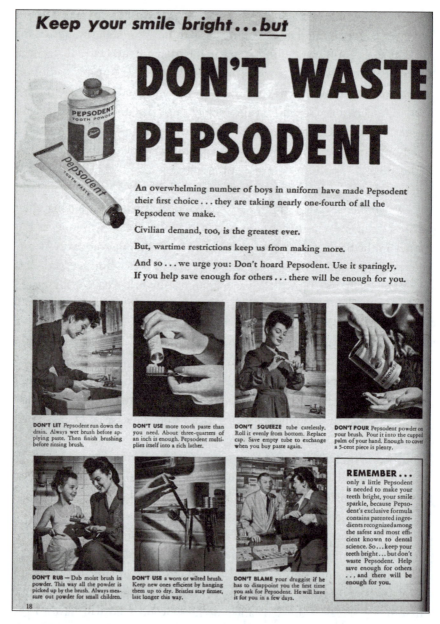

Figure 5.4 Conservation, not consumption, was a common message in ads during wartime.

Source: Image from the January 1943 issue of *Motion Picture* courtesy of University of Southern California Cinematic Arts Library.

with pattern numbers, encouraging readers to sew their own dresses and mix and match them with store-bought items.[42] The cloth shortage also meant no frills on clothing, and skimpier bathing suits (the first bikini appeared right after the war, in 1946).[43] An ad for Nonspi deodorant reminded readers that "Fabrics are getting scarce!" and their product was fabric safe.[44] Kleenex could be used to save stockings from getting dirty inside galoshes and to clean razors to extend their use, according to an ad, which asks readers to write in with their examples of how "Kleenex Tissues saves you money and helps win the war."[45]

Just as the Depression made food harder for many to come by, rationing during World War II meant that food would remain scarce. Limiting food intake became more than a personal goal, but a national necessity. Perhaps not surprisingly in this climate, ads for weight loss became more common than those for weight gain during the war. In a time of strict food rationing, particularly for items such as sugar, meat, butter, and oil, being overweight symbolized eating more than one's fair share. Ads admonished readers not to buy food from the black market or more than they absolutely needed. A 1943 *Motion Picture* article provides tips on how to avoid waste; luxuries such as sugar and butter were to be savored but used in moderation for the country's war effort.[46] As the holidays approached in 1943, a bulletin reminded readers that "if you can't get turkey at the legally established ceiling prices, serve roast chicken or pork shoulder rather than buy from the black market."[47]

Even if food was scarce, it was still necessary to have a well-nourished population to maximize the war effort. The National Nutritional Defense published ads encouraging daily consumption of "magic foods." "Without meat, milk, eggs, fish, America could never have an efficient army."[48] "Your Government Says U.S. Needs Us Strong," an ad by the Office of Defense Health and Welfare Services reminded readers, encouraging them to eat enough dairy, vegetables, meat, and bread to get sufficient nutrients.[49] Even an ad for Baby Ruth candy bars stressed that they were "rich in dextrose, vital food-energy sugar," and would help little boys grow up strong.[50] Likewise, an ad for Karo Syrup suggests that it provides "valuable food energy" for sailors and soldiers. "So let's be patient. Occasional shortages of Karo are only temporary," the copy reads, suggesting that doctors contact the manufacturer directly if their patients need the corn syrup for their health.[51] Additionally, *Modern Screen* began running features about food in 1942, providing suggestions of how to prepare healthy meals to maintain one's strength, to keep the American war machinery running.[52]

Women, Wartime, and Upward Mobility

As noted earlier, America's entry in the war finally drove unemployment rates down. In 1942, the rate had dropped to just below 5 percent, nearly half of the 1941 rate.[53] The draft drained the labor pool of young men, and the new labor shortage gave women opportunities that would have been unimaginable during the depths of the Depression. While the G.I. Bill would dramatically increase upward mobility for (mostly white) men after the war, working women became symbolic of national service. Instead of warning against the threat of "new women," as in previous times, the celebrity industrial complex promoted them as patriots.

"If you can qualify as a U.S. Cadet Nurse, you can look forward to a professional life that gives you a wide choice of interesting work," promises an ad for the U.S. Cadet Nurse Corps, which included free tuition and a monthly allowance between $15 and $30. More than just a way to earn money or contribute to the war effort, this ad suggests that nursing provides entry into a career and future opportunities (although the ad assures readers that married students can apply and that "the marriage rate among nurses is unusually high.")[54] A similar ad to join the WAC (Women's Army Corps) echoed the promise of an exciting career, with the copy "Of course . . . you may marry!" in bold type.[55] Being a career woman was one thing, but being married was still considered a woman's primary goal.

Other appeals for women to work in support of the war appeared in ads for all sorts of products that one might not directly associate with military victory. "Your Country needs you in a vital job!" an Ipana toothpaste ad noted, encouraging women "to release more men for wartime duties," and "Check the Help Wanted Ads" in their area.[56] A Beautyrest mattress ad not only encouraged readers to buy war bonds, but featured a sleeping woman above the caption, "She'll do a man-sized job tomorrow!" and will be well rested for her "full-time regular job, [and] her after-hours war work."[57] An ad for a feminine hygiene product featured women in military garb, and stressed that their product enabled women to do anything that they needed to do during this time of sacrifice. "Every

Figure 5.5 Unlike before the war, strong, independent women were not seen as threatening, but as patriotic.

Source: Image from the December 1942 issue of *Motion Picture* courtesy of University of Southern California Cinematic Arts Library.

woman is a war worker today!" the Modess ad proclaims.[58] Likewise, an ad for Chesterfield cigarettes featured Rosalind Russell as an air raid captain, in uniform clutching a whistle. Women and power were no longer a threat to men, but a necessity for the war effort.[59]

The movie magazines' ads also attempted to reconcile traditional femininity with new wartime responsibilities. "It's a good idea for women in the war to be 'just women' every once in a while," a Camel cigarette ad states.[60] Unlike Gladys Brockwell, the World War I era actress *Motion Picture* said was "doing 'his' bit" in 1918, the same magazine's World War II ads made it clear that women could be part of the war effort and stay feminine. "I scramble 'EGGS'—of enemy bombardiers," says Betty Rice, featured in the Camel ad in an evening gown with a "Prince Charming escort."[61] "America's Smart Flying Women Choose Favorite Cutex Shades," an ad for nail polish announces, picturing women in uniform wearing shades named "On Duty," "Alert," and "Off Duty." "It keeps me looking feminine even in a man-size job," the caption under a photo of a training pilot reads. Pilot Elinor "Irish" Fairchild calls her shade "marvelous with flying togs or date dresses."[62] Lest readers fear that war work is unfeminine, a lipstick ad reassures, "We are still the weaker sex," despite "serving shoulder to shoulder with America's fighting men," while including pictures of women in the uniforms of all service branches.[63]

Ads characterized civilian women as strong and independent too. A feminine hygiene ad features a woman in a Red Cross uniform changing a tire,[64] while a Tampax ad promotes itself as the choice of smart women who are not afraid of change. "The younger set does not hold back from trying new ideas," the copy states, noting that both college and "progressive women" favor this new form of feminine protection.[65] In addition to ads, the magazine articles wrote of opportunities for "career girls." A 1942 fashion layout of women's business suits for "school, the office, for USO meetings or volunteer defense work."[66] Another fashion spread includes outfits for the "Perfect Secretary," which feature broad shoulder pads that create a more masculine line and connote power.[67]

Changes in women's status went beyond clothing. A *Photoplay* article, "Who Said Women and Men Aren't Equals?" directly addresses the changing status of women during the war. In the article, actress Rosalind Russell challenges comments actor George Sanders made in an earlier issue claiming that "woman's place is in the home—and nowhere else."

Figure 5.6 Ads frequently emphasized how women's war service was compatible with traditional notions of femininity.

Source: Image from the September 1943 issue of *Motion Picture* courtesy of University of Southern California Cinematic Arts Library.

This comment drew angry responses from readers as well.[68] The next month's issue of the magazine ran an article called "Don't Be a Doormat!" with quotes from actress Lana Turner, who said, "Why not assert oneself—in a ladylike way" and a story of how Rosalind Russell demanded a meeting with a studio executive to find out why she was not cast in a role she wanted.[69] In some regard, working women could look to actresses as examples of how not only to hold a job, but to create a career.

But make no mistake, Hollywood was not by any means a place where women were equal to men, as Sanders feared. Gender discrimination was very much a part of the movie industry during the war years. A *Motion Picture* article details the difficulties of working in Hollywood, from directing and acting to publicity and hairstyling. Not only does the story warn how hard it is to get jobs of any kind, but in a section titled "Beware!" it warns of drawbacks such as, "ulcers, nervous breakdowns and unhappy married lives."[70] Script "girls," publicists, and scenario writing were open to women, but the magazine warns of a glass ceiling. Some writers, if male, go on to direct, and female publicists nearly all have to start in the secretarial pool, unlike men. Hairdressing was a field traditionally open to women, but the article describes this vocation as very competitive, with long hours, and warns, "Very few hairdressers are married."[71] While war might have brought new career opportunities for women, the war threatened to upend women's traditional path to upward mobility: marriage.

Marriage and Mobility

Besides patriotism, World War II era movie magazines focused even more on celebrity romances—including courtships, advice from stars about dating, rumors, and celebrity divorces—than in previous years. *Modern Screen* even included a monthly feature, "Matrimony in Movieland," a roster of Hollywood marriages that included the wedding date, any previous marriages, children, and the updated status of the marriage, much like a scorecard.[72] Stories of celebrity romances served in part as a romantic escape during the war. Articles included quotes describing how stars prepared for dates, the inside scoop on dating various Hollywood men, and their thoughts on what made relationships successful—much as today. A profile of Ann Sheridan describes "how it feels to go out with the glamour boys." Sheridan names some of the men she has dated and the famous night spots where the dates took place.[73] "If you were to visit

Hollywood and could 'step out' with ... any of filmdom's 'eligible bachelors,' whom would you choose?" asks a *Photoplay* story describing the places each of the men would probably like to go on a date.[74] Male stars gave interviews about what sort of woman they found most attractive, with quotes from leading ladies about their sex appeal.

Why did celebrity culture focus so much on romance and marriage during the war years? When the United States entered World War II, men became a scarce commodity, ramping up fears of losing one or never finding a man in the first place. As perhaps the most romanticized war in U.S. history, celebrity culture of the time promoted both support for the war and romance, often interweaving the two. But at the same time, being drafted and shipped out to foreign lands, perhaps never to return, could also promote shorter courtship and premature pronouncements of unending love. Ironically, the war served to increase both marriages and divorces. In 1942, the marriage rate rose to its highest level since records were first kept in 1887, from a low of 7.9 marriages per thousand during the depths of the Depression in 1932 to 13.1 per thousand in 1942.[75] Divorce rates rose more gradually, from 1.3 per thousand in 1932 to 4.3 per thousand in 1946.[76] But between 1940 and 1946 divorce rates more than doubled from 2 per thousand to 4.3 per thousand.[77] Separation during the war didn't always make the heart grow fonder.

Just as advertisements warned readers during the Depression that inattention to their appearance would cause divorce, war era articles suggested to women that holding a marriage together during the war was their responsibility. Articles encouraged women to question whether they were being good wives. An article by actress Kathryn Grayson, "Are American Women Good Wartime Wives," recounts her observation of women seeing men off, and then going out drinking with other men, which she attributes to "war hysteria." "And the treatment for hysteria is a good, resounding slap in the face."[78] Actress Bette Davis wrote in *Photoplay* that women would be responsible for "hold[ing] intact the home as an institution." She goes on to say that "women have a tendency to become self-centered" during times of peace and prosperity, and that women have the responsibility "to avoid ... endangering American morals" during wartime.[79] In a later article, Davis wrote that women should not accept proposals driven by the draft. "DON'T BE A DRAFT BRIDE!" Davis begs, suggesting women ask themselves, "Is this man honestly in love with me or is he just using me?" since married men would be less likely to be sent overseas in the event of war (emphasis in original).[80]

The end of the war did not end the anxiety. In fact, it created more; articles such as "What Kind of Woman Will Your Man Come Home to?" and "Will He Want to Come Home?" suggested that women consider whether the end of the war would cause them to face new challenges staying married.[81] "Will the man want to come back to her and the routine of peacetime living?" asks Mary Astor in an article she wrote for *Photoplay*. "Just because you've got your man doesn't mean you'll hold him," cautioned *Motion Picture* in an article about keeping one's figure.[82] Male and female stars weighed in with advice for married couples in order to stave off the threat of divorce.[83] With service members returning home in large numbers, a lot of questions remained about what the future held.

The End of the War and the End of Collectivism

America's triumph in World War II was more than a military victory; it appeared to validate the American way of life so celebrated in movie fan magazines and in the war propaganda the film industry produced. Ironically, future generations would romanticize the spirit of collectivism the war brought, but aside from fleeting moments in time, would not recreate a sustained sense of unity similar to this era. Nor would as many Americans share in the sacrifice of war as they did during this time, thanks in part to the economic prosperity the postwar period would usher in. Collectivism would not just give way to a return to individualism, but in a few short years the fear of communism would make any suggestion of common purpose bait for "red" hunters. In the postwar era, the American Dream would once again reinforce the supremacy of the individual.

Americans had experienced a decade and a half of Depression and war, and what came next was unclear. When the millions serving in the armed forces returned, would the Depression come back with them? The two crises destabilized families, who had to begin anew when service members returned or manage without them if they did not. The postwar era would require families to regroup and the independence women experienced while earning sustainable wages—perhaps for the first time—threatened to shift the balance of power further. African Americans who fought for democracy overseas returned home expecting to be part the American Dream, not merely observers of prosperity. The seeds of a second wave of the feminist movement and the civil rights movement would germinate after the war as well.

Rather than dramatic changes, both celebrity culture and the broader social context in the years immediately after World War II would reflect a focus on middle-class security. Many Americans had finally been able to save during the war, thanks to low unemployment rates and rationing, and after the war were ready to spend. The military machine that supported victory in Europe and the Pacific could be converted to producing the accoutrements of a comfortable middle-class life. In 1945, the income gap between richest and poorest shrank dramatically; the bottom 90 percent held nearly 70 percent of the nation's wealth. By contrast, during the boom years of the 1920s they held just 50 percent of America's wealth.[84] If ever there was a time when the American Dream seemed like it could become reality, it was the years after the war when purchasing power was strong and new suburban developments came to symbolize the new American Dream. As the United States ascended to the role of world superpower and economic powerhouse, millions of Americans would experience upward mobility that their grandparents might have only dreamed of. Despite numerous public policies and public investment that made this new lifestyle possible for millions, the notion that success came solely from individual effort returned.

6

SUBURBAN UTOPIA

THE POSTWAR
MIDDLE-CLASS FANTASY

Near total employment and the rationing of goods during the war meant that many Americans were flush with cash when the war ended, perhaps for the first time in their lives. The combination of personal savings and public investment in creating the infrastructure for new suburbs, new schools, and subsidizing the college educations of millions of returning G.I.s created sweeping changes in the United States. Just as millions of Americans became homeowners in the new suburbs, fan magazines' celebrity features emphasized domestic bliss. Rather than describing celebrities' massive wealth, as magazines did during both the boom years of the 1920s and bust years of the Depression, coverage in the late 1940s and 1950s suggested that celebrities had moved to the suburbs too. Celebrity homes seemed modest, mirroring the tract homes many readers had likely just bought. Middle-class life allegedly arrived for all; in reality this was still an illusion, as racial and other forms of inequality persisted. To this end, the fan magazines' suggestion that all Americans enjoyed suburban bliss diverted attention from significant social and economic inequality. At the same time, these feel-good stories offered a sense of social cohesion by suggesting we could all enjoy the spoils of victory, and these stories perhaps helped less well-off readers believe that their prosperity would be coming soon, too.

Prosperity led to early marriage and children, often for young women in their late teens. As the baby boom started, fan magazines gushed over births to celebrities, much as they do today. In direct contrast to the war years, celebrity stories fawned over women who stayed at home and suggested that women who allowed their careers to come first would find themselves alone, missing out on domestic bliss. Romanticizing domesticity suggested a return to more traditional notions of gender—in some ways a reactionary response to women's economic and social gains made during the war.

Ironically, just as Americans seemed ensconced in middle-class domestic bliss, fears about the stability of the country emerged as the Red Scare began. Fear of communism was a drastic contrast to the war years, when fan magazines stressed collective sacrifice and other notions that would arouse suspicions just a few years later. This chapter explores the following questions: How and why is middle-class bliss central in celebrity stories after the war? Who is excluded from the suburban utopia? And finally, why did these utopian fantasies require women to devote themselves primarily to the domestic sphere?

The Good Life Arrives

After the end of World War II, a large proportion of the American population could lay claim to a new version of the American Dream, one that featured a comfortable home in expanding suburbs and increasing leisure time. The national unity felt during the war effort trickled into domestic policy, with the passage of the Servicemen's Readjustment Act, commonly known as the G.I. Bill. This bill provided millions of returning veterans the opportunity to attend college, dramatically expanding the middle class. G.I.s could also obtain low-interest loans to purchase homes in the expanding suburbs. As historians have thoroughly detailed, these benefits were seldom as generous for African-American and Latino G.I.s, who were effectively closed out of enjoying the spoils of postwar prosperity.[1] This inequality would eventually help fuel the civil rights movement, but for many (white) Americans it seemed as though the American Dream had come true.

Most Americans who wanted to work could. Despite the failure of Congress ever to implement fully the Employment Act of 1946 (meant to ensure maximum employment), unemployment rates remained mostly low in the postwar era, albeit with brief spikes during recession years of 1949–1950 and 1958–1959.[2] Unemployment reached postwar lows of less than 3 percent in 1952 and 1953, reflecting the new prosperity. After the war, the income gap between the wealthiest 1 percent and the bottom 90 percent also reached an all-time low.[3] Coupled with high personal savings rates during the war—estimated at over 25 percent of disposable income—this enabled mass consumption to flourish at a time when manufacturers turned their attention from the war effort to consumer goods.[4] The good life seemed to have arrived.

As the postwar economy expanded, the concept of the American Dream promoted suburban lifestyles, which included plenty of leisure time and increased consumption. Hollywood parties came back in style, no longer only possible under the pretense of a charitable purpose. Fan magazines included more ads for vacation and travel, inviting readers to see America. *Photoplay* offered regular photo tours, suggesting spots for tourists to visit. Pictures of the Beverly Hills Hotel surrounded by palm trees beckoned readers to vacation there and star gaze at the hotel's famous pool.[5] One article even lists airfares from various major cities and suggests restaurants to visit where tourists are likely to see their favorite celebrities. "Almost everyone in the world yearns for a Hollywood vacation. During the war, California asked tourists to stay at home," but in postwar America travel was a new way to experience celebrity culture.[6]

Tourists who had already been to Hollywood could visit other destinations to get a glimpse of movie stars. An article about Palm Springs invites readers to "do as you please in this dreamy resort," where stars such as Spencer Tracy, Lucille Ball, Paulette Goddard, and others are "frequent visitors." "Without a sojourn to this dreamy resort no visit to California is complete."[7] Whether water skiing at Lake Arrowhead,[8] yachting to Catalina,[9] or sunning in the Caribbean,[10] the boom years meant more leisure time, and even a chance to see the stars up close.

Another issue of *Photoplay* includes a photo spread of a group of young actors hanging out on the beach in Malibu, spending the day in the water and sitting around a bonfire at night. It was not only okay to have fun again, but fun seemed to be a new imperative. "When spirits are high let the wind blow—add a dash of youth, sunshine, healthy appetites—and the grand and glorious total is A WONDERFUL TIME" (emphasis in original).[11] Robert Wagner wrote "Today—I'm Living it Up" for *Photoplay* in 1954, with pictures of him enjoying a swim. "If I give the impression that I'm enjoying life every minute, it's strictly on the level. I am."[12] With

Figure 6.1 After the war ended, fan magazine ads and articles encouraged readers to travel and enjoy more leisure time.

Source: Image from the June 1946 issue of *Motion Picture* courtesy of University of Southern California Cinematic Arts Library.

war and the Depression in the past, celebrity culture led the way in promoting life as constant fun.

Postwar prosperity did not curtail the prevalence of celebrity rags-to-riches stories. Happy days were here again, and so were Horatio Alger-type stories of individuals rising to fortune and fame from nowhere. Prosperity might have been in abundance, but it still required work and sacrifice. Hollywood tales of hard work leading to fame continued to pepper fan magazines. Marie McDonald, nicknamed "The Body," detailed her struggle for fame, rising from chorus girl to become a singer and actress.[13] Gregory Peck found himself homeless and penniless as a struggling actor in New York, according to a 1947 *Photoplay* article, which describes how he and a friend "often survived on small easily-taken cans of food that fitted into overcoat pockets."[14] That Peck was allegedly a thief did not tarnish his reputation—most of his film roles embodied a sense of wholesome virtue—but rather highlighted his noble struggle from poverty to stardom. Assuming that the good life was now available to all willing to work for it, the dream seemed theirs for the taking. Even in Hollywood, hard workers could become stars, according to a 1948 article, "You Don't Have to be Beautiful." "Looks aren't everything in Hollywood, say Eve [Arden] and Kirk [Douglas]—and they glory in the fact that they've never won a beauty contest."[15]

Fame could even lead to the ultimate upward mobility: marrying royalty, as Errol Flynn did with Romanian princess Irene Ghika, and Grace Kelly famously did with Monaco's Prince Rainier in 1956. But most tales of postwar celebrity success would seem much more attainable to the average American, as fan magazines promoted the American Dream as a decidedly middle-class, suburban experience.

The Middle-Class Dream

Celebrity stories again emphasized that stars were a lot like everyone else, implying that all Americans could live as well as many of their favorite stars, much as magazines do today. Foreshadowing contemporary gossip magazines that love to snap pictures of celebrities going about their daily lives, a 1957 *Photoplay* spread includes images that heighten the sense that celebrities are "just like us," doing well, but not fabulously wealthy. In turn, we could be just like them. "Seems these movie stars are nothing but plain old people," the caption reads under a picture of

Jayne Mansfield sleeping on an airplane. A picture of Paul Newman eating a snack, "playing tourist on Los Angeles' Olvera Street," implies he is just an average guy.[16]

While pictures from Hollywood nightspots still harkened to an age of glamour, the magazines seemed to go out of their way to present celebrities as middle class; comfortable, but hardly rich. Famed gossip columnist Hedda Hopper attempted to dispel the belief that "All stars are rich as Croesus and spend their millions like sailors on a spree" in a 1949 *Modern Screen* article. "Maybe you'll be shocked to know that a good half of Hollywood's gold-plated guys and gals figuratively hock the family silver along about February of each year so they can pay their income tax."[17] A 1952 article, "Flat on their Bank Accounts," reveals which stars "forget that tomorrow will bring a bill from the tax collector." To finance the war, tax rates lingered between 82 and 92 percent for the highest earners—for families with incomes over $200,000, the equivalent of nearly $2 million in 2010 dollars. In 1948, the income ceiling rose to $400,000, the equivalent of more than $3.6 million today.[18] Rita Hayworth allegedly required a $100,000 loan from her agents and didn't own her own home despite being married to a prince. Movie stars allegedly struggled to pay for their fabulous gowns and jewels, which the story describes as a necessary business expense.[19]

"Who can save a dime these days?" Asks a 1950 *Photoplay* article, "Where Does the Money Go?" which reveals that stars often borrow money from their studios or delay vacations.[20] A 1953 article about Janet Leigh describes her as having sensible tastes—"she firmly believes that a penny saved is a penny earned"—and describes her memories of receiving her modest first film paycheck of $43.80 a week (the equivalent of about $358 in 2010 dollars).[21] In another interview that same year, Leigh described how she and husband Tony Curtis had to decide whether to purchase a new car or go on a trip to New York. "We couldn't have both right then," Leigh explained.[22]

Actor Rory Calhoun seems just as thrifty in an article published that same year, titled "Glamour on a Shoestring." In the story, Calhoun points out his $2 plaster frames on the wall and the furniture he made himself, such as the canopy over his bed and the curtains his wife made. "Rory and Lita Calhoun furnished their home inexpensively yet with sentimental touches and a dramatic flair," the story goes, adding that the couple was currently renting a boxy apartment (albeit in Beverly Hills) while they saved for a house.[23] A 1955 story on Calhoun described him as an "electrician, plumber, [and] carpenter" who finds "working with his hands . . . a physical kind of independence."[24]

Frugality—real or alleged—was a virtue that many young couples just starting out in the postwar years could relate to. "By most standards, Audie Murphy is overly cautious in financial matters," according to a 1953 *Motion Picture* article. Murphy describes how his wife has him on a tight budget: $10 a week for lunches (the story's author observed him counting seventy cents at the studio commissary), and how they purchased a modest home in the middle-class San Fernando Valley suburb of Van Nuys instead of Beverly Hills. This despite him earning $1,100 a week (the equivalent of nearly $9,000 per week in 2010 dollars).[25]

Single stars could work their way to material success as well, but at first they lived modestly, according to fan magazines. A 1951 article on young single stars notes that many young women rent apartments, often at rooming houses that provide meals and have a curfew. "Very few have maids," the story notes, revealing that the average rent is $105 per month (the equivalent of about $880 in 2010 dollars).[26] The story includes a picture of future first lady Nancy Davis hanging up laundry on a line outside at one such rooming house, with a caption that she is currently dating Ronnie Reagan. Actor Ben Cooper's modest apartment appeared in *Modern Screen* in 1955, furnished "on a shoestring." He cooks for himself, and his roommate sister cleans. Another young actor, Hugh O'Brian, rents part of a house, the article notes, picturing O'Brian on the phone in what appears to be a small and crowded room.[27]

The Dream of Homeownership

Many readers could also relate to the experience of becoming a homeowner for the first time. Following the trauma of the Depression and total war, the postwar years led to a cocooning period for many Americans. A housing shortage followed the end of the war, and the construction of the suburbs helped millions move out of cramped apartments they might have shared with family members. New homes for little or no money down helped to fuel early marriage and the baby boom, since more Americans than ever could afford the purchase of a home. Aided by federal policies like the G.I. Bill and the influx of public funding to build roads, sewers, and other infrastructure, tax dollars subsidized a mass

movement from America's cities and made homeownership easier than
ever, particularly for whites. Many new developments explicitly banned
nonwhites from purchasing homes, a practice that was legal until passage
of the 1968 Fair Housing Act. Not only did these practices limit opportunities for homebuyers, but the growth of the suburbs also increased
residential segregation after the war.

Before the war, buying a home was an onerous task. Purchasers
generally needed to put upwards of 50 percent down and pay off their
mortgage within five years when a balloon payment came due. This process priced most people out of the market; according to census data, in
1930 less than 48 percent of Americans were homeowners. This number
declined during the Depression to under 44 percent in 1940. But by 1950,
55 percent of Americans owned their own homes, which continued to
grow to nearly 62 percent in 1960.[28] (The percentage continued to rise
to present-day levels; just under 70 percent of Americans are homeowners
today.) This collective nesting dominated celebrity magazine articles
throughout the postwar era. The whiteness of the new suburbia would
be invisible in fan magazines, which remained bastions of whiteness
themselves.

A 1947 issue of *Photoplay* featured actor Guy Madison in his home.
Madison had served in the Coast Guard, and so presumably readers
could relate to the shift from serving during the war to the new comforts
of home. Citing his time overseas in the military as central in his independence, he describes how he cooks for himself to save money, as he
says many men in his situation do. "Almost every guy I know is able
to cook ... A lot of them, like me, learned to cook while out hunting,"
he notes, assuring his readers that his domestic skills were the result of
traditionally masculine endeavors of being a soldier and a hunter.[29]

Owning one's own home served as a tangible example that the
American Dream was real. "Vera Ralston's home," a 1948 *Motion Picture*
article detailed, "might well be called an American dream come true."
Vera was born in Czechoslovakia, "with blonde good looks and an inherent
talent for skating ... [which] brought her inevitably to the United States—
and Hollywood." She found a home of her own in the San Fernando
Valley section of Los Angeles County, a region author Kevin Roderick
refers to as "America's suburb" in his book *The San Fernando Valley*. Its
population nearly quadrupled between 1940 and 1950 from 112,000 to

over 400,000 as new developments sprang up across this 260-square-mile area. A caption to a picture of Vera emerging from her modest pool reminds readers that, "Swimming pool and all, Vera's home represents the fruits of long, hard work." The clear message was that entering the new prosperous suburbs still required hard work.[30]

Actress Debra Paget's elaborate home made the pages of *Modern Screen* in 1954. "For as long as she could remember, her ... mother ... had promised the five children that if they were good, watched their weight and worked hard, some day they'd live in a big house with a swimming pool," the article noted. Paget didn't just follow her mother's advice, but worked hard to renovate a deserted home that "looked like something out of an old Boris Karloff movie," with broken windows and overgrown weeds.[31] For the article, her house symbolizes the hard work buying a house requires, and also the labor needed to turn a house into a home.

A 1958 issue of *Photoplay* made the dream of homeownership available to fans, as part of a twelve-page section called "How I can Have a Hollywood Dream House," including decorating tips, "plans for 'Hollywood' homes you can afford," and a contest. The article included simple suggestions for finding and retouching small furnishings that "reflect your personality." In an extended advertisement for builders, the pictorial includes pictures of children's bedrooms and a master bedroom with a one-way window for parents to peek in on the kids. Readers could choose to add an indoor pool, which "requires little or no work" and could be converted "into a handsome dining room and garden" when the kids grow up. Five floor plans are available for readers to choose from, all guaranteed to "fit on even 75 × 100 ft. lots."[32] Dream homes were not just for Hollywood celebrities in the prosperous postwar era.

Celebrities posed in front of homes that looked a lot like the modest new suburban family homes that millions moved into after the war. Stars frolicked on manicured yards, often with dogs, with pictures focused on a small area made to look like the size of their yards matched those in new subdivisions. Backyard pools highlighted the home as the primary site of leisure, as space became increasingly privatized.[33] Jack Lemmon's home and simple kitchen appeared in *Photoplay* in 1955, with the caption saying that he and his wife "share an unpretentious ... home [and] exhibit no longings for marble halls." "He doesn't look like a comic or live like a star," the article adds.[34]

A HOME

Mrs. Tufts and Sonny, with Cocoa, the French poodle. See the oranges? The wheel is from an old desert freighter. You'll be seeing Sonny in Paramount's new comedy, The Well-Groomed Bride

Waco, flying watchdog of the Tufts ranch, is a rough customer. His "love pecks" leave Sonny torn and bleeding

The living room, as well as the rest of the house, contains many antiques picked up by Mrs. Tufts all over the United States. That big coffee table was once a library table, cut down under the guidance of Mrs. T.

Figure 6.2 Photos such as these suggested that celebrities lived in modest suburban homes.

Source: Image from the June 1946 issue of *Motion Picture* courtesy of University of Southern California Cinematic Arts Library.

Celebrity decorating tips included pictures of modest rooms that might accommodate a non-celebrity's budget. Jane Russell's home is on display in a 1953 issue of *Motion Picture*, including a photo of the actress smiling as she gardens.[35] June Allison posed at home that same year in a house *Motion Picture* describes as a "charming new farm-home" that appears modest and even cramped in the magazine.[36] These homes and their seemingly happy inhabitants suggested that the postwar American Dream was one of middle-class stability, with the home as centerpiece.

Fashion spreads encouraged women to bring glamour home, to dress up while lounging on a sofa or during a backyard barbeque. Pictorials of a day in the life of a star provided a decidedly non-glamorous view of them at home too. In 1948, *Photoplay* featured "Photo Day" with Ava Gardner, from her early morning coffee that she brews herself, her drive

Kitchen Barbecue

Recipe for a perfect evening—two bright hosts like the Don De Fores and a kitchen big enough to mix in

Women at work: Large kitchen kept Marie Lund, Marion De Fore and Betty Hutton out of Don's way

Marion De Fore, Marie Lund, Ted Briskin, Don, Betty Hutton and John Lund at tavern-type table made by a visiting uncle

Figure 6.3 Celebrity photo spreads emphasized their family lives in the postwar years.

Source: Image from February 1950 issue of *Photoplay* courtesy of University of Southern California Cinematic Arts Library.

Figure 6.4 Home became the site of glamour after the war.

Source: Image from February 1955 issue of *Photoplay* courtesy of University of Southern California Cinematic Arts Library.

to work, shopping and lugging her new purchases, to a glamorous night on the town with a date.[37]

Celebrity features still included hints of aspirational consumption now and then; some celebrity homes were clearly beyond the grasp of middle-class readers. Pictures of Italian tenor Mario Lanza's Bel Air mansion appeared in a 1953 issue of *Modern Screen*. Described as a "rambling, Mediterranean-style mansion" that "cost $250,000 to build" years before, with fountains and walls two feet thick. "Few people can afford to build homes like this anymore," Lanza said. "All of their fourteen rooms over-flow with children, guests, and singing—and just plain happiness!" according to the magazine.[38]

The Suburban Family Dream

Happiness, according to this version of the American Dream, could be found in a home you own, shared with a spouse, and filled with children. Low unemployment and the rise in earning power meant that a single earner could support a growing family. Although divorce rates spiked in the years immediately following the war, they soon dipped again and birth rates famously boomed. The family was central both in Americans' postwar focus and celebrity culture. Fan magazines emphasized the idealized "nuclear" family just as nuclear weapons caused the word to take on nightmarish meanings. Focusing on one's home and family represented a trend of turning inward after a period of intense focus on the war and international affairs. Beyond safe, the family seemed to represent the new, idealized form of leisure.

Celebrity culture was well positioned to represent this new "fun morality" of family life, as sociologist Martha Wolfenstein described it midcentury.[39] Fan magazines characterized celebrity marriages, families, and households as the site of wholesome happiness. "Marriage is Such Fun," according to a 1948 *Photoplay* article about the marriage of Veronica Lake and husband Andre de Toth, who divorced four years later.[40] A 1952 Noxema hand cream ad includes a young wife washing dishes with the caption "Home-making in our new apartment is lots of fun."[41] While wartime was a time of material sacrifice for a common cause, the postwar common cause was to enjoy the bounty of victory.

The median age of first marriage dipped to its lowest level on record during the postwar era; half of all women were married by age twenty in 1950; by contrast, in 2009 half of all women were married by age twenty-six.[42] Ads for feminine hygiene products pictured mothers giving young daughters lectures in order to maintain a happy marriage. The economic boom and a postwar culture that fetishized domesticity promoted early marriages, as did a backlash against the need for women's labor during the

Figure 6.5 Many women married in their teens after the war.

Source: Advertisement from August 1947 issue of *Photoplay* courtesy of University of Southern California Cinematic Arts Library.

war effort. Promoting marriage and family served as a call for women to return home. Despite the challenges marriage poses for young people, celebrity stories largely promoted a romantic fantasy of dating and marriage.

Celebrities seemed to embody the postwar ideal, cast as having fantasy relationships and families that their fans could only dream of having themselves, rather than as mortals who often struggle to maintain their own relationships. "Enchantment" awaits Hollywood's young stars as they date each other, according to a 1948 *Photoplay* article.[43] Celebrity stories focused on relationships for decades, but after the war, coverage of teen celebrities, such as Elizabeth Taylor and Shirley Temple, revealed both the romanticization of early marriage, as well as its pitfalls. The postwar economic boom meant that a high school diploma could lead to a steady job that paid well enough to support a family, in contrast to today when teen and young adult jobs tend to be lower paying and less stable. Many teens married and started families at ages that seem extremely young today.

When Temple married in 1945 at age seventeen, fan magazine stories depicted her life as a fairy tale come true. She offered her "Ten Rules for a Happy Honeymoon" in 1947, recounting the fun vacations she took with her husband and stating that "All this makes me feel slightly like an authority on this subject" at the age of nineteen.[44] Temple frequently provided advice in *Motion Picture* to teens hoping to marry, such as how to get parental permission, the challenges of living with in-laws, and whether young brides should continue with their education.[45] *Motion Picture* later asked several celebrities whether they thought young people should attend college, and while most agreed they should, Loretta Young said "for girls I think it is a waste of time," and that "a year of travel is more valuable to a girl than is college."[46]

Actress Claudette Colbert answered questions about relationships for *Photoplay*, frequently from teens such as "Sara G.," a nineteen-year-old who wrote in 1947 asking for advice on how she could make her boyfriend "get serious with me and marry me now . . . Can you tell me how to get this boy to realize how happy we could be?"[47] Colbert also gave advice to a twenty-year-old already having problems in her year-old marriage. When she asked her husband to help with housework, he slapped her. And while Colbert replies that she did not know how she "could continue to love that man if he abused her," her advice was to stop asking him to help around the house.[48]

Colbert received other letters from teens struggling in their relationships and from people in their early twenties already separated from their husbands. Other articles alluded to the difficulties readers might face in their marriages. Young marriages are particularly prone to turbulence and divorce. In a 2002 report, the group most likely to divorce within ten years of marriage are those under twenty.[49] Concerns about teen marriages did emerge in celebrity fan magazines eventually. A 1949 issue of *Modern Screen* catalogued a long list of celebrity teen marriages that had failed, in contrast to another list of celebrities that married in their twenties or thirties whose marriages had "succeeded" (at least at press time). "Do teen-age marriages lead to happiness? Or are they the shortest road to despair?" the article, "Are Odds <u>Against</u> Teen-Age Brides?" asked (emphasis in original). The answer: "nervous breakdowns, prolonged ill health, search for escape in use of narcotics. Sometimes—yes, sometimes even death!"—the last warning was a reference to actress Carole Landis's suicide at age twenty-nine (she had married for the first time at fifteen).[50] *Motion Picture* published "Teen-age Tragedy" in 1953, noting that, "Almost without exception, every star who has married in her teens has faced disaster in marriage."[51]

Teen bride and former advice columnist Shirley Temple divorced her husband at the end of 1949 as well. *Photoplay* might have taken it harder than Shirley, noting that "When Shirley announced she was divorcing John Agar, she ended more than a marriage. She also ended an American Dream." A caption next to a photo of the couple and their toddler daughter claimed they "presented a happy picture in public only."[52] By contrast, fan magazine articles characterized Elizabeth Taylor, who married in 1950 at age eighteen and divorced a year later, as spoiled and immature. A 1951 *Photoplay* article, titled "Liz: Spoiled Brat or Mixed-Up Teenager," took her to task for ending her marriage. "When she rushed headlong from one romance to another, people excused her because of her youth. But when she ended her marriage, that was different." "The fairy tale's over," laments the author.[53]

The Good Wife

A successful marriage in the postwar celebrity culture was cast almost exclusively as a woman's responsibility. Articles praised the wives of male stars who knew their place. "We Applaud Mrs. Robert Taylor," a 1957 *Photoplay* story announced, citing her decision to make "his career more important than hers" and "for giving up 'sophistication' to be a housewife and mother." She even went with him on camping trips. "Someone has to cook," said Mrs. Taylor, formerly Ursula Thiess. "Besides, I carry the coffee thermos, the cigarettes, and sometimes the gun."[54] The good wife was dutiful, subservient, and created a blissful domestic life for her husband and family, at least according to fan magazines. "Behind every top actor you'll find a woman—living in the shadows of success and giving freely of courage, love, and devotion," wrote Hedda Hopper in a 1949

Modern Screen article. Good wives, according to Hopper, sometimes even pretend not to exist if news of marriage would thwart a young leading man's career prospects. They would patiently abide arrests, as Robert Mitchum's wife Dorothy did, and even infidelity, as Spencer Tracy's wife Louise apparently had to endure when he took up with Katharine Hepburn. While Hopper does not mention Hepburn in the article, she focuses on how Mrs. Tracy devoted herself to raising their deaf son.[55]

If a good wife wants a career, she could work to support her husband's. Alan Ladd's wife Carol Sue Ladd served as his agent. Even movie star wives could act as their husband's assistants. According to a 1951 *Movieland* article, actresses Jeanne Crain and Gene Tierney acted as helpmates for their spouses' design careers. Actress Mona Freeman married a car salesman, and "she talks up Ford cars at Paramount . . . [and] posed prettily with new auto models."[56] Stars who "made him her life's work," as Lauren Bacall allegedly did of Humphrey Bogart, would give husbands "the kind of push a man needs to send him soaring," according to a 1952 *Photoplay* story. "The husband couldn't possibly be where he is today . . . if the little woman hadn't been right behind him."[57]

By contrast, women who seek their husband's support pursuing their careers are "Hollywood's Biggest Headaches," says a 1953 *Motion Picture* article. The story describes having an actress wife as "fatal" and a big "dilemma" for men to negotiate; his wife can be "a thorn in the side of a star's career" if she "goads" him to help her get parts. Actor Cornel Wilde's career supposedly began to decline when his attempt to get his first wife acting roles "was getting on everyone's nerves." "Happiness is only possible with his wife at home," the story notes of marriage to his second wife, who was apparently less ambitious.[58] Betty Grable provided "Rules for Wives," claiming that she and husband Harry James "have never quarreled" (although they eventually divorced in 1965). Grable's rules were mostly about how to accommodate one's husband by learning to take criticism, and learning to "give in" without completely giving up "your personality."[59]

These failed marriages seem to be about more than the young women involved, but reflect the notion that marriage represented the ultimate achievement of postwar success. Luella Parsons discussed Hedy Lamarr's divorce in equal disbelief. "When the gods got around to Hedy, they . . . gave her beauty with such abundance," and yet somehow her beauty,

Figure 6.6 Marriage once again took center stage in advertisements for women's cosmetics.

Source: Advertisement from March 1952 issue of *Motion Picture* courtesy of University of Southern California Cinematic Arts Library.

her husband's millions, and their three children could not lead to happiness.[60] Success seemed to have a downside, at least for a woman's marriage. A 1947 *Photoplay* article, "Till Work do Us Part," suggested Judy Garland and Vincente Minnelli's impending breakup was due to "their twenty-four-hour-a-day job."[61] Some "ambitious Aphrodites" allegedly used marriage as a career move, according to the article "Hollywood's Marriage Morals."[62] Marriage break-ups seemed worse if they violated the public's image of a celebrity, particularly if the public perceived an actress to be an exemplar of domesticity. Jane Powell's career "hangs in the balance" after "the ideal of young motherhood" not only

As Laura read Jim's old love letters she had no idea
what had broken their engagement. She spent many a
lonely evening before she discovered that sometimes
there's a breath of difference between "ex" and "exquisite."
Once she corrected her trouble*, she gradually won Jim
back. And exquisite she was as he carried her across
the threshold . . . a girl with breath as sweet as the blossoms
in her bridal bouquet.

Listerine Antiseptic not only stops *halitosis (bad breath)
instantly . . . it usually keeps it stopped for hours on end. This
superior deodorant effect is due to Listerine's ability to kill germs.

Figure 6.7 Advertisement from the July 1953 issue of *Motion Picture*.
Source: Courtesy of University of Southern California Cinematic Arts Library.

sought divorce but began a new relationship. She, and Ingrid Bergman
before her, are "fallen idol[s]," women the fans might not be able to forgive.
Powell's primary offense seemed to be challenging the postwar era's image
of the happily-ever-after marriage.[63]

Hollywood divorces threatened the postwar celebration of suburban
domesticity, which the magazines and perhaps their readers might not
have been ready to accept just yet. Rumors of trouble between actress
Barbara Rush and her husband Jeffrey Hunter prompted one fan to write
them of how much their happy marriage meant to her. "We have the

added responsibility of not letting anyone else who believes in us down," Rush told *Photoplay* in 1954 (the couple divorced the following year).[64]

Postwar prosperity led to more elaborate weddings, propped up in part by celebrity coverage of these fairytale events. *Motion Picture* described actress Ann Blyth's 1953 wedding in such detail that the reader could have placed themselves at the ceremony, and even recite the vows along with Blyth. "Her blue-blue eyes are shining through the mist of [a] long white veil ... Her gown is of white satin, the bodice tightly fitted with a yoke of rare lace."[65] *Photoplay* described her as "intensely happy ... she had beside her not only the man whom she would worship forever, but

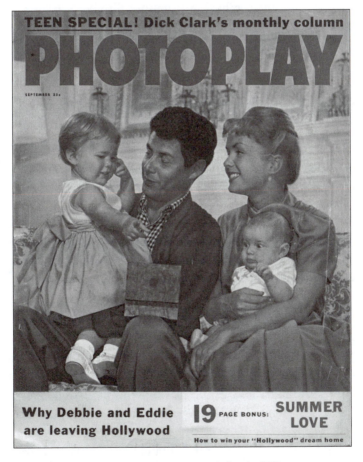

Figure 6.8 Family life was central to celebrity coverage during the 1950s.

Source: Image from September 1958 issue of *Photoplay* courtesy of University of Southern California Cinematic Arts Library.

she had his family too."[66] Called "Hollywood's marriage of the year" by *Motion Picture*, Blyth and her husband remained married until his death in 2007.

Hyping marriage was—and continues to be—a way to sell magazines, with gossip providing early glimpses into possible upcoming nuptials. Famed columnist Luella Parsons was not shy about taking congratulations for breaking the news that Debbie Reynolds and Eddie Fisher were an item while covering their star-studded engagement party in 1955.[67] When the couple had their first child, the magazines quickly ran photos of the happy couple, now apparently even more perfect with a baby. "Children *are* the home," according to actress Susan Hayward in a caption to a photo of her and her husband running through a park with their twin sons.[68]

The Baby Dream

The postwar era was in many ways a perfect storm for babies and children in the United States. Birth rates spiked from a low of about 2.5 million births per year during World War II to more than 4 million per year during the late 1950s.[69] The combination of the end of the war, prosperity, massive construction of new housing, and the heightened emphasis on domestic life for women created more than a baby boom, but a baby craze. Babies and children served as symbols of the new American Dream, a clean break from the recent past of war and Depression. These children would, ideally anyway, grow up never knowing the struggles their parents and grandparents lived through, and would be the most prosperous, best educated generation yet. In short, the children of the baby boom generation would embody all of the potential of America, the emerging superpower.

The celebrity baby buzz began soon after war's end. A 1946 *Motion Picture* story suggests ways that new moms can "have your baby and keep your beauty," featuring Ann Sothern's advice on how to lose weight soon after delivery through dancing and playing tennis.[70] "It's nursery time in Hollywood," a *Photoplay* article proclaims, featuring stars such as Hedy Lamarr, Dorothy Lamour, and Rita Hayworth with their little ones.[71] Coverage of celebrity baby showers and public proclamations of love for babies became commonplace, as were highly sentimental descriptions of newborns and pregnancy itself.[72]

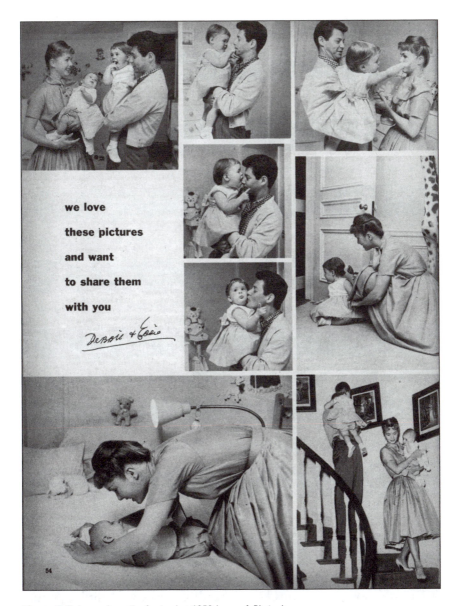

Figure 6.9 Image from the September 1958 issue of *Photoplay*.

Source: Courtesy of University of Southern California Cinematic Arts Library.

Betty, of "The Perils of Pauline," considers Lindsay Diane her greatest production to date

Figure 6.10 Stories about celebrity baby showers and pictures of nurseries became common after the war.

Source: Image from March 1947 issue of *Photoplay* courtesy of University of Southern California Cinematic Arts Library.

An article about actress Betty Briskin's newborn describes the "typical" way in which a wife informs her husband of her news: "knitting of tiny garments, to be discovered by a surprised spouse with a 'you mean?' accompanied by a modest dropping of eyelashes," or "walking out of a doctor's office with stars in her eyes, bumping into buildings and plucking daisy petals" on the walk home.[73] The December 1947 issue of *Photoplay* includes a Christmas prayer, describing an infant as "In starfish hands, and flower-textured face/In rosy flesh, by innocency blest," supposedly inspired by a photo of actress Jeanne Crain Brinkman and her baby.[74]

A 1952 article declares that "Hollywood is Hometown, U.S.A." on the "magic day" of Christmas. Featuring photos of mostly doting celebrity moms and their happy offspring, the story details how the stars' kids will learn "the true meaning of Christmas" and donate many of the fans' presents.[75] The sentimentalized image of children was also used in many magazine ads, such as the one pictured in Figure 6.11 for Ivory soap. Other ads, such as a 1958 spot for Mum deodorant, featured a smiling mother hanging up a sign advertising an upcoming P.T.A. meeting—a huge departure from Depression-era ads warning women they might never

Figure 6.11 Image from the January 1955 issue of *Photoplay.*

Source: Courtesy of University of Southern California Cinematic Arts Library.

marry. Marriage and mothering were portrayed as the keys to women's happiness, especially for celebrity moms who seemingly had it all.

Upon the birth of Shirley Temple's first baby, columnist Luella Parsons described the flurry of emotions that overtook her as she interviewed the new mother and baby. "Suddenly, I felt more sentimental that I have ever felt before on an interview. Sentimental, happy and even a little sad that this beautiful happiness that is Shirley Temple's life story cannot happen to every girl in the world." Of the new mother, Parsons said, "She shines with happiness and her newly acquired maturity."[76]

A baby could do wonders for marriage too, according to the celebrity stories. New parents Jane Powell and Geary Steffen could experience "more than just the magic of being in love. There was the magic of being married and being parents. About them, there was the glow of past as well as present happiness—and of future years together and children still to come." All this was apparently evident from a picture of the couple dining at a Hollywood restaurant, included with the article.[77]

Just as photo spreads regularly provided a look into the stars' seemingly middle-class homes, they also highlighted the everyday family lives of celebrities by photographing them with their young children, from having fun in their backyards to sending them off to school. Their smiling faces and impeccable outfits highlighted the happiness that children are supposed to bring to growing American families.

Babies would make a troubled star happy, according to the magazines. Bing Crosby had lost his first wife, Dixie Lee, to cancer in 1952 and remarried actress Kathryn Grant in 1957. The next year, just months before their first child was due, *Photoplay* described "why Bing and Kathy *need* this baby so much" to help cement their new union (emphasis in original).[78] A *Photoplay* story described Judy Garland as "shy and sensitive," and associated "with the wrong people," but after baby Liza Minnelli was born Judy's troubles had supposedly ended. "Every day is Mother's day" for Judy now, who is pictured with Liza in a multi-page spread.[79] Debbie Reynolds said, "I've got my children . . . all I need to be happy," after her highly publicized split from Eddie Fisher, who left her to marry Elizabeth Taylor.[80]

Selling Domestic Bliss

Christina Crawford's 1978 expose, *Mommie Dearest*, chronicles the dark side of the happy Hollywood child image. Describing adoptive mother

Joan Crawford's abuse, the younger Crawford suggests that her very adoption was an elaborate publicity stunt. She and her three other adopted siblings frequently appeared in Crawford's publicity photos, including a 1948 issue of *Photoplay*. In the interview, Crawford describes Christina as "an angel," and proclaims that though the actress had a full life before adoption, she adopted "for the pure and simple reason that I just literally love kids."[81] A *Photoplay* photographer described visiting their home and finding Crawford playing on the floor with the children, in what he called a "true-to-life portrait" of the fun the family often had together.[82]

Perhaps a thrice divorced woman with no children in her forties might have had trouble connecting to fans in this new age of the child; staying competitive in Hollywood—especially for an "aging" star—would require a new public image as a mother for a woman best known for her roles as powerful, independent women. Unfortunately for her (and perhaps for her adopted children), that image had gone out of style.

Female celebrities weren't the only ones using their families for publicity, even if their onscreen personae were anything but domestic. No celebrity dad seemed to appear in fan magazines with his kids more than Alan Ladd, best known for *This Gun for Hire* (1942) and other crime noir movies. He is shown at home with his children, on his ranch with his children, and introducing his new baby. "A barefoot boy has joined the cast of 'The Happy Family'," *Photoplay* announced in a feature about the birth of Ladd's son. He told the magazine about how he helped his four-year-old daughter deal with her jealousy of the new baby by having dinner alone with her for the first time. "It made her proud as Punch."[83]

The "domestication" of leading men seemed to reflect the new tranquility of postwar life. Decorated veteran-turned-actor Audie Murphy embodied the embattled young man who finds happiness through marriage, family, a home in the suburbs, and a career in Hollywood. He saw combat for 27 months during the war, and as *Photoplay* describes, "In his ranch home in the San Fernando Valley, Audie Murphy is staking his claim to the happiness he's earned." Photos show him happily playing with his young son in their manicured backyard.[84]

A "Photolife" of Glenn Ford shows him in uniform as a Marine, as a groom in full military regalia, and then holding up his infant son with his wife smiling beside him.[85] A photo of Robert Mitchum reading bedtime stories to his young sons counters the actor's hardscrabble movie image (and later arrest for possession of marijuana). "He has at times been called a 'trouble-maker,'" but is apparently just a misunderstood family man, said *Photoplay* of Mitchum.[86] "Life was uneven as a roller-coaster for Mark Stevens," according to another *Photoplay* story, picturing the actor appearing to change a diaper with the caption, "Baby Mark is their good-luck piece—[and] made his debut as 'perfect' child." Stevens, who also appeared in film noir roles, was made to seem happy-go-lucky since marrying and having a child.[87]

"Sometimes, a man has to live a lot, learn a lot, before he knows what he wants out of life," said a *Photoplay* article describing actor Ray Milland's newfound happiness as a family man. "I learned to . . . sit and do nothing . . . sit and feel calm and peaceful inside," Milland told the magazine. Peacetime was now a state of mind.[88] "Seven years ago I was Hollywood's prize square," said actor Dick Haymes. "Seven years ago, I knew from nothing. But, brother, I sure thought I did . . . That was . . . before Joanne." Haymes goes on to describe how empty his life had been, despite "catching many a mitt full of pennies," before marriage and children, in an article he wrote for *Photoplay*, complete with pictures of him happily enjoying domestic life with his wife and children. "You'll be finding 'Us' living under the Haymes brand a good many years from now," he wrote. Despite this feel-good family story, the couple split two years later and Haymes went on to marry four more times.[89]

Emphasizing his role as a father helped Harry Belafonte, one of the first black performers to achieve critical acclaim, in his early publicity. "Just Where Do I Belong," a *Modern Screen* article about the singer-actor asks for him, and then answers its own question: "I belong with my kids." The story goes on to describe the loving exchanges he had with his daughters, and how he removed a splinter from one of their feet. Although the article largely casts him as exotic—describing his heritage as a "trail leading from Africa, to the French possessions—Haiti, Martinique— ending in a year and a half in Harlem. And then Jamaica,"—by emphasizing his family, the article might have made him seem more "relatable" to white audiences. "He belongs to his family—his wife and his children," the story goes on, adding that "When you sing from the heart and you're standing in front of the people, negro [*sic*] and white . . . then you're grateful to God because: *you know where you belong!*" (emphasis in original).[90]

Babies and children could also be powerful symbols of vulnerability in the growing cold war with the Soviet Union. "I have far less patience with those who jeopardize our American way of life by idealizing less rooted and proven forms of society," Shirley Temple wrote in 1948 in an article titled "For My Baby." "These thoughts and hopes and fears of mine have always been common to mothers and prospective mothers, I am sure . . . I want my child to uphold the American way of life with heart and mind, words and actions," she concludes, suggesting that her child's future as an American is in jeopardy because of the growing threat of Communism.[91]

The Dream at Risk: The Postwar Red Scare

Just as the postwar era seemed to provide evidence that the American Dream could be achieved by the masses, the Cold War fanned fears that the spread of Communism could threaten the newly realized American Dream, with its suburban homes, happy families, and multitudes of young children. The attention communist-hunters such as the House Committee on Un-American Activities (also called the House Un-American Activities Committee, or HUAC) paid to Hollywood reflected both the significance of the industry and its celebrities, but also a radical departure from the impression that celebrities represented the height of patriotism during World War II. Despite serving as cheerleaders for the American Dream's various forms for decades, celebrities fell under suspicion as possible subversive elements as the Cold War began. If celebrities at once represented the fantasy of achieving the American Dream, they could also be used to heighten the fear of communist infiltration: even icons could not be trusted. They might seem just like us, but maybe that was part of the ruse. In an age of spies and sleeper cells, celebrities might not be as "American" as they seemed.

Fears of Communism emerged well before the start of the Cold War, or even U.S. entry into World War II. U.S. Representative Martin Dies, chair of HUAC, visited Los Angeles and spoke to a number of actors in 1938, determining that none were communists.[92] But many red-baiters remained suspicious of celebrities who had been early critics of Nazi Germany. In March 1940, *Photoplay* ran a story "Exposing Hollywood's Red Menace," casting stars as victims of manipulative communist forces that "plundered" money from unsuspecting and gullible celebrities, claiming donations would be for humanitarian purposes and to fight fascism. "Hollywood has learned a terrible lesson. It'll never need another," the article concludes.[93]

The red-baiting often associated with the postwar era grew during the war. A *Modern Screen* gossip columnist checked the voter registration rolls to see if any celebrities registered as Communist party members. "We don't for a minute believe any of these imputations," the magazine notes.[94] Others weren't so sure. "Is Melvin Douglas a Communist?" asked a *Photoplay* article, citing his anti-fascist sympathies during the Spanish civil war. "Are you a radical, then Mr. Douglas?" the interviewer asks. "If you choose to call the New Deal radical," Douglas responded.[95]

Douglas had espoused views that might have seemed radical at the time, but certainly wouldn't draw much attention today. He criticized the Roosevelt administration for its failure to aid more refugees from Nazi Germany and for not passing an anti-lynching bill. Douglas subsequently became active in Democratic Party politics in 1940. He and others in Hollywood dared to mention the persistence of racial inequality in the Jim Crow era, policies and practices that flew in the face of the notion of the American Dream providing opportunities for all who were willing to work for them.[96] As historians Larry Ceplar and Steven Englund detail in *The Inquisition in Hollywood*, for decades many in Hollywood had supported leftist causes that criticized American inequality; none of these causes, however, posed a serious threat to the government. Some did in fact join the Communist party, or felt sympathetic to some of the party's positions during the Depression years of the 1930s. Those that HUAC labeled "premature anti-fascists" fell under suspicion as well. Ceplar and Englund note that many Hollywood leftists became disenchanted with Communism after the Soviet Union signed a non-aggression pact with Nazi Germany in 1939, but in the context of the rising tide of red-baiting these beliefs seemed menacing.

"Now the stars live in constant dread of being unjustly branded as un-American," another *Photoplay* story noted, while naming stars such as James Cagney and Humphrey Bogart among those under suspicion. "These stars have since been cleared of this charge . . . unfortunately, the stigma still lingers," the author observes, while clearly adding to the suspicion by mentioning that celebrities have donated money to charities suspected to be communist fronts.[97]

While the economy had improved by 1940 and unemployment declined significantly, the persistence of the downturn could have easily challenged both the American Dream and capitalism itself. Prewar red-baiting was a useful tool to combat criticisms that the American economic system was broken; any suggestion could be labeled unpatriotic communist propaganda. Publicly flogging celebrities served a powerful purpose: if those in the fantasy-land of Hollywood could be targeted, anyone who questioned the American Dream might be at risk for derision and downward mobility.

After the war the anxiety about communism grew to a fever pitch; in 1947 HUAC opened a new investigation at the behest of conservative industry insiders, irked after labor disputes in 1945 and 1946. The newly created Motion Picture Alliance for the Preservation of American Ideals (MPAPA) charged that Hollywood unions had been infiltrated by communists, whom they blamed for stirring up tensions.[98] "Is Hollywood Red?" a 1947 *Photoplay* editorial asked. Without directly answering its question, the editorial concluded that "There can be areas where even the most fanatical Red can properly keep hands off, and where even the most well-intentioned counter-Red activities can easily verge on the absurd."[99] This very idea would play itself out over the next several years, as writers, directors, and actors found themselves under scrutiny during the postwar red scare. Those that HUAC named as possible communists often made their case in the pages of fan magazines.

The committee summoned actor Larry Parks to a 1947 hearing, and though he was not called to testify, he attempted to clarify his point of view in a 1948 issue of *Photoplay*. Parks assures readers that his ancestors fought in the American Revolution and he was:

> as average an American in my background as could be found anywhere ... As far back as I can remember I learned from my father and my mother and from the preacher in my church that America was the best and greatest land on earth.

He goes on to add that because of his beliefs in freedom and equality:

> I believe that every Negro [*sic*] child has the same right to food and shelter and health and education and opportunity that was

granted me at birth. I believe that anti-Semitism is a crime against humanity, and that all men [*sic*] have the right to worship in private without interference and without abuse.[100]

It is likely these beliefs in equality, which would be unremarkable today, marked Parks as a "lefty" and perhaps a radical in the pre-civil rights era. Celebrity magazines seldom mentioned African Americans and inequality during the Jim Crow era. And the many Jews in Hollywood either downplayed their backgrounds or changed their names to mask their heritage, preferring to blend in rather than directly challenge anti-Semitism.[101] HUAC subpoenaed Parks again in 1951, and this time he admitted having past communist ties. He begged the committee not to force him to name names, but ended up naming ten alleged communists. Parks lost acting roles and only appeared in three more films, ejected from the realm of celebrity.[102]

Humphrey Bogart was perhaps the biggest celebrity to find himself under suspicion after someone leaked his name in 1939 testimony. In 1948, Bogart felt compelled to write "I'm No Communist" after he flew to Washington with a group of other celebrities, such as Lauren Bacall, Lucille Ball, Henry Fonda, Judy Garland, Katharine Hepburn, Gene Kelly, Myrna Loy, and Edward J. Robinson among others, to protest HUAC's tactics as part of the newly formed Committee for the First Amendment (CFA). "I'm about as much in favor of Communism as J. Edgar Hoover," he wrote in *Photoplay.*

> Our plane load of Hollywood performers who flew to Washington came East to fight against what we considered censorship of the movies . . . we were there solely in the interests of freedom of speech, freedom of the screen and protection of the Bill of Rights.[103]

After advice from friends, Bogart toned down his opposition to HUAC, and the CFA disbanded after numerous threats to participants' careers and reputations.[104]

In an era of suspicion, maintaining celebrity status meant upholding a patriotic image. Fan magazines helped to promote an almost maudlin notion of celebrity patriotism. Describing his return to the U.S. from Europe, "Rock Hudson's Love Affair with the USA," notes that Hudson got choked up as he saw the Statue of Liberty as he sailed into New York harbor.

> Rock had forgotten . . . how much this all meant to him, forgotten how lucky he was that he was an American who could come back to this country . . . a country where a lad from the wrong side of the tracks could afford to dream, dream anything he cared—to become a movie star in this case—and have the chance to make the dream come true.[105]

Stardom clearly reinforces the notion of freedom and upward mobility, and Hudson's "reminder" serves as a reminder to readers of opportunities presumably available to all fortunate enough to be Americans. This and articles like it suggest that these opportunities would be threatened by communism.

The intensity of HUAC's focus on Hollywood peaked in 1956, but the damage had been done to many whose careers were ended and reputations ruined, not to mention those who spent time in prison.[106] The accusations, true or not, also shifted the public's perceptions of celebrities: what dark secrets did they harbor? In the years to follow, celebrity fan magazines and the growing gossip industry would devote much of their resources to trying to uncover details about stars that they and their publicists might not want the public to know about. While the American public might have let go of the notion that celebrities might be secret communists, HUAC's investigations helped to encourage the public to take further interest in celebrities' private lives.

The End of an Era

It is quite possible that had Will Hays, selected in 1922 to quell the rising tide of criticism against Hollywood, still been the industry's Washington emissary that he might have been able to control the damage done by the HUAC hearings, but he retired in 1945. Besides HUAC, another important shift would forever change the production of celebrity culture: the collapse of the studio system. A key blow came from a 1948 Supreme Court ruling. *United States v. Paramount* required the studios to relinquish their theater chains, citing a violation of the nation's antitrust laws. This removed a very profitable aspect of the industry and ultimately provided independent filmmakers more of an opportunity to compete. By the end of the decade, the contractual structure whereby celebrities would be employees of a studio began to fall apart. Coupled with the rise of television and the decline in box office revenues, studios eventually lost possession of what were once among their greatest assets: their celebrities.[107] Many of the major studios' biggest non-acting celebrities—moguls like Louis B. Mayer (MGM), Harry Cohn (Columbia), and Jack Warner (Warner Brothers)—died or retired between the 1950s and early 1970s, leaving Hollywood studios without the powerful leaders who helped shape the film industry in the early years of the century.

After the studio system ended, celebrities essentially became free agents rather than studio property. They gained more control over their careers and could negotiate their salaries by project, rather than under a general contract that would obligate them to take assignments the studio deemed appropriate. But they also lost access to the tightly run publicity machine, which not only controlled their images, but also protected them from bad publicity. If a fan magazine printed an unflattering story that offended the studio, the magazine could potentially lose access to the studio's other stars. At the same time, a studio could choose to release embarrassing information to punish a recalcitrant celebrity/employee, or threaten to do so during contract negotiations. So when the studio system fell apart, the celebrity gossip industry gradually reinvented itself. Publicity departments began to focus mainly on promoting movies, not celebrities. That role would be taken by private publicists, the most powerful of whom could elicit some control over what information about their clients went public.[108] But after the end of the studio contract system, the studios' investment in celebrities was much more limited, and they had less financial incentive to protect against potentially damaging information.

Beyond reduced information control, celebrity itself would take on a different meaning in the coming decades. Not only would the industries that produced entertainment undergo a tremendous shift, but the country itself would enter a period of change that would call into question the meaning of the American Dream. For some, the suburban oases no longer represented the utopian dream the postwar era promised.

7

IS THAT ALL THERE IS?

CHALLENGING THE SUBURBAN FANTASY IN THE SIXTIES AND SEVENTIES

The American Dream might not have turned out to be as utopian as promised in the heady postwar years. Just as many young Americans questioned the goals of materialism and suburban prosperity, celebrity stories focused on tales of unhappy, suffering celebrities during the 1960s and early 1970s. The magazines no longer described fame and fortune as a shortcut to happiness. Marriage would not necessarily bring a lifetime of bliss either, as celebrity divorces and rumors of unhappy relationships became a regular feature. Cohabitation, bearing children outside of marriage, and interracial relationships all challenged the accepted social order at a time when shifts in the racial and gender order took place. At the very same time these major changes occurred, the studio system also collapsed, seriously altering the production of celebrity culture. The symbiotic relationship between movies and fan magazines faded, and coverage of other kinds of celebrities widened: television stars, athletes, and political figures became more common subjects in the magazines. Celebrity coverage also included more information the studios might have previously prevented from running, such as news of drug use and arrests. Gossip and more invasive stories became more common, and the coverage became much more similar to the no-holds-barred coverage we have today.

This chapter explores how the celebrity culture of the sixties and seventies reflects both criticism of the postwar version of the American Dream, as well as the uncertainty about what would follow in an era of

149

social change. The celebrity stories of this era reflect both a sense of alienation—the feeling of disconnection from one's true sense of purpose amidst the pressures of consumer capitalism—as well as anomie—a lack of certainty about social norms during a period of flux, leading to feelings of disconnection to the broader society. In addition, this chapter addresses the following questions: How did celebrity coverage reflect the social changes taking place in the 1960s and 1970s? What led to the changes in tone in stories about women, relationships, and families? How did these changes lead to the start of a conservative backlash and a return to more traditional values?

Questioning the American Dream

Postwar prosperity and all it brought—a corporate job, marriage, children, a house in the suburbs—sometimes seemed empty to the generation coming of age during a time of plenty. By the 1960s there had already been cultural rumblings about the midcentury version of the American Dream. In the 1950s, the so-called beat writers challenged the social order, writing about topics such as drug use and sexual experimentation, considered unseemly in an era dominated by polite suburban middle-class family life. William H. Whyte's 1956 book *The Organization Man* raised questions about conformity and the loss of individuality that the new prosperity seemed to bring, both in the workplace and in the expanding suburbs. Homemakers such as Betty Friedan, author of *The Feminine Mystique*, admitted that their lives often felt empty and lonely in these new suburban communities. Soon after the postwar dream came to fruition, many questioned whether there wasn't more to life than a suburban tract home and all the newest appliances.

For many young Americans whose basic economic needs felt secure, other concerns arose, particularly as the conflict in Vietnam expanded. A credibility gap emerged; despite officials' claims of the war's success, losses after the 1968 Tet offensive suggested otherwise. Young people who grew up during the postwar era enjoying the benefits of material security and who were then drafted and sent to Vietnam sometimes questioned the nature of the American Dream as no other generation had before. The counterculture movement that emerged in tandem with the student anti-war protests of the era called into question many previously taken-for-granted assumptions about American life: that the government was trustworthy; that chastity, marriage, and monogamy were ideal; and that consumption of material goods was central to happiness. Not coincidentally, many individuals and married couples began asking questions like this too, through consciousness raising groups, marriage encounter workshops, and other self-help activities. During the economic struggles of the Depression and war years, marriage seemed tantamount to success in celebrity stories and products advertised along with them. Perhaps as an outgrowth of continued prosperity, happiness was no longer seen as being as simple as getting married, finding a house in the suburbs, and having children. Where exactly happiness came from is a quest that thousands would seek through the burgeoning self-help movement. According to sociologist Micki McGee, author of *Self-Help, Inc.*, the economic downturn of the 1970s created a sense of scarcity that led to a concerted move toward individual self-improvement and away from collaborative social change.[1] It is equally likely that the prosperity of the 1960s caused people to look for meaning beyond material wealth.

The New Hollywood

No longer did celebrity culture reflect and reinforce a dominant version of the American Dream; now, rather, it highlighted antiheroes who challenged the social order. Television shows such as *The Smothers Brothers Comedy Hour* provided regular cultural and political criticism during its brief 1967–1969 run. *Rowan & Martin's Laugh-In* (1968–1973) also relied on countercultural and sexually suggestive references, pushing the cultural boundaries on television. Just as critics challenged the premise of how Americans defined success midcentury, the celebrity industry itself was shifting. The celebrity machine, once well-honed and under studio management, would change during the tumultuous decades that lay ahead. No longer employees of large media conglomerates, performers gained independence and were free to choose projects that they preferred at salaries their increasingly powerful agents would negotiate. And yet their once carefully crafted—and protected—images would no longer be under the control of a handful of powerful studio bosses.

This opened the door for fan magazines to print more unflattering details about celebrities' lives, be they real or imagined. The door had been cracked open by magazines such as *Confidential*, first published in 1952, which specialized in revealing the seamy side of celebrities and public figures. Rather than appeasing the studios by publishing star-friendly features, *Confidential* paid informants for dishing salacious details that frequently countered celebrities' manufactured images. But a barrage of lawsuits from the studios helped put the magazine out of business in 1957.[2] Just a few years later, the magazine would have likely been able to continue; the *National Enquirer* began focusing on sex scandals in 1957 and became a mainstay in revealing dark celebrity secrets in the years that followed. The traditional fan magazines would also adopt some of the "gotcha" qualities of *Confidential*, increasing their reliance on anonymous sources and by using exclamation points in headlines to suggest scandal.

Confidential expanded its coverage beyond traditional celebrities to include politicians, gangsters, royalty, and high-society figures. Likewise, both tabloids and, increasingly, mainstream fan magazines broadened their definition of celebrity. The diminished power of the movie studios meant less pressure to devote as many pages to promoting movie stars, which in turn broadened who became part of the public imagination, a precursor to the near free-for-all that the definition of celebrity has become today. The election of a movie-star handsome president in 1960 was a perfect match for this broadened definition of celebrity. He and his storied family became fodder for celebrity fan magazines, although by contemporary standards the coverage treaded lightly when it came to the president.

Both the entertainment industry and celebrity culture would reinvent themselves during the 1960s and 1970s. Hollywood's original fan magazines would gradually fade into oblivion during the 1970s, to be replaced by *People* and *US Weekly*. Weekly movie attendance had nosedived with the introduction of television, from nearly 60 percent of Americans in 1946 to just 10 percent in 1964, a level that would hold steady over the next four decades.[3] With the arrival of the baby boom, millions of families now had young children to look after at home; migration to suburbs might have meant that many families were now farther away from movie theaters as well.

A "new Hollywood" would emerge, focusing on antiheroes who challenged the establishment, and became increasingly critical of postwar conformity, as author Peter Biskind describes in *Easy Riders, Raging Bulls: How the Sex-Drugs-and Rock 'n' Roll Generation Saved Hollywood*. The content of movies became grittier to compete with television and the influx of so-called "New Wave" films from Europe, which included more overtly sexual themes. Several American-made films of the late 1950s and 1960s openly violated the Hays production code, but their release and audience attendance indicated that the 1930s-era code had lost its influence over filmmaking.[4] By 1968 the movie industry abandoned the code, putting a rating system in its place. Movies began to feature nudity and profanity regularly, and explored issues earlier films would not have approached for fear of violating the code. Likewise, celebrity stories would venture into new territory, describing many celebrities' nontraditional lifestyle choices, including their sex lives and drug use. Just as moviemaking became more graphic, showing the darker side of life, stories about celebrities were no longer always sanitized and fan magazines did not idealize celebrity lives to the degree they had in the past.

Prosperity and Ennui

If the postwar years symbolized the birth of a newly realized American Dream of prosperous families living in new suburban developments, the 1960s and 1970s represented an adolescence of sorts. Celebrity culture both reflected and reinforced this growing disillusionment. The dark side of fame emerged as freelance photographers began seeking more surreptitious shots of stars beyond the image machine of the weakened studios. The 1960 film *La Dolce Vita* brought the term "paparazzi" into the mainstream, a film that focused on the hedonistic life of a celebrity photographer. Cultural studies scholar Ellis Cashmore cites the invention of the zoom lens as a defining moment in the history of celebrity culture. The 1962 shot of Elizabeth Taylor and Richard Burton kissing on a yacht, though married to others, marked a turning point according to Cashmore. Celebrities from this point forward would have a harder time maintaining a barrier between their private life and their manufactured public life.[5]

While in the past attaining celebrity status seemed to confirm that an individual had arrived and enjoyed not just financial success but happiness, celebrity stories of this era often dwelled on their loneliness and unhappy lives. Even children of the famous, feted just a few years earlier in fan magazines as living charmed lives in impossibly perfect photo spreads, were not immune. David Cassidy, son of actor Jack Cassidy and star of *The Partridge Family*, had "an insatiable need for" love after an unhappy childhood, according to *Movieland and TV Time*.[6] Children of actors were

Oh, what a beautiful adventure —thought John J. Kennedy, Jr. He rode with his dad via helicopter to Andrews Air Force Base, trotted along behind the President to the big plane waiting there; scampered up the ramp to join the travelers—then got hauled down and sent home with his nurse. Poor little fella—he thought he was going on the trip, but it was only goodbye again—and tears!

31

Figure 7.1 Traditional fan magazines expanded their coverage beyond movie stars after the studio system's collapse. The Kennedys became a favorite subject.

Source: Images of John F. Kennedy Jr. from October 1963 issue of *Photoplay* courtesy of University of Southern California Cinematic Arts Library.

not the only ones who apparently suffered if their parents were famous. While much of the press celebrated the photogenic first family, characterizing them as idyllic, fan magazines focused on the Kennedy family's sadness—even before the November 1963 assassination. In October 1963, one month before his father's assassination, *Photoplay* described three-year-old John Kennedy, Jr., as a "sad little fellow. Pouting. Lonely-looking. As if already conscious of the enormous problems that lie ahead for him (and there are many)."[7] *Modern Screen* in a January 1963 issue described John's mother, Jacqueline Kennedy, as sad and lonely, desperate for privacy. No longer able to make a simple visit to the grocery story or go shopping for her children, photographers and Secret Service meant that the First Lady always had throngs of people following her, the magazine noted in "The Hidden Life of Jackie Kennedy."[8]

Jackie was a frequent subject of gossip magazines after her husband's assassination and her second marriage to Greek shipping magnate Aristotle Onassis. "Beauty, fame, wealth, total freedom about where she goes and whom she sees. Surely Jackie must be the luckiest woman alive! *Is* she? . . . No," declared a 1970 *Movieland and TV Time* story. The article emphasizes her lack of privacy and how her life had become something of a freak show, with photographers following her, trying to get pictures of the former first family. "The Pain Remains!" a gossip item noted, picturing both Jackie and Robert F. Kennedy's family visiting his grave on the anniversary of his assassination in 1972. "Perhaps . . . now that she has made a whole new life for herself she is able to be herself and give in to her natural feelings."[9] Following the death of Onassis's son Alexandros in 1973, the magazine also reported on the grief-stricken couple, with a photo of a solemn Jackie with her head down in mourning.[10]

The end of Hollywood's "Golden Era" created many opportunities for public mourning. As celebrities from the early days of filmmaking aged, fan magazines regularly reported on news of their illnesses and deaths. Charles Laughton was suffering from cancer, Luella Parsons noted in a 1963 *Modern Screen* column.[11] A 1964 *Photoplay* story describes "Mrs. Peter Sellers' Deathwatch," as Britt Ekland, wife of the British comedian, sat helplessly outside of intensive care waiting to see if he would survive a series of heart attacks (he did, at least until 1980).[12]

Celebrity deaths, or even their fear of death, became a common fan magazine topic, suggesting that the famous were swimming in sadness. "I'm going to die young," Connie Stevens told *Photoplay* in 1961. "She lives impulsively," the magazine claims. "There's a side she keeps so well-hidden that only her father dared comment: 'I think Connie is the loneliest girl in the world.'" The article includes a photo of the actress alone at a table, apparently having just eaten a meal by herself.[13] An even more solemn story about Brigitte Bardot describes her has depressed, "afraid of getting old" (at twenty-six), with "moods that change by the moment." According to a "confidential" story in *Photoplay*, Bardot was suicidal over the trouble in her marriage to Jacques Charrier. "For the little girl who had everything, there seemed no happy ending. Just those she finds in her movies."[14]

A 1972 article claimed that Richard Burton suffered from "thanatophobia," or fear of death. "I have this terrible fear of dying, of being forgotten, of being nothing," he told *Movieland and TV Time*. He was also afraid of crowds, like "most international celebrities," a psychiatrist told the magazine, which delved into Burton's family history of premature deaths.[15] Despite international news of Elizabeth Taylor's illness during the filming of *Cleopatra* (1963), *Photoplay* claimed she was "in physical agony" from a "serious illness she [hid] from the world."[16] Celebrity lives in these and other stories seemed lonely, painful, and neurotic.

Following Marilyn Monroe's death, described as a suicide in a 1963 issue of *Modern Screen*, the magazine pictured the late actress reaching out, with the caption "Help Me." "Marilyn Monroe begged throughout her thirty-six years. Her outstretched cup did not ask for money or fame. It did plead for love. No one gave it to her, not for a long enough time . . ." The story goes on to describe her difficult childhood in foster care, her mother's mental illness, and her own failed marriages. "Drugs helped blind her hurt . . . darkness claimed her," the article concludes.[17] More than a year after Monroe's death, *Photoplay* ran a story about her mother, who allegedly escaped from a mental hospital. The article describes the woman as "contemplating the great maw of black and darkness."[18]

Movieland and TV Time covered George Sanders' 1972 suicide in similar fashion. In a story titled "He Died Alone!" the magazine describes how his nude body was found in a Spanish hotel room with a suicide note that said "I am bored." He apparently had talked of having a suicide party. "Nobody came to George Sanders' farewell party and in the end he didn't even toast himself." The article alluded to aging, failed marriages, financial difficulties, and loneliness as reasons Sanders took his life. "I have no friends . . . I just want to be left alone," he allegedly said in his suicide note.[19] That same year the magazine also covered actress Gia Scala's apparent suicide at age thirty-eight. She "was a very promising actress years ago when she married Don Burnett," but the marriage ended and roles came only sporadically for Scala, perhaps contributing to her death.[20] Achieving celebrity might have brought fame and even wealth, but as these celebrity stories suggested, any happiness success may bring is only fleeting.

Integration and the American Dream

Ironically, while those presumably reaping financial benefits often wondered if there wasn't more to life than fame or suburban prosperity, civil rights movement leaders demanded entrée into the middle class. The spoils of the postwar era were not shared equally. In 1959, 18.5 percent of American families lived below the federal poverty line; by 1970 that rate had dropped to 10 percent, but the poverty rate for black families in 1970 remained stubbornly high, at nearly 30 percent.[21] The rising expectations of equality following World War II helped galvanize the civil rights movement during the 1950s, challenging both the racial order and the meaning of the American Dream. When the Reverend Martin Luther King, Jr., declared in his famous 1963 speech "I have a dream," he argued that the American Dream that so many Americans apparently had realized after the war was meant for everyone.

Historically, both the American Dream and celebrity status were considered the purview of whites. Fan magazines focused almost exclusively on white performers. Despite a thriving African-American film community in Los Angeles in the early decades of the century, African Americans rarely appeared in fan magazines. Coverage all but ignored international stars such as Dorothy Dandridge, rendering their lives and careers invisible.[22] Performers who changed their names, like Margarita Cansino (Rita Hayworth) and Raquel Tejada (Raquel Welch) could "pass" as Caucasian and garner coverage. Those who could not pass were typically relegated to stereotypical roles or kept out of celebrity culture entirely. But the growing prominence of civil rights activism, coupled with the demise of the studio system, began to curtail the Anglicization of would-be celebrities.

When nonwhites did appear before the 1960s, the magazines either portrayed them as caricatures or exotic foreigners, particularly in the 1920s. For instance, drawings and photos of Asian women occasionally appeared in ads for beauty products, claiming to share beauty "secrets of the Orient" in the 1920s. The occasional coverage African-American performers did receive prior to the 1960s would rely on stock racist imagery. For example, a 1929 *Photoplay* story called "A Jungle Lorelei" describes actress Nina May as tawny, eye-rolling, and primitively sexual ("a little colored spasm ... she rolled them hips ... [and performed] back-to-jungle movements") despite the fact that May was just fifteen at the time. The interview furthers the Jezebel stereotype of the scheming black woman who uses her sexuality for money, by quoting May in stereotypical black dialect, no less: "No suh ... When I marry it's goin' be for money. Yes suh, I think that's a good idea."[23]

Figure 7.2 During the 1920s and 1930s, images of African Americans relied on racist stereotypes.
Source: Image from February 1934 issue of *Photoplay* courtesy of University of Southern California Cinematic Arts Library.

A 1934 *Photoplay* article, "Drums in the Jungle," describes filming the 1936 movie of the same name in Haiti and the challenges of working with the native people. The article describes the native performers as "singing in primitive, jazz-like rhythms," and casually mentions the "two darkies" who guided the article's author around, as well as how he happened upon "an ugly half-naked black man" during a voodoo ceremony. One picture from the movie features African-American actress Fredi Washington (who famously passed as a white woman in the 1934 film *Imitation of Life* with Lana Turner) as a sorceress who controls the natives and "compel[s] them to help her kill the white women."[24]

A 1941 profile of Eddie Anderson explicitly notes that his success was the result of "a colossal supply of goofer dust," or dumb luck. In a baldly racist story, Anderson seems to embody the worst racial stereotypes. "Hard work? Don't be silly," says the *Modern Screen* article about the comedian who became famous playing Jack Benny's valet. While Anderson allegedly

When you see King Vidor's "Hallelujah," watch for the tawny Nina May. Nina longs for dresses like Gloria Swanson's and "diamonds dribblin' all over my physique—um-um!" And she wants to go to Paris to be a hit like Josephine Baker. Nina isn't quite eighteen. She went on the stage at fifteen, in a Harlem negro revue

Figure 7.3 Image from the July 1929 issue of *Photoplay*.
Source: Courtesy of University of Southern California Cinematic Arts Library.

scrounged for his next meal just a few years prior to his success, the article impugns his work ethic. Referring to Anderson as Rochester, his character's name, throughout the article the magazine describes how he "invariably shows up late, won't go to work until the milkman arrives on his late rounds . . . Then he struts in . . . showing not the slightest regret that he is late."[25] And yet he owned a fourteen-room house, thirteen horses, a yacht, and a nightclub. In contrast to the scores of Horatio Alger tales about white performers, Anderson's wealth seems undeserved. These and other pre-1960s stories about people of color in fan magazines suggested that nonwhites were illiterate at best and frightening savages at worst.[26]

Coverage began to change with the civil rights movement, and the increased awareness about the serious inequities in postwar America. As the American Dream expanded to include more than just whites, celebrity stories did as well. By the early 1960s, the civil rights movement was in full swing, but mostly still absent from celebrity magazine stories. A 1964

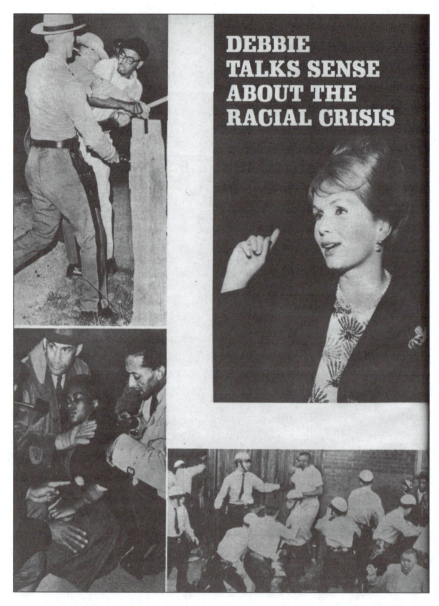

Figure 7.4 The civil rights movement barely earned a mention in fan magazines; here the focus is on white actress Debbie Reynolds' views on the subject.

Source: Image from May 1964 issue of *Photoplay* courtesy of University of Southern California Cinematic Arts Library.

Photoplay article is a notable exception, featuring numerous photos of black protesters being beaten by police. And yet the story itself focused on Debbie Reynolds' views on the "racial crisis," which is not surprising, since the magazines continued to focus nearly all of their coverage on whites.[27]

During the 1960s, coverage of African-American entertainers increased from virtually non-existent to occasional features, but never without mention of race. Notably, fan magazine stories began to cover African Americans as individuals struggling to combat racism, although they never criticized the Hollywood establishment itself for discriminating against nonwhite performers.

For example, a 1963 *Photoplay* ran a story on Sammy Davis, Jr., and Dick Gregory called "How Two Negro Showmen Fight for Integration." The article names several celebrities, including Paul Newman, Joanne Woodward, and Rita Moreno, who attended a Los Angeles civil rights rally led by Martin Luther King, Jr., and offers a sympathetic discussion of the impact racism has had on Davis and Gregory. Both describe their service in the U.S. Army and the discrimination they faced from fellow soldiers. The story implies that Hollywood provided opportunity that the rest of American society did not, and casts show business as a meritocracy. Their talent set them apart, despite the persistence of racial inequality, according to the story. Sympathetic celebrities helped too. "Frank [Sinatra] helped me overcome my greatest handicap, my inferiority complex about being a Negro," said Davis.[28]

African Americans could also count on coverage if they were romantically linked with whites, such as a 1964 story about Chubby Checker describing how his mother was apparently distraught because of his marriage to a white woman, a former Miss World winner.[29] "Why is Mommy White?" asks an article that same year, allegedly a question that Sammy Davis, Jr.'s children had about their Swedish mother, May Britt.[30] A 1970 gossip item noted how Pat Morrow (a white actress who appeared on *Peyton Place*) "admits" to dating Mike Warren (an African-American basketball player). The item describes how "it takes courage for her to date him and him to date her. Nobody seems thrilled about it in either family."[31] These stories focused on the perceived potential problems of interracial families; Checker's mother was allegedly concerned it would end his career, and the article on Davis's family presumed that his children experienced confusion about their identity.

Real life or onscreen interracial relationships served as a source of curiosity. A story about Raquel Welch focused on her role in the film *100 Rifles* (1969), one of the first Hollywood films to feature an interracial love scene.[32] Likewise, a 1968 *Movieland and TV Time* article discusses actor Sidney Poitier's European vacation with his children. An Italian reporter asked the star of *Guess Who's Coming to Dinner* (1967), a story about an interracial relationship, whether he would "marry a white girl." Poitier answered that he would, and was also asked to comment about race relations in the United States.[33] While being included by fan magazines was a significant advancement for African-American performers, Davis, Gregory, and Poitier's blackness preceded their celebrity in the stories.

In the coming years, interracial relationships began to lose their newsworthiness, particularly after the landmark 1967 Supreme Court ruling *Loving v. Virginia*, which decriminalized interracial marriage. A 1971 *Photoplay* story about African-American actor and former football player Fred Williamson's son with his Swedish ex-wife focuses on how Williamson teaches the boy to be proud of his diverse heritage. The article describes how he "he has been blessed with some of the best features of each of his parents," with "golden hair, clear gray eyes and a caramel tan."[34] By 1972, photos of interracial couples began appearing in gossip pages without any specific commentary.[35]

A notable exception was white actress Peggy Lipton's relationship with African-American music producer Quincy Jones. Jones was married when Lipton became pregnant in 1973. And yet the title of a 1974 *Modern Screen* article, "Peggy Lipton tells about the Joy and Pain of Having a Black Baby," suggests that the interracial nature of the relationship was the most significant issue, not that he was married to someone else. "I never knew how cruel some people could be until now," she told the magazine, "why do people look down on me for having an affair with a black man?" Lipton's parents, according to "a close friend" were also "sick about the whole thing," according to the story. Lipton did address the marriage issue, telling the magazine, "Quincy and I can't marry until he gets a divorce ... but neither of us sees the need to marry. It might destroy our whole relationship." And yet the majority of the focus was placed on the issue of race, rather than their reluctance to marry.[36] When Lipton and Jones did marry in 1974, *Movieland and TV Time* swooned:

From the beginning [they] wanted to have a baby together (they didn't want an illegitimate baby, but circumstances necessitated it). They wanted a symbol of their own *pure* love for each other, knowing that a baby would make their union complete . . . Their love for each other was never a *sin* to Peggy and Quincy, only to those who wouldn't choose to do as they did. They only knew that they were two people loving and caring for each other.[37]

Rates of interracial marriage grew modestly in the general public as well. According to economist Roland G. Freyer, Jr.'s analysis of historical census data, rates of intermarriage between blacks and whites were flat between 1880 and 1970, and rose slowly after that time. By 1980 about 1 percent of all marriages involved an interracial couple, rising to 3 percent in 2002.[38] According to the Gallup Poll, 73 percent of Americans disapproved of marriage between blacks and whites in 1968; by 1978 that number fell to 54 percent. In 2007, just 17 percent of respondents disapproved.[39] The growing visibility of interracial marriage in celebrity stories signified changes taking place in ideas about marriage. At the same time, marriage itself was no longer regarded as central to the American Dream as it had been in the years immediately following the end of World War II.

Marriage in Trouble

If a happy marriage was synonymous with success after the war ended, by the 1960s this would fall into serious doubt. Divorce rates rose over the next twenty years until divorce itself became commonplace; in 1969 California became the first state in the nation to institute no-fault divorce proceedings to ease a growing caseload. A 1963 ad for a book called *How to Find a Husband After Forty* reflects the increase in divorce and second marriages, including chapters on both premarital sex and how to win over each other's children.[40]

Vince Edwards, who played TV doctor Ben Casey, told *Photoplay* that marriage-minded girls should "cool it" in an article titled "Teen Marriages are Ridiculous!"[41] An article in *Modern Screen* titled "How to be Married" concedes that the two celebrity couples featured were not always happy. "What is wrong with young Hollywood marriages?" the author asks, detailing the large number of unsuccessful marriages of stars such as Lana

Figure 7.5 Ads such as this one reflect shifts in marriage and divorce during the 1960s.

Source: Advertisement from January 1963 issue of *Modern Screen* courtesy of University of Southern California Cinematic Arts Library.

Turner and Rita Hayworth. "They are young, they marry early, have babies early, settle down in apartments or little houses and they want their marriages to resemble, as closely as possible, those of the ubiquitous 'couple next door'. But they can't always do it."[42]

This statement could apply to any one of the thousands of young people who married in the years after the end of World War II. Many of the newly divorced were likely part of the teen marriage trend of the postwar era. The year 1960 marked a peak in the percentage of Americans married: 67 percent of women and 71 percent of men over fifteen had been married.[43] The median age at first marriage for women dipped under twenty-one between 1950 and 1970; divorce rates gradually climbed from just under 8 per thousand in 1955 to 20 per thousand in 1975.[44]

Even being a queen was no guarantee of a successful marriage and happiness. A 1961 *Modern Screen* article details the divorce between the Shah of Iran and Queen Soraya, despite her beauty and love for her husband. She had failed to produce a male heir, according to the story:

"Heartbroken, cast off, Soraya wanders the world in lonely exile."[45] Eddie Fisher was also "cast off" by Elizabeth Taylor after their scandalous affair and subsequent marriage dominated headlines. Fisher discussed his struggle after learning of Taylor's affair with *Cleopatra* co-star Richard Burton, stating that, "A kick in the teeth makes a guy who was too lucky in the first place re-evaluate life. I never had to struggle; always got the right breaks at the right time. Everything was too easy."[46]

Celebrity stories no longer characterized marriage as a state of infinite bliss, as it often was characterized in the prior decade. Instead, marriage seemed more like a struggle. "Our Marriage Wasn't Made in Heaven— But It's Getting There!" a 1964 *Photoplay* article on Rod Taylor's marriage admitted. "The idea that a man and a woman can live together in complete harmony is not only a difficult notion, it's preposterous," Taylor wrote after being married for less than a year. He described how "A man likes to feel that the little woman regards him as a mountain of muscle, always on hand to shield her, but evidently Mary doesn't regard me as anything faintly similar." Taylor also noted that although his anniversary was a date that was easy to remember, he probably would forget it (he would stay married to Mary for five more years).[47] A 1972 article on Shirley Jones and Jack Cassidy's troubled marriage describes how they have had "many agonizing moments" and that while "most people divorce without any second thoughts when things aren't as harmonious as they thought love would be," the couple was attempting to reconcile. Besides discussing their volatile personalities and many fights, the article suggests that her success might have bruised Cassidy's ego. Jones is "woman enough to handle both a career and family," and told the magazine that she might have been naïve about marriage initially. "I'm not saying it's the greatest of all institutions," she said, adding that "the commitment alone is worth it to me." The couple divorced two years later.[48]

By this time, magazine articles began using anonymous sources and wrote stories inserting themselves into couples' alleged conflicts. No longer were these confined to brief mentions in gossip columns, but magazines crafted entire stories around what amounted to speculation. A 1974 *Modern Screen* story attempts to dispel a rumor that Sonny Bono beat wife Cher so badly that she was hospitalized. "They *are* fighting; bitterly and heartbreakingly. But probably not violently," the magazine surmised. According to the story, their marital difficulties seemed to emerge from

ELIZABETH MONTGOMERY DIVORCING?

The end of "Bewitched" seems to have also heralded the end of the marriage of its star and her husband—Liz Montgomery and Bill Asher!

Figure 7.6 Rumors of pending celebrity divorces were common during the 1970s.

Source: Image from September 1972 issue of *Movieland and TV Time* courtesy of University of Southern California Cinematic Arts Library.

their success. Cher was exhausted from their schedule, thus the hospital stay, according to the magazine. Sonny "has a driving need to prove himself again and again with each new challenge," and their variety show meant that they were together too much. "They wear on each other's nerves."[49]

According to a 1972 *Movieland and TV Time* story, another couple who worked together—actress Elizabeth Montgomery and her producer-director husband, William Asher—might also be headed for divorce. "They seemed very happy at home and working together," a caption read, next to pictures showing the couple holding hands. "She and Bill bicycled and played tennis and shared real togetherness. What happened?" asked another caption. The magazine proposes an answer to its own question: "The end of *Bewitched* seems to have also heralded the end of the marriage of its star and her husband."[50]

It wasn't just marriage that was in doubt; perhaps celebrity itself was a recipe for unhappiness. An item about Lana Turner's alleged marital trouble with fifth husband Fred May, "Fifth on the Rocks," describes how her famous discovery in the Hollywood soda shop might have been the beginning of her undoing. "If Lana hadn't worn a sweater that day she might be happier today."[51] Likewise, Elvis Presley's stardom and massive financial success seems to have derailed what was once considered a storybook marriage to Priscilla Beaulieu. "Priscilla . . . has become disenchanted with being the wife of one of the world's most famous and secretive men," according to a 1972 story:

> She is relegated to sitting with the wives of his pals and bodyguards, or perhaps his father . . . Yes, she can go shopping and buy anything she wants . . . She can get tired of possessions to replace a husband . . . There are just so many houses you can decorate, so many cars you can ride in, so many courses you can take without being sated to death by all that opulence.[52]

Despite "mansions in various parts of the country, servants for day and servants for night so that, at any hour, her every wish was granted, [and] unlimited checking accounts," she left her marriage to live in "a small apartment, without servants, without unlimited money and for an ordinary man." Elvis's frequent travel was a factor, according to a 1973 *Modern Screen* story. Besides touring, Elvis made a string of movies during their relationship, yet she mostly stayed in Memphis. "Priscilla was . . . lonely, with too much time on her hands," the article concludes.[53]

This story serves as a larger cautionary tale, one that many people were learning after their own disillusionment with materialism during that time. Many who had achieved the postwar version of the American Dream asked themselves, "Is this all there is?"—particularly the generation coming of age during prosperous times. During the 1960s, national unemployment rates fell from a high of 7.1 percent in May 1961 down to a low of 3.4 percent in August 1968.[54] Median household incomes rose about 27 percent during the decade, adjusting for inflation, and college enrollment doubled between 1961 and 1970.[55] Upward mobility seemed practically inevitable, and it did not always bring happiness. Perhaps marriage was no longer a prerequisite, either, for upward mobility.

Fan magazines did not completely stop romanticizing marriage, and celebrity weddings could still yield gushing magazine coverage. "Deborah Walley said I do to Chet McCracken and things just couldn't be happier!" according to a 1968 story about their relationship. "Debbie feels now that love is lovelier the second time around," the article claims, next to a photo spread of the affectionate couple at home. "They talk together almost all of the time, read together and listen to music together."[56] And yet on the very next page of the magazine, the gossip pages describe how all is not what it seems with Hollywood marriages. In describing an alleged affair, gossip columnist Victoria Cole opines, "What's wild is that the image they present is that of such a goody-goody all-American couple," perhaps like Walley and McCracken's on the previous page.[57]

A 1970 gossip page focused on "a month for marriages" in Hollywood, picturing five newly married couples.[58] When *Room 222* star Denise Nicholas married, *Movieland and TV Time* described her and her songwriter husband as "being wonderfully, gloriously in love," and "have hopefully embarked on a lifetime of wedded bliss."[59] Royal weddings received attention too: a 1974 *Modern Screen* gossip page included Princess Anne of England's wedding pictures as well as "our own royal family," with Robert F. Kennedy's daughter Kathleen's marriage to David Townshend.[60] "Married Love is Better than Ever!" according to a 1973 story about Karen Valentine and Mac McLaughlin. *Modern Screen* describes how Valentine "in her breathless little girl voice" talks about their new home:

> further demonstration of the roots they've planted in their marriage. When they were wed four years ago, friends were afraid they were heading for instant problems because Karen was the money-maker . . . and Mac could scarcely get work as an actor.

The couple divorced that year.[61]

Regardless of whether their disparate incomes were the cause or not, women did enter the labor force in large numbers at this time. While in 1950, 34 percent of women worked in the labor force, that number rose to 43 percent in 1970 and has continued to rise, according to the Bureau of Labor Statistics.[62] And yet it would still be very rare for a wife to be the primary money maker at that time. In 1970, just 4 percent of wives out-earned husbands, compared with 22 percent in 2007.[63] Valentine's situation might have been unusual, but as women gained ground in the job market they became less financially dependent on marriage for survival.

Just as women were entering the workforce in larger numbers, they were having fewer children. The Food and Drug Administration (FDA) approved the first oral contraceptive in 1960, and within two years doctors prescribed "the Pill" to more than a million American women.[64] The baby boom officially ended in 1964, and celebrity magazines no longer romanticized children as they had when it began in 1946. The birth rate peaked in the late 1950s at about 120 births per thousand women; by the early 1970s the rate was nearly half that, at just over 60 per thousand.[65] Families were less likely to appear in highly produced publicity spreads with immaculately groomed children. When children of celebrities did appear in magazines, informal snapshots were much more common. And while fan magazines still covered births to celebrities as highly anticipated events, typically babies and children were less central to stories than they had been in the baby boom era. "Connie [Stevens] and Eddie [Fisher]

Figure 7.7 During the 1940s and 1950s carefully staged pictures of celebrities and their children like this one regularly appeared in fan magazines.

Source: Image from July 1948 issue of *Photoplay* courtesy of University of Southern California Cinematic Arts Library.

ON A TRIP!

The Osmond brothers went to England to do a Royal Command Show to aid British Olympic team fund. They loved the trip and the show and meeting the Queen of England. Here are Jay, Wayne, Merrill, Donny and Alan and little Jimmy, 8 in the foreground. They were big hits over there as they are here.

Figure 7.8 During the 1970s images of celebrity children were much less formal than in previous decades.

Source: Image from September 1972 issue of *Movieland and TV Time* courtesy of University of Southern California Cinematic Arts Library.

were rumored to be having marital trouble in a big way but then Connie announced they were expecting again," according to a 1968 caption under a photo of the couple looking less than blissful.[66] The presence of children, both within celebrity marriages and in the general population, no longer prevented divorce.

Rumors of celebrity marriages in peril were by no means new during this time, but they grew even more commonplace. This brand of gossip about troubled marriages emphasized a general sense of unhappiness surrounding even the most celebrated marriages. "The gossips said they'd part again and go their separate, lonely ways," said a 1960 issue of *Photoplay* about Princess Grace and Prince Rainier of Monaco.[67] That same issue included a story about Marilyn Monroe and Arthur Miller, simply headlined "Divorce." Monroe was allegedly infatuated with co-star Yves Montand, and according to the story, he was ignoring her repeated efforts to see him.[68] No longer would dating while still married to someone else be a scandal. Instead it appeared to be practically inevitable at a time when marriage seemed doomed to fail.

The Joy of Divorce

By the 1970s, the fan magazines stopped characterizing divorce as a tragic end to a romantic fantasy, but rather as a liberating beginning to a new and improved life. "Joey Heatherton is a free woman again now that her divorce from Lance Rentzel has come through," according to a 1972 gossip item.[69] Gossip about marriages in trouble went a step further. No longer did gossip columns coyly allude to new relationships, but both the magazines and celebrities themselves owned up to extramarital affairs. Besides Elizabeth Taylor and Richard Burton's famous courtship while still married to others, dozens of stars admitted that they too hoped to wed a new love when a divorce was final.

Gossip columnist Hedda Hopper asked Elizabeth Ashley if the rumor of a relationship with George Peppard was true. She confirmed it was, adding that "neither of us is divorced, so marriage will have to wait."[70] Cybill Shepherd and Peter Bogdanovich appeared in a 1972 photo under the headline, "To Marry Soon!" The copy added, "as soon as the divorce is final, they'll tie the knot."[71] "Sandy Duncan has admitted that she and her doctor friend will be married when her divorce comes through," according to a gossip item that same year.[72] Susan Dey, then starring on *The Partridge Family*, was allegedly dating an ABC assistant producer, but when they were not photographed together at a party, an article noted that the producer ". . . was married and is getting a divorce, so perhaps he preferred not posing with Susan yet."[73]

Divorced celebrities also seemed to be reveling in their freedom. A 1974 *Modern Screen* story explains that Barbra Streisand supposedly "doesn't want marriage" after her 1971 divorce from Elliott Gould. Citing an "industry confidante" as the story's main source, Barbra was allegedly dating around Hollywood, and "her proud, enigmatic smile seems to say" she no longer desires marriage and "one man is not enough for me now!"[74]

A 1974 *Modern Screen* article presented a celebrity relationship from the other woman's perspective. The story described 56-year-old Dean Martin's engagement to 25-year-old Catherine Hawn as "a never ending soap opera" due to:

> . . . the suspense of not knowing when Jeanne Martin [Martin's wife of twenty-four years] was finally going to get her divorce

and how many zillions she'd get as a "settlement". But Cathy was patient. Good for Cathy. She knew a good thing when she saw one.

The article goes on to describe the relationship as a dream come true for the young woman, with "diamonds and homes and unlimited charge accounts," without further mention that Martin was still a married man. When their dream wedding did come, it cost $50,000–$100,000 ($220,000–$440,000 in 2010 dollars) according to the magazine, which described the lilacs flown in from Paris and twenty-two cages of white doves in the ceremony. The story even claims that Frank Sinatra called it "the most beautiful wedding I've ever seen." And yet, for all of this drama, "the wedding night was very anti-climatic," because apparently Martin had a painful ulcer and asked to sleep in a separate room. The marriage lasted three years.[75]

Mobility Beyond Marriage

While many marriages such as Martin and Hawn's did not last long, stories similar to the one above still gushed over celebrity weddings. And yet fan magazines did not always characterize getting married as the height of success and happiness as they did in the years immediately after World War II. In fact, many celebrity stories told of the exciting lives young, single female stars led in Hollywood. *Modern Screen* interviewed Connie Stevens in 1963, and she told the magazine that she "date(s) many boys," and that "it's fun to date . . . I don't want to get married now. I'm all for marriage, but I'm a Catholic girl and don't believe in divorce." She added that when she went on a date she made it clear that she is not promiscuous, and that just because she dates a lot does not mean that she is sexually active, citing her religious values.

Beyond promoting abstinence ("I don't object to necking . . . But it should be done wholesomely"), Stevens' comments focus on her sense of independence. "I like the feeling of being free which I can achieve in my single state," she says, describing how being single can mean making your own decisions and worrying less about your appearance:

I think one of the tragedies of teenage marriages, is that the girl misses the fun and experience of knowing a lot of boys. What a small world it is for a girl when she marries the boy who's sat in the next seat to hers since she was twelve![76]

While teen marriages were a mainstay in celebrity magazines immediately after the war—most notably Shirley Temple and Elizabeth Taylor's early marriages—stories about young celebrities promoted delaying marriage now. A 1968 *Movieland and TV Time* article called "Two Boy Friends are Better Than One!" notes how television star Elizabeth Baur, then twenty years old, was in no rush to get married. She told the magazine, "I just cannot imagine myself being married . . . there are so many things I want to do before settling down to marriage and a family." She also added:

> I wouldn't want to give up my career for marriage . . . when you're married you should be a freer person than when you're single— and I don't think you should dictate to somebody you love what they can and cannot do.

Baur did note that she wanted to be married and have children eventually, but that she would not be "tie[d] . . . down" to dating just one man.[77]

For Stevens, Baur, and many others coming of age during the 1960s, delaying marriage meant a few more years of focusing on one's own needs before a husband and children would become the center of a woman's life. Just one month after Stevens' interview ran in *Modern Screen*, Betty Friedan published the iconic *The Feminine Mystique*, chronicling the "problem with no name" many suburban homemakers felt in the postwar era. Friedan's depiction of marriage and motherhood called into question the assumption that they were inevitable pathways to happiness for women. Just as Stevens, then twenty-four, seemed to revel in her single status, *The Feminine Mystique* suggests that marriage could be mind-numbingly dull for young women, virtual prisoners in their new tract homes filled with the latest conveniences. In 1962, Helen Gurley Brown published *Sex and the Single Girl*, which gave advice to young unmarried working women about sex and dating, and suggested that working before marriage was not only more common, but could be exciting and a good way to meet men.

Figure 7.9 Ads offered women opportunities for careers and, in this ad, "a glamour job where the pay is far above the average."

Source: Image from December 1968 issue of *Movieland and TV Time* courtesy of University of Southern California Cinematic Arts Library.

Fan magazines offered tiny glimmers of the feminist movement in the 1960s. Ads promoting jobs pictured well-dressed "career girls" and promised glamorous and exciting careers in the corporate world. One booklet, advertised in 1973, promised information on "12 careers where today's woman takes a back seat to no one."[78] And yet ads and articles still characterized work as a temporary prelude to marriage; ads for books such as *How to Win and Hold a Husband* continued to appear, and gossip pages frequently referred to married women by their husbands' names, particularly if she was not famous (e.g. "The John Smiths enjoy a night on the town").[79]

Delaying marriage and childbirth, in stark contrast to the postwar years, began to define the new mode of success for women. The growing availability of birth control meant that family planning became more possible, although it was not until the 1968 Supreme Court ruling in *Griswold v. Connecticut* that married women would be assured access to birth control in all fifty states. And even then, only married women were legally guaranteed access at first. The ad below suggests that limiting the number of children (referred to as "the right number") would lead to happiness.

The right number of
CHILDREN
MAKE THE
HAPPIEST
FAMILIES

"the right number of children"

is as many as you can individually

love, guide, support — educate.

Over 80 family planning associations, each with its own Medical Committee, now recommend EMKO FOAM for mothers who plan the number and spacing of their children. From thousands of doctors in private practice who favor EMKO FOAM, come reports of its effectiveness. One report, for example, is based on use by 102 patients. Their opinion, in general, after 1,011 months of experience, was that EMKO FOAM was the best product they had ever used.

Figure 7.10 Family planning ads began to appear in fan magazines in the 1960s.

Source: Image from April 1964 issue of *Photoplay* courtesy of University of Southern California Cinematic Arts Library.

While reporting on the possible reconciliation of two high-profile couples—Natalie Wood and Robert Wagner, and Connie Stevens and Eddie Fisher—a 1972 *Movieland and TV Time* story suggested that marriage might not be necessary for a couple's happiness. "More and more we are hearing of people who say they feel more married without a license," the author observes, "it is far too soon to tell if all the young people who refuse to marry, but will have children and then move on to new loves will be able to say it was good for the children." The article suggests that the two couples' marriages might have ended in divorce, but really didn't "fail" since the couples were still apparently in love, distinguishing legal marriage from a sort of spiritual union.[80] "Obviously, in this day and age, Natalie and Bob could have just continued to be together, not bother to marry. But they wanted the commitment," according to the magazine later that year, after they had remarried. "Marriage is better the second time around," the article exclaims.[81]

However, some celebrities expressed no interest in marrying even if they were in presumably monogamous relationships. "We have no plans to marry at the moment," said Jacqueline Bisset of her live-in boyfriend in a 1971 issue of *Modern Screen*. She added that "if the time comes when we both want children, we will, of course, make it legal. I don't believe in bringing up children illegitimately."[82] "Marriage seems to be a word that finishes a relationship. It doesn't start it," she told the magazine in 1974 after her live-in relationship ended. According to "friends" quoted in the article, despite their modern arrangement it seems the problem was that her boyfriend insisted that she cook for him and do as he said, "subservience, pure and simple," according to *Modern Screen*.[83] In contrast to the 1950s, when a relationship failure seemed related to a woman's ambition, celebrity stories such as this one allude to patriarchy as a central problem of marriage. And while Bisset might not have wanted to have children outside of marriage, some cohabiting celebrity couples were vocal about their lack of interest in marriage, even if they were having children.

Bucking Tradition: Children Outside of Marriage

By the 1970s, with the postwar fantasy of happiness through marriage and family beginning to unravel, coupled with the end of the studio system and its contract morality clauses, having a baby outside of marriage was no longer as scandalous. Unmarried women who had babies during the heyday of the studio system would have to cover it up or risk termination. For instance, actress Loretta Young went on "vacation" in 1935 and returned with an "adopted" daughter she had given birth to, fathered by a married Clark Gable. The public only learned of the affair when their daughter, Judy Lewis, published her autobiography in 1994. Otherwise, their careers (or at least Young's) would have most certainly ended in scandal.

While celebrity divorces and subsequent single parenthood were by no means new in the 1960s, adopting outside of marriage would have been unusual. In 1964, *Photoplay* claimed that Stefanie Powers "wanted to be a mother before [she] became a bride" and was considering adoption. "My agent, the studio, everybody thinks I'm crazy," she told the magazine.[84] While it's unclear whether Powers ever went ahead with the adoption, in the years to come many celebrities spoke openly about becoming parents outside of marriage. Pregnancy often preceded marriage in the past, but typically this was a family secret rather than discussed publicly—especially by the mother-to-be herself.

Instead, fan magazines described news of an impending birth to an unmarried couple cheerily by the 1970s, even if one of the parents-to-be was married to someone else. "Larry Harvey admits to siring a daughter . . . with gorgeous Britisher Paulene Stone and says they'll marry as soon as his divorce to [*sic*] Joan Cohn comes through," according to a 1972 issue of *Movieland and TV Time*.[85] A 1970 gossip item notes that "Mia Farrow and Andre Previn are walking on air—Mia's expecting a baby, and Andre's seeking a divorce from Dory."[86] Later in the same issue of the magazine another columnist writes that, "neither he nor Mia seem uptight about whether or not they'll be married in time to welcome their little heir or heiress."[87] Allegedly even Farrow's mother, actress Maureen O'Sullivan, was quite excited about the development, despite being a devout Catholic.

Yet the next page of the magazine contains an extremely critical rebuke of Vanessa Redgrave's refusal to marry the father of her baby, claiming that it could "make his life harder." But perhaps the real reason for the condemnation has less to do with Redgrave's marital status than her political beliefs. "You protest against America . . . No, we aren't perfect, Vanessa, but neither is England or any country for that matter," wrote columnist Victoria Cole.[88] (Redgrave went on to marry her son's father, Franco Nero, thirty-six years later in 2006.)

Fan magazines offered little scrutiny of other unmarried couples. A 1972 gossip item in *Movieland and TV Time* under the heading "Another Baby!" says that "Jennifer Bogart and Elliot Gould are said to be awaiting their second child. Like so many modern couples these days, they have not married yet."[89] A gossip item in the same issue notes that Barbara Hershey and David Carradine would be having a baby but had no plans to wed.[90] That this was a small mention (under the caption "Mod Duo!") suggests that their relationship was far from scandalous. She told the magazine in a later issue that "marriage is dumb," and "love cannot be imprisoned." A 1979 *People* story described her as "the archetypal Hollywood hippie," and the 1972 article also characterized her as such.[91] For a time she insisted on being called "Barbara Seagull" after a seagull was killed during a movie shoot. "They don't believe in dressing up, socializing, just in being free and doing what they feel like doing," according to *Movieland and TV Time*, and their lack of interest in marriage reflected their countercultural values.[92] In fact, their son was named Free (though he apparently later changed his name to Tom).

Not all unmarried pregnant celebrities got glowing coverage, especially if the mother-to-be wasn't in a relationship. A 1971 article about Patty Duke, then pregnant and unmarried, cast her behavior as bizarre and erratic. The previous year she abruptly eloped with a man "she had known casually" and filed for divorce seventeen days later. "One of the most disastrous things in the world is boredom," she told the magazine.[93] Duke has subsequently been open about suffering from bipolar disorder, which would explain her impulsive decisions. But at the time her behavior seemed part of a hedonistic youth culture that flouted convention.

A Shift in Mores

Aside from changes in mores about marriage and family, box office competition from television and risqué European New Wave films meant that standards surrounding nudity were changing. "What a difference a decade makes!" proclaimed a 1962 issue of *Modern Screen*. Ten years prior, when nude photos of Marilyn Monroe surfaced, observers thought her career would be over. But the magazine's August 1962 issue (published just before her death that month) featured an article titled "Marilyn Bares All!" which described her nude scene in the film *Something's Got to Give*. Nude scenes and photos would become more acceptable, "as movies become more adult and daring."[94] Nudity gradually became less scandalous, although the photos and film clips that remain from the film she would never complete are anything but revealing. A year later, *Photoplay* ran a story "Now Liz Poses Nude!" about Elizabeth Taylor's appearance in *Playboy* magazine in January 1963. The author asks whether she is "'modern' or 'immoral,' 'emancipated' or 'exhibitionistic?'" for appearing in the magazine, but makes clear that her bathing scene from *Cleopatra* was justified and that "no European showing of an American-produced film is successful without at least one episode in which a female star swims or bathes in the altogether."[95]

With the collapse of the studio system, there was no longer a powerful organization to kill stories that might present celebrities in an unflattering light. Celebrity arrests might have been kept out of the pages of fan magazines during the studios' heyday, but no longer. When German actor Horst Buchholz, who had recently appeared in *The Magnificent Seven*, was in a drunken driving accident in Munich in 1961, *Photoplay* not only reported on the story but included a full photo essay reminiscent of today's tabloids.[96] A few years later, in 1964, the magazine ran a series of photos of Elizabeth Taylor and Richard Burton standing with what appears to be beers outside of a pub. "How long can Burton hold Liz—and his liquor, too?" *Photoplay*'s headline asked.[97] Taylor and Burton became a cottage industry of speculation about their alleged life of excess. From reports of massive spending (A "69 carat million-dollar Cartier diamond; the $305,000 Krupp diamond; the $37,000 Peregrina Pearl, merely a handful among others"[98]), affairs,[99] and even an open marriage,[100] the couple came to represent a new era of "gotcha" celebrity coverage, where the more personal the story, the better.

During the heyday of the studio system, publicists would have tried hard to ensure that celebrity drug use remained secret. In fact, drugs became a topic of fascination during the 1970s. *Movieland and TV Time* fully covered David Carradine's 1974 arrest for trespassing, malicious mischief, and attempted burglary, along with tales of his unhappy childhood and frequent use of peyote and LSD. "Something is at war in his soul," the author concludes.[101] Jack Nicholson spoke openly of his drug use to *Photoplay* in 1975, in a story called "Jack Nicholson Tells What It's Like to Get Stoned on Pot, Cocaine and LSD." He told the magazine that he was "really quite old-fashioned," and that he was really just a social drug user who knew when he had had enough.[102]

Figure 7.11 Fan magazine stories began including more scandals in the 1960s, frequently featuring Elizabeth Taylor and Richard Burton.

Source: Image from April 1964 issue of *Photoplay* courtesy of University of Southern California Cinematic Arts Library.

In 1971, Jane Fonda was arrested for drug smuggling and assaulting an officer after failing to declare 105 vials of capsules to customs when re-entering the U.S. from Canada. *Modern Screen* described the actress-turned-political-activist's life as "chaotic" in a less-than-flattering story about her arrest, which included a picture of Fonda in handcuffs.[103] *Movieland and TV Time* characterized Fonda as being used by "drifters eating Jane out of house and home" just weeks after her highly publicized visit to Hanoi in July 1972.[104]

Fonda's visit to Vietnam marks a stark contrast between Vietnam-era celebrities and their World War II counterparts a generation before. While celebrity support for the war effort was compulsory during World War II, with studio-organized benefits and the likelihood of reprimand by studio heads for stars who seemed not to be doing their part, by the height of the Vietnam War studios no longer had control of either celebrities or what the magazines printed about them. And at the same time, fan magazines almost completely ignored the war in Vietnam. There are probably many reasons for this, but unlike the World War II years, when the prevailing notion of the American Dream sparked a sense of collectivism, the 1960s and 1970s version of the dream was far more fractured. According to a Gallup Poll, support for the war was strong in 1966 but began to erode soon after, remaining under 50 percent after July 1967, and falling to a low of 28 percent in 1971.[105] Selling the increasingly

Figure 7.12 Fan magazines covered stories and included photos that might have been covered up during the heyday of the studio system, such as Jane Fonda's 1971 arrest for drug smuggling.

Source: Image from February 1971 issue of *Modern Screen* courtesy of University of Southern California Cinematic Arts Library.

controversial war would not be a boon to celebrity culture, nor would many of the antihero stars do much to gain public attention for the war effort either.

If anything, collectivism in this era would form through the anti-war movement. Those involved in the counterculture movement came together, however briefly, to challenge both the war and the values represented by postwar prosperity: conformity, materialism, and militarism. The social activism of the 1960s mutated, however, into more introspection in the 1970s, with people coming of age then frequently labeled the "me generation," as self-help began to overtake social change as a central focus. A 1977 *Photoplay* article features actress Valerie Perrine's "confession" that she sometimes sees a psychiatrist.[106] Whether through collective encounter groups, therapy, or reading one of the many best-selling self-help books of the era, many baby boomers coming of age then would seek alternatives to materialism for personal fulfillment during the 1970s.

Finding Religion

Despite the common characterization of the sixties and seventies as a time of hedonistic, pleasure-seeking behavior, fan magazines increasingly emphasized how celebrities' faith helped them during difficult times. It might seem contradictory that during a time when celebrities became more open about drug use, cohabiting, and having children outside of marriage that religious faith would become a topic fan magazines would cover more. Historically, the Catholic Church in particular was highly critical of both movies and fan magazines; it is the Catholic League of Decency that successfully lobbied for the Hays Code, and in 1935 the Church supported a boycott of fan magazines, complaining that the photos they contained were highly revealing and unsuitable for families.[107] Celebrity stories sometimes reflect the antithesis of religious piety, and instead can be viewed as morality tales of personal excess. But during the 1970s, celebrity stories included more discussion of the connection between celebrity's faith and success.

When singer Kathy Lennon had a hysterectomy despite her desire to have children, *Movieland and TV Time* described how "Kathy's prayers for a child have gone unanswered," but she maintained her strong belief in God, according to an article titled, "Kathy Lennon's Faith!" "All of the Lennon sisters are Catholic—they think of babies as God's blessing of a marriage, and Kathy still hoped and prayed that she . . . too would be blessed."[108] The same magazine also discussed how Connie Stevens was fervently praying for not only her unborn baby when complications left her hospitalized, but also for her husband's ex-wife, Elizabeth Taylor. Stevens is "a very devout girl," according to the story, who "thanks Him for all the good things she has received."[109]

Rita McLaughlin, an actress on *As the World Turns*, told of the importance of prayer in her life as she navigated the challenges of show business. In the 1975 article, "She Prays a Lot!" McLaughlin notes how she "couldn't get through the day without talking to God." She had turned down a movie offer that included a nude scene, saying, "I utilize my religion in everything I do."[110]

Apparently she was not alone. A 1972 article in the magazine, called "I Owe You, God!" detailed dozens of stars and their faith. "Hollywood is always getting surprises from those in its midst whom it may think it knows well and does not know at all," notes the article, which includes anecdotes about stars ranging from Lana Turner, Sophia Loren, and Rosalind Russell to Danny Thomas, Glen Campbell, Dick Van Dyke and John Wayne. Bob Crane, the star of *Hogan's Heroes*, told the magazine that his "wife and I do our best to bring up our youngsters to pray, to attend church and to seek God's help with their troubles." The article includes both quotes from celebrities and stories of their days of struggle before stardom. Rather than simply hard work, their success appears to be the result of their faith and the mercy of God who answered their prayers.[111]

A *Movieland and TV Time* feature on soap star Nancy Karr details the challenges of being a working mother of four young children in a 1972 article. She describes how she became discouraged and exhausted while trying out for acting roles and credits her success with a return to her parents' home. "While regaining my bodily strength I also regained my spiritual faith," she said, adding that "those doors did start to open for me."[112] A 1972 gossip item tells of Johnny Cash's faith: "his good deeds are legend . . . Religion has played a large part in his life and he practices it every day of his life," according to *Movieland and TV Time*.[113] Ads such as the ones below, proclaiming, "God, I am Troubled!" appeared frequently in the 1970s, offering religious solutions for readers' troubles.

Figure 7.13
During the 1970s, stories about celebrities' faith appeared regularly in *Movieland and TV Time*, as did ads for religious paraphernalia.

Source: Advertisement from May 1973 issue of *Movieland and TV Time* courtesy of University of Southern California Cinematic Arts Library.

While at first it may seem counterintuitive that celebrities of the 1970s would share their religious beliefs more frequently, this coincides with the growth of the conservative movement and the birth of the so-called "Moral Majority" in 1979, which sought to provide an evangelist influence to the national political agenda. A growing backlash to the perceived excesses of the era led to increased support for a shift towards conservatism, both personally and politically. The vast social changes—for people of color, women, and increasingly for gays and lesbians—would create a sense of anomie for some, who looked around and wondered what had happened to the Normal Rockwell pictures they held in their imagination when they thought about the meaning of America. And while the American Dream seemed unclear during this time of flux, conservatives suggested returning to an older version of the American Dream as a solution, one focused directly on family and indirectly on economic gain.

The roots of the modern conservative movement also predate the 1960s, with the writings of William F. Buckley, who founded *The National Review* in 1955. His work would help galvanize those on the right, leading to Barry Goldwater's 1964 run for president as "Mr. Conservative." While Goldwater was unsuccessful, one of his strongest supporters, Ronald Reagan, would be successful in 1980. With a conservative economic agenda, Reagan ran on a platform that promised to bring back the postwar version of the American Dream, one that seemed simpler and clearer. America elected its first movie star president, merging celebrity culture and the American Dream into one iconic figure.

8

MASSIVE WEALTH AS MORAL REWARD

THE REAGAN REVOLUTION AND INDIVIDUALISM

The iconoclastic movie and television stars of the 1960s and 1970s seemed to do little to inspire the fantasy of the American Dream in the way that their predecessors once had. Film scholar Anthony Slide partly attributes this failure to the eventual demise of fan magazines such as *Photoplay* and *Modern Screen*, as their subjects no longer served to stoke the public's imagination of what life might be like if only they too made it big.[1] If anything, the magazines' focus on unhappy celebrities rejecting mainstream society left a void in the fantasy. In a desperate attempt to increase circulation, the old fan magazines re-ran stories about stars from the 1930s and 1940s, hoping to revive nostalgia for Hollywood's Golden Age. It didn't work, and the traditional fan magazines had folded by or during the 1980s, to be replaced largely by *People*, a spinoff of a mainstream weekly news magazine.

Instead, it was an actual celebrity from the Golden Age who would combine celebrity culture with a renewed version of the American Dream, one that harkened back to the postwar era. Ronald Reagan would use nostalgia for the American Dream of plenty not only to win the presidency in 1980, but to help create a new fantasy about the possibilities this dream could hold. As we will see in this chapter, this fantasy had its roots in the 1970s, reflected in *People*'s mostly celebratory coverage of heirs, entrepreneurs, and titans of industry whose personal lives peppered stories of how their hard work led to their fortunes. Stories often created sympathy for the super-wealthy when they suffered a tragic loss or experienced personal difficulties at the same time as fiscal policy favored tax cuts for the highest earners.

Celebrity culture once again glamorized massive wealth, reflecting the Reagan-era vision of the American Dream, ironically at the same time that the average American's economic outlook would dim. Not since the Great Depression had celebrity culture promised wealth of this scale; perhaps not coincidentally, in 1982 unemployment rates would rise to levels not seen since the Depression. Celebrity stories helped prop up the illusion that a glamorous lifestyle was not only possible, but moral, despite the counterculture movement's calls for reduced consumption and finding meaning outside of materialism. Articles regularly revealed dollar amounts of big paydays and described the lush lifestyles of the rich and famous. Marriage would once again seem glamorous, especially for those who married rich. Hard work could pay off practically overnight, and seemingly anyone could get lucky, no matter how humble their beginnings. And yet not all coverage was positive. Several stories offered morality tales of people who cheated investors or appeared excessively greedy at a time when the wealth gap began to widen, but for the most part being rich seemed like a moral reward for hard work.

By ignoring the growing wealth gap, these stories encouraged readers to identify with the wealthy while providing examples suggesting that wealth could be just around the corner for those who were lucky and hard working. Such stories both helped divert readers from the increasing economic disparity while also encouraging a renewed fantasy of the American Dream following an era of social upheavals. This chapter addresses the following central questions: How and why did celebrity stories return to focusing on material success? In what way did this shift reflect a change in the production of celebrity culture? And finally, what do these stories imply about the limits of individualism?

Morning in America

In many ways, it is understandable that the conservative movement would resurrect the dream of plenty, and that the public would respond. Following a period of social change and upheaval, material comforts make sense, particularly after a time of scarcity. For the first time since the Depression, Americans had been forced to do with less: the oil embargo of 1973 led to severe fuel shortages and helped spark high rates of inflation. In what would become known as President Jimmy Carter's 1979 "malaise speech" (although he never used that particular word), the president chided the nation for wanting more materially:

> In a nation that was proud of hard work, strong families, close-knit communities, and our faith in God, too many of us now tend to worship self-indulgence and consumption. Human identity is no longer defined by what one does, but by what one owns. But we've discovered that owning things and consuming things does not satisfy our longing for meaning. We've learned that piling up material goods cannot fill the emptiness of lives which have no confidence or purpose.[2]

Perhaps the president was right in substance, but this speech likely sealed Reagan's victory. Peppered with admissions of his administration's shortcomings and the failure of the American public to conserve resources, the speech was more of an angry sermon warning of future damnation. Although many of his warnings proved to be valid—particularly as we face the same challenges regarding energy and environmental damage more than thirty years later—Carter's pessimistic remarks failed to invoke the mythology of the American Dream that Reagan was able to use so well throughout his career. Carter's suggestion that we must make do with less offered no clear fantasy of the future in contrast to Reagan's nostalgia-laden reply four months later, where he invokes the notion of the American Dream indirectly:

> They tell us we must learn to live with less, and teach our children that their lives will be less full and prosperous than ours have been; that the America of the coming years will be a place where—because of our past excesses—it will be impossible to dream and make those dreams come true.
>
> I don't believe that. And, I don't believe you do either . . . Our leaders attempt to blame their failures on circumstances beyond their control, on false estimates by unknown, unidentifiable experts

who rewrite modern history in an attempt to convince us our high standard of living, the result of thrift and hard work, is somehow selfish extravagance which we must renounce as we join in sharing scarcity.[3]

Thus, "selfish extravagance" becomes redefined as part of the American birthright, a shift that came to shape both celebrity culture and national policy in years to come. While inflation, unemployment, and poverty rates would rise during the early years of the 1980s and purchasing power would decline for the average American, the powerful mythology of the American Dream of abundance would replace feelings of scarcity in the absence of a clear notion of the dream.

In reality, many of the social upheavals associated with the 1970s continued and, in some instances, worsened in the 1980s. Divorce rates nearly doubled between 1970 and 1980; in 1970 4 percent of American women over fifteen had been divorced compared with 7 percent in 1980, rising to nearly 10 percent of all women in 1990.[4] Double-digit inflation continued through 1981, and average weekly earnings fell nearly 18 percent between 1972 and 1982 when adjusted for inflation, reducing workers' purchasing power.[5] Median family incomes rose only modestly between 1970 and 1990, just under $7,500 (in 2001 dollars) during the twenty-year period, according to census data. This is despite significant increases in educational attainment: of Americans over twenty-five in 1970, 55 percent had graduated from high school compared with 74 percent in 1990; 11 percent had graduated from college in 1970 compared with 20 percent in 1990.[6] Any family income gains were likely the result of a greater number of women entering the paid labor force, rising from 43 percent in 1970 to 58 percent in 1990.[7]

Poverty rates remained at double-digit levels, surpassing 12 percent during 1982 and 1983, their highest rates since 1965 and the War on Poverty. For families with children, poverty rates would exceed 15 percent after 1981 and remain higher until 1998. African-American families' poverty rates would rise to nearly one out of every three families in 1982.[8] The income gap between the wealthiest 1 percent and the rest of the population began to rise in the 1980s after remaining stable since about 1950.[9]

Yet both the political culture and celebrity culture emphasized the plight of the wealthy. During a time when policies reduced welfare benefits and other domestic social programs while cutting tax rates by more than half for the highest earners between 1980 and 1990, the wealthy became celebrities themselves.[10] With the newly launched *People* magazine, royalty, heirs and heiresses, politicians, and corporate leaders would join a new version of celebrity culture, one that highlighted the trials and tribulations of the rich, while emphasizing the rags-to-riches stories of entertainers and athletes. As many Americans experienced personal and economic instability, celebrity culture provided a fantasy that enabled the public to partake, at least vicariously. These celebrity stories served to justify the new economic agenda while seeming to offer visible proof that a return to the American Dream would not just create prosperity, but would allow Americans to feel good about materialism again. If anyone could rise to the top through hard work, then poverty was just a temporary setback and inequality the result of personal failures.

A Shift in Celebrity Production

The shift in celebrity culture was about more than political change; the structure of both Hollywood and fan magazines underwent serious organizational changes in the last decades of the twentieth century. The end of the studio system likely triggered the demise of the traditional fan magazines, although it took decades before the last would fold. Studio publicity departments once provided fan magazines with a steady stream of content, and it was a relatively open secret that some studio publicists also wrote for the magazines, supplying favorable coverage of the studio's biggest stars. These connections sometimes led to "white lists," meaning some studios would only allow their stars to give interviews to favored magazines.[11] This synergy ended with the studio system, but was reborn with the growth of super agents and powerful publicists. Agents were not new to the industry, but large talent agencies could sell the services of their clients—actors, writers, and directors—as packages to maximize the agency's profits and power. And publicists who amassed rosters of stars could leverage their control over their clients' images to shape the kinds of stories told. Crossing a publicist could mean the end of access to their entire clientele.

As in the studio system days, this meant that magazines covering celebrities had to craft their content carefully to avoid offending the wrong people, but a celebrity's image was increasingly their own to create. One major difference between the agent/publicist arrangement and the studios' is that the entertainer employed the agent and publicist, while the studio employed the entertainer. Therefore, it is the celebrity who can hire and fire a publicist or agent, and ultimately they have more power in the relationship. It's not that uncommon for stars to change agents and publicists as they become more famous, further weakening the agents' and publicists' power in comparison with the studio system.

The old fan magazines would have had to reinvent themselves in this new environment, which they ultimately failed to do. Circulation declined, in part because television began to cover "celebrity news" and so the monthly magazines' deadlines would mean that they would be scooped every month by television.[12] Starting in 1969, Rona Barrett began her national television career, softening news broadcasts with celebrity gossip during a time when gritty Vietnam War coverage dominated the news.[13]

A few years later, in 1974, Time Incorporated sought to revive its struggling magazine fortunes with the launch of a new weekly magazine designed to tap into the market share of *TV Guide* and the *National Enquirer*. Time Inc.'s photo-heavy weekly magazine *Life* had just folded in 1972, and its assistant managing editor Richard Stolley became the founding editor of *People*.[14] Rather than launch a fan magazine in the tradition of *Photoplay* or *Modern Screen*, *People* would combine celebrity stories with general human interest, what Stolley described as "OPP": other people's problems.[15] He also sought to stretch the boundaries of celebrity, including features on more than just entertainers, which garnered criticism from other news organizations, including *New York Times* columnist William Safire, who derided Time Inc. for presuming their readers to be "tasteless fadcats."[16] And yet "celebrity journalism" would only grow in the coming years; in 1977 the New York Times Company founded *US Weekly* to compete with *People*. *Rolling Stone* founder Jann Wenner bought *US* a few years later and continues to run the magazine today. Celebrity coverage expanded far beyond magazines, with the birth of *Entertainment Tonight* and *The Barbara Walters Special*, both starting in 1981. The quest for ratings meant that celebrity stories would find their way into more and more traditional news programs as well.

"Personality journalism" would change not just the production of celebrity culture, but the culture itself, as the concept of celebrity expanded and information pertaining to celebrities became more ubiquitous.[17] Many of the same people likely to be featured in *Time* would occasionally find themselves in *People*; political figures such as Henry Kissinger and heirs of great fortunes such as Nelson Rockefeller not only expanded the definition of celebrity but broadened the definition of news to include personal details. Perhaps in search of an identity, many of *People*'s early stories focused on lifestyles of the wealthy and their personal problems. Editor Richard Stolley created a formula for what worked best with newsstand sales. A partial list includes: "Young is better than old, pretty is better than ugly, rich is better than poor."[18]

At a time when many Americans faced tough times of their own, reading about the rich—and their many problems—was likely a convenient escape. While *People* magazine expanded its coverage beyond movie stars and entertainers, it retained many of the same features of the old fan magazines: profiles of entertainers, with details of their private lives and photos of stars behind the scenes. Much like the fan magazines, *People* obtained significant cooperation from celebrities, and thus many of the stories were celebrity-friendly in contrast to tabloids such as the *National Enquirer*, which focused more on scandal.

Unlike traditional fan magazines, *People* included a few stories about non-famous individuals who had accomplished great feats or who overcame major tragedies. By incorporating these stories about people who presumably had much in common with the magazine's readers, celebrities seemed more like everyday people and everyday people might appear to have something in common with celebrities. While we might normally associate the expansion of celebrity with the internet and reality show age (which I discuss in the next chapter), the introduction of *People* helped hasten this shift. With the demise of traditional fan magazines and the success of *People*, the same kinds of fantasies spun around movie stars would extend to athletes, politicians, heirs, business leaders, and anyone else whose story might sell magazines.

The Rich are Different from You and Me

Just as in the fabled jazz age of the 1920s, when F. Scott Fitzgerald suggested that the rich were different from the rest of us, the end of the twentieth century brought a return of tales of the wealthy in the popular imagination. Many of these stories reinforced the Horatio Alger myth by emphasizing the hard work of their subjects. The stories suggest that material wealth is a just reward for those who have earned it, a conservative message in direct contrast to the counterculture movement's emphasis on the virtues of living with less.

Perhaps symbolizing the changing of the guard from old-style Hollywood fan magazine, *People* invited former *Photoplay* writer (and onetime Fitzgerald mistress) Sheilah Graham to write one of the first articles the magazine ever published. Graham wrote disparagingly about her move to Palm Beach, focusing on its lack of social mobility and what she saw as petty battles for social position. "The big difference between Palm Beach and Hollywood is that Hollywood is a working city," Graham claimed. "There you can open every door with talent . . . But you don't have to marry someone rich to make it. Society is the only industry in Palm Beach."[19] While reaffirming the notion that show business was a meritocracy, Graham's critique of elites would not match the generally positive coverage they would receive on the pages of *People*.

Creating personal stories of those with wealth and power highlighted their importance and set the stage for defining success through the accumulation of massive wealth. Wealth meant constant leisure and happiness beyond imagination in most of the stories. During a time when many young people sought meaning through non-traditional channels, the message in *People* was simple: being wealthy was still a worthy goal.

The magazine's stories suggested that the international jet-set were not just richer than everyone else, but had more fun. Describing the opening of the Las Hadas resort in Mexico in 1974, *People* noted that, "There may have been a stray baron or two who got lost and ended up in Costa Rica, but just about everybody else in the way of nobility and global society was in Mexico for the weekend." A heart surgeon who visited said, "Las Hadas may not make you live longer, but you will certainly live happier."[20] Advertisements stressed their product's supposed links with the super-wealthy, implying that eating the right ice cream or using the mustard of the elite would confer higher status on you, too.

Secretary of State Henry Kissinger seemed to be having lots of fun hanging around the wealthy crowd. The magazine treated this controversial Watergate figure not as a public servant and intellectual, but as a member of the elite, covering his courtship and wedding to Nancy Maginnes, with details about the couple's ceremony and Mexican honeymoon.[21] "A party only a Rockefeller could afford," was held for the couple when they returned, attracting guests from as far away as Europe for the elegant affair. The story also describes the home that the couple would rent in Washington, previously inhabited by a Supreme Court justice and a member of the Chase family.[22] A 1975 article reports that Vice President Nelson Rockefeller and his wife, Happy, vacationed with Kissinger and his wife in Puerto Rico, where Laurence Rockefeller owned a hotel. The foursome golfed, swam, and dined at a "swanky plantation restaurant" according to *People*.[23] Rather than an implication that political leaders were out of touch with everyday people's lives—particularly during a time when public trust in government had plummeted—their adventures seemed proof that wealth would be bestowed on those in high places, and that this was inevitable and acceptable. The privilege of mingling with society's elite appeared to connote an individual's worth, much as wealth itself would seem to go to those most deserving.

The Virtue of Wealth and Hard Work

A precursor to Robin Leach's television show *Lifestyles of the Rich and Famous* (1984–1995), *People* stories about the wealthy allowed readers to live vicariously through its subjects, which presumably could be used as guideposts for how to become fabulously wealthy yourself. *People* often turned its attention to heirs of great fortunes, describing their vast wealth and in many cases emphasizing their hard work, suggesting that their success was not simply an accident of birth but the result of their own efforts. A 1975 article titled "World's Richest Man" described J. Paul Getty. "In deepening solitude, like some melancholy Dickensian recluse, Jean Paul Getty offers the frailest of shoulders on which to rest the title of World's Richest Man," the article begins, listing the billionaire's many ailments before enumerating his vast wealth. Getty embodied the value of thrift, according to the story, which noted that he kept a pay phone in his palatial home for guests to use and that he kept track of who last paid when he dined out with a friend. Most notably, the article suggests that Getty, then 81, amassed his fortune through hard work and was not yet ready to retire despite his tremendous fortune, frailty, and advanced age.[24]

Likewise, a story about Barron Hilton, son of Hilton Hotel founder Conrad Hilton, describes how he started as a doorman at the El Paso Hilton and worked his way up to run the company. After a stint in the Navy, his father offered him a $150 a week position as a management trainee. He rejected this offer and started his own company before becoming president of the hotel chain, which had grown in profitability with his leadership. Hilton had "no pinkie ring, no tan from a bottle," according to the story, but instead was a "benign-looking man in gray pinstripe." The article goes on to detail that despite his relatively "modest salary" of $150,000 (the equivalent of just over $600,000 in 2010 dollars), Hilton lived lavishly with a "Holmby Hills estate [and] . . . a money-green Rolls-Royce . . . a tennis court, a small movie theater, a large pool and a putting green." The message was clear: it wasn't nepotism that made him rich, he had earned it.[25]

The self-made man is such an iconic figure in popular culture that *People* features implied that even scions of wealth apparently made it on their own. A 1987 story on perhaps the most famous of contemporary celebrity moguls, Donald Trump, describes his rise during the 1970s as based on thrift, smarts, and hard work. "Ten years ago Donald Trump was just another millionaire, the son of Fred Trump, a developer who made his fortune building moderate-income housing in Brooklyn and Queens." Donald went to the Wharton School of Business and then moved into a "tiny studio apartment." "Fred Trump hadn't gotten rich throwing money around," the article adds. "Then it began. With no real track record, Trump persuaded banks to lend him money, New York City officials to give him tax breaks, property owners to sell to him cheap." Trump later began developing high-end properties that attracted celebrity buyers. The article estimated his wealth as between $850 million and $3 billion (the equivalent of $1.6 billion to $5.8 billion in 2010 dollars) and noted that he donated regularly to charities. Yes, the story acknowledges, he had been criticized for pressuring tenants to leave buildings he hoped to develop for high-end clientele, but despite the story's title, "Too Darn Rich," the article largely celebrates his rise to wealth and fame.[26]

While Trump, Hilton and Getty were born into wealthy families, *People* often featured tales of actual self-made millionaires. The magazine profiled Arthur Murray, the dance studio mogul, in a 1974 story describing his life of affluence. He and his wife, Kathryn, "live in a condominium penthouse hard by the surf of Waikiki. Their walls are lined with silk and a minimuseum of Renoirs, Monets and Bonnards." Despite his retirement, the article notes how he would wake up for the morning bell of the New York Stock Exchange to watch how his investments fared.

The story describes how Murray started giving dancing lessons in 1913, charging 15 cents while he was a student at Columbia University. The article also includes a tale of the couple's first date over an ice cream soda, making the pair seem much like any other.[27] Hard work could presumably lead anyone to a Hawaiian dream retirement, regardless of where they started.

Stories commonly focused on executives' salaries, with descriptions of how they rose to the top from humble beginnings. *People* magazine helped invent the celebrity CEO, who (typically) worked his way to the top:

> The son of a Los Angeles car mechanic, Lynn A. Townsend worked his way through college by peeling potatoes, scrubbing floors and washing dishes in a frat house. Thanks to the Horatio Alger routine—and pointers he picked up around dad's garage— 54-year-old Townsend is now chairman of the Chrysler Corp., at $393,440 a year. [The equivalent of more than $1.7 million in 2010 dollars.]
>
> High school summers John D. deButts worked on a railroad track gang. After graduation from Virginia Military Institute, he turned down a glamorous Marine Corps commission for a lowly training job with Ma Bell. By last year deButts was earning $325,738 [the equivalent of more than $1.4 million in 2010 dollars]—hardly a wrong number for the chairman of the American Telephone and Telegraph Company.[28]

While many of *People*'s stories focus on how titans of industry made it big, there is also a recurring theme of the possibility of the average American becoming wealthy by both skill and luck. One article tells the story of a Houston couple who refused to sell their home to developers, even when offered a price significantly higher than market value. Eventually they sold their home for $525,000—a handsome profit, since they had purchased it for about $20,000. The article describes their modest three-bedroom home with discount furniture, noting that after their windfall they, "plan to indulge themselves a little." "I'll buy a newer home; I'll serve better whiskey and I'll buy better steaks," the homeowner told *People*.[29] Many readers might not envision themselves as CEOs, but the idea of wealth via homeownership is one that many can relate to.

Poor Rich People

As *People*'s founding editor foresaw, readers could also connect with other people's problems. Stories about wealthy families that faced ongoing tragedy helped create public sympathy for those at the top of the income hierarchy. In direct contrast to challenges from the left, stories about the elite's personal struggles helped humanize a group often criticized as greedy and having too much political influence. Stories about wealthy people's problems could often be very dramatic and sell magazines. The Kennedy family's well-documented tragedies were tailor-made for the magazine; dozens of *People* covers have featured a Kennedy and explored the human side of the political dynasty. The message in these stories is clear: life is not necessarily easy for those in wealthy families, and they suffer just like anyone else. As with the so-called "Kennedy Curse," the wealthy might even experience greater losses than the rest of us and deserve our sympathy. Although not necessarily intentional—after all, the goal of a magazine is to sell copies—such stories of loss and pain help readers sympathize with the super-wealthy. Readers could take pity on royals or heirs to great fortunes, rather than question the growing gulf between the wealthiest percent and everyone else.

Along with the Kennedys, the tribulations of the wealthy Onassis family became a *People* staple. When Jacqueline Kennedy married shipping magnate Aristotle Onassis, she symbolically united two families whose tragedies would provide stories for *People* well beyond both of their deaths. Aristotle's daughter from his first marriage, Christina, was a frequent subject of *People*. Cast as a poor little rich girl, with wealth beyond imagination but a disconnected family life, the magazine described her life as "a Greek tragedy" in 1975 when her father was gravely ill. Problems plagued her much of her life, from her parents' divorce and her alleged dislike of stepmother Jacqueline Kennedy Onassis, to her brother's and parents' deaths within a two-year period, and her alleged suicide attempts. Christina supposedly struggled with her appearance and had cosmetic surgery, "overshadowed by her mother's beauty."[30]

After her father's death she took over the family business and sued her mother's widower for $320 million.[31] Her second marriage to Alexander Andreadis meant that "the Greek economy is now concentrated in the hands of one family," according to an unnamed banker. Andreadis himself described the marriage as "like being made king for the rest of your life."[32]

Christina would marry four times and ultimately die at 37, leaving her three year-old daughter the sole heir to the Onassis fortune. A 1989 article describes Athina's third birthday party, attended by many children and featuring two massive cakes. This somber story notes that despite Athina's wealth, her fourth birthday would be without her doting mother.[33]

Stories such as these perhaps helped middle-class readers feel better about their own social position. While Christina wondered if friends and suitors sought her out for her money, a problem most of us never face, her vast wealth seemed to cause more problems than it solved. And yet these stories of sadness never question the implications of the high concentration of wealth in the hands of so few. Other stories described how the wealthy led reclusive lives while spending their vast fortunes on lavish palaces decorated with original artwork and filled with private recreation rooms so they would have no need to venture out of their self-imposed exile. If the wealthy were to be pitied rather than envied, the public might feel less animosity towards them during a time of growing economic division.

Coverage of wealthy royals also attempted to humanize them and portray them as regular, even humble folks. A story on Saudi Arabia's King Faisal described his religious devoutness and noted that he belonged to an "ascetic" sect of Islam, suggesting an austere lifestyle.[34] Another story describes how a duchess faced down a wasp while sitting out on her Paris veranda.[35] "Just the Royal Folks Next Door," begins by describing a family trip to see grandma and grandpa . . . at a castle in the Ardennes Mountains. Princess Grace and Prince Rainier of Monaco were busy, like many other families, but their to-do list included an ascension to the throne anniversary party and their daughter's coming out party.[36] A story about the Duchess of Windsor, Wallis Simpson, described her sadness after the death of her husband, who had famously abdicated the throne to marry her.[37] While most people could never imagine what it might be like for a king to leave his throne, their romantic story and the sadness of loss is something readers could identify with and thus see royal lives as similar to their own.

It Could Happen to You

If wealthy people were a lot like us, it stands to reason that we might one day be a lot like them and enjoy the bounty of wealth. Becoming famous seemed to offer a chance to anyone with talent willing to work hard to get rich. Especially in its early days, *People* features were nearly always positive assessments of how its subject rose from obscurity to fame, emphasizing their hard-earned success and reinforcing the idea that America is a meritocracy. Baring a strong resemblance to celebrity tales of the 1920s and 1930s, these stories suggested that talent would bring wealth and the chance to mingle with the upper crust. A 1975 mention of Gstaad, the Swiss skiing resort, describes how the likes of Jack Nicholson, Roman Polanski, Richard Burton, and Audrey Hepburn might see the Kennedys, the Onassises, and royalty while vacationing there.[38] Being a celebrity could produce rapid upward mobility and acceptance by the elite.

And apparently it could happen to anyone, according to *People*'s many rags-to-riches stories. A twenty-two-year-old goes from nursing student to modeling for Halston and Oscar de la Renta within one year, and now frequents the most exclusive New York clubs.[39] An eighth-grade dropout earns big money on the roller-derby circuit.[40] A once drug-addicted Las Vegas showgirl lands a movie role opposite Dustin Hoffman.[41] A modeling agency discovers a seventeen-year-old when her boyfriend, an aspiring photographer, takes her picture.[42] An ex-groupie becomes a singer herself.[43] A young man goes from pumping gas to owning an auto body shop to financing a hit movie.[44] An immigrant who speaks no English and was once a self-described "80 pound weakling" joins the YMCA to bulk up and becomes a wrestling star and real estate investor.[45] For those hoping to give their children opportunities to become famous, a 1984 article, "Kids for Sale," describes how children can go from diapers to diamonds, listing several child stars' earnings.[46] These kinds of stories pepper the pages of *People*, emphasizing seemingly endless Horatio Alger stories.

Fame would bring wealth, too. The magazine regularly gushed over the rumored salaries and accumulated wealth celebrities had, as well as what they might have paid for their homes and other luxury items. For instance, a 1983 story made no pretense of being about anything other than Paul McCartney's wealth. "A Fab Fortune" includes speculation on his income the previous year (from a low of $300,000 to $129 million), and compares his wealth to Rockefeller and Carnegie.[47] "Who Makes What $" rattles off salaries in 1985, in what became a regular feature, with the "all-time moneymakers hall of fame." After the end of the article, an ad for high-end cognac appears.[48] The 1986 version of the hall of fame suggested that money could come quickly: singer Sade earned $10 million in two years. Michael J. Fox was hungry, unemployed, and $30,000 in debt; four years later he drove a $200,000 car and commanded $1.5 million per movie. Whoopi Goldberg was on welfare two years before she reportedly commanded $1 million per movie after her success in *The Color Purple*.[49] Bruce Willis went from "balding bartender" to earning $50,000 a week on television, and then $7 million through pitching wine coolers, movie deals, and HBO specials within three years.[50]

Horatio Alger Goes to Hollywood

People stories tended to follow a template when profiling celebrities' paths to success: typically the story highlights a recent accomplishment, notes their humble beginnings, emphasizes their hard work and tenacity, describes their lucky break, and ends with a description of their hard-earned massive wealth. Singers, actors, designers, athletes, and other public personalities all appeared to have worked their way to success and continued to exhibit a strong work ethic. Partying and the good life would be a reward, but for the most part these Horatio Alger stories focus on work. The takeaway message: celebrities are examples of what happens when people are willing to sacrifice and work hard.

Charles Bronson, famous tough guy and star of the *Death Wish* series, appeared to be a bona fide rags-to-riches tale. Described as the top grossing actor of 1974, Bronson had come a long way to reach international movie stardom:

> The 11th of 15 children born to an illiterate Russian-immigrant coal miner named Buchinsky in Ehrenfeld, Pa., Bronson savors his success as only those who have experienced rock-bottom poverty can. His family was so poor that he remembers being sent off to school in his sister's hand-me-down dresses.

The article continues, describing his struggles from working in a coal mine, picking onions, and serving time for robbery before finding work as an actor in Philadelphia. Despite setbacks, Bronson "kept at it . . . [he] worked on his speech at the Pasadena Playhouse and slowly began to win parts", eventually earning $1 million per movie and purchasing "a 33-room Bel Air mansion and a 1791 Vermont farmhouse set on 260 acres."[51] If a poor ex-con can make it to the top, apparently anyone can.

A 1975 profile of singer Barry White fits this pattern as well. From his childhood "on the mean streets of East Los Angeles," White "learn[ed] his music by playing the organ in church and then directing gospel choirs." His big break: "clapping in the background at a studio recording session." The article notes that over the previous two years his records had grossed $22 million (the equivalent of more than $89 million in 2010) and concludes by describing his "21-room house in Sherman Oaks—which includes one of L.A.'s most opulent pool houses, a 30-seat movie screening room, plus badminton and basketball courts."[52]

Country singer Charlie Rich had been dropped by five record labels and struggled in the music business for twenty years before having platinum and gold singles, as well as a Grammy, an American Music Award, and a Country Music Award in the early 1970s. A 1974 story emphasized his humble beginnings:

> Born on a cotton farm in Colt, Ark., his childhood was a tug-of-war between a Bible-brandishing Baptist mother and an alcoholic father. At 7, Charlie saw his brother killed by a tractor and hid in the woods for three days.

Rich went on to study music theory in college (albeit for only a year) and joined the Air Force before becoming a farmer. He decided to take a chance on his dream and after years without success could now cash in, buying a luxury home outside of Memphis and "having withdrawal symptoms from poverty," according to his wife, who also wrote one of his hits.[53]

Fellow country music star Kenny Rogers' father never owned a home, according to a 1982 article. But Rogers was "hard-driven" and worked constantly to expand his wealth, breeding horses, starting a clothing line, and appearing in films. Not only was Rogers building a "columned 8,000-square-foot Grecian-style house complete with a wraparound porch in Italian marble, [and] a 60-foot living room," but also a 90,000 square foot stable for his Arabian horses. His efforts had afforded him a household staff of twenty-two employees as well.[54]

As in the case of Rogers, *People* celebrated stars who came from humble beginnings and then went on to live in lavish surroundings. Singer Elton John's rise from "a dingy London flat, playing for fish-and-chips money on the semi-pro circuit in jeans" to earning more than $7 million a year in 1975 (the equivalent of more than $28 million in 2010) is chronicled, along with his lavish spending. "Nobody but the hero of a 19th century romantic novel has ever lived his childhood fantasies as elaborately as the ugly duckling from Middlesex," the article notes, going on to describe how John practiced the piano diligently and won a scholarship to the Royal Academy of Music at eleven years old.

But his success is not punctuated by happiness—in fact, the story mentions on several occasions how insecure John is—but by wealth and the elites he can now call friends:

> He pops in for cocktails with David Frost, plays tennis with Billie Jean King and Jimmy Connors, parties at Cher's . . . He owns two Rolls-Royces and a Ferrari, a new house in Benedict Canyon and is buying an English manor house in Windsor. He collects art; his prizes are several Magrittes and a few Rembrandt etchings. He has bought a Rolls-Royce for his agent, a fox fur for an assistant at Rocket Records, and . . . gifts from Cartier.

John also purchased homes for his parents, whom the story describes as having "sturdy middle-class values" and being uncomfortable with his newfound wealth.[55] His spending habits may not embody the virtue of thrift, but the story characterizes his hyper-consumption as a just reward, even something that makes John unique. A picture with what appears to be hundreds of pairs of shoes emphasizes this abundance, and also his eccentricities—which by implication are central to his success as an entertainer who wore elaborate costumes at the time.

Having a high-end wardrobe was also a marker of well-earned success. Designers who outfitted celebrities became celebrities themselves and frequent subjects of *People*, often with similar stories of working their way to the top of the profession. A story about designer Yves Saint Laurent describes how he and his partner "built their business from nothing," and after a nervous breakdown he "was broke and out of work," despite having worked at Christian Dior. Yet his efforts led him to run the second-largest couture house in the world, with the wealth to match.[56] Fellow designer Calvin Klein also rose from modest beginnings, according to a 1982 story. Klein grew up in the Bronx, as the son of a grocer and who almost went into the grocery business himself, but his parents encouraged him to keep pursuing his dream to be a designer. A year later, when his business partner inherited $10,000, they started selling Klein's designs. Just over a decade later, the two had become fabulously wealthy, with investments in oil and hotels, not to mention several homes in Manhattan as well as beach properties. His clothing line grossed $750 million in 1981 (the equivalent of $1.8 billion in 2010 dollars), the year before the article's publication. Klein became a celebrity himself, hounded for his autograph on the streets of New York. But the story reinforces the idea that Klein is just like anyone else, concluding that he sometimes feels uneasy with his massive wealth. "Coping with success is very difficult. You start thinking maybe you don't deserve it," Klein told *People*. "Then you come to realize how hard you've worked." A caption to a picture of him reading in bed notes that he "worked eighteen hours a day, seven days a week when he started," emphasizing a central tenet of the Horatio Alger story.[57] The profile makes clear that his wealth was a direct outgrowth of talent and hard work.

Horatio Alger and the Athlete

People's expansion of coverage beyond traditional entertainment personalities opened the door to coverage of many more rags-to-riches stories. Athletes seemed to provide a treasure trove of examples of hard work yielding massive wealth; their physical labor was visible, and their salaries were becoming legendary with the advent of free agency during this time. Athletes had been celebrities in the past, but the combination of their growing wealth and coverage next to movie stars and CEOs would catapult players' fame, and present readers with another supposed path to massive wealth.

Basketball player Moses Malone was nineteen when he signed a million-dollar contract in 1974. Raised by a single mother earning $100 a week, an article describes the desperate conditions of their home, a "decaying row house . . . the beige paint on the walls is peeling . . . a thick layer of dust clogs the louvers of an ancient oil heater." Despite these bleak conditions, the story describes Malone's collection of trophies representing his efforts: "most valuable player, highest scorer, best rebounder." Not only did he walk away with a big contract, but his mother would get a new house and stipend, cast as a reward for the single mother's devotion and sacrifice.[58] Stories such as this one suggest that many low-income families have a way out of poverty if they too work hard, particularly as being an athlete paid increasingly well. The article mentions Malone's low grades in school as just another obstacle he overcame in realizing his own Horatio Alger story.

Also from humble beginnings, a harness racer from a "poor French farm family" in Quebec who dropped out of school after the fifth grade would gross $2 million in 1974 (the equivalent of more than $8.8 million in 2010) thanks to his non-stop schedule training and racing horses. *People*'s feature on Herve Filion mentions the value of his home in an exclusive suburb on Long Island, and says that he and his family live modestly. However, to avoid the New York rush hour traffic he typically travels to work, the article notes, by private helicopter.[59] That same year, *People* featured Miami Dolphins star Larry Csonka, describing him as a "budding tycoon in shoulder pads." Pictured holding a bottle of champagne and standing in his convertible Bentley, the story emphasizes his hard-scrabble start as a farm boy from Stow, Ohio. The physical farm labor presumably gave him the strength and wherewithal to dominate opponents on the field.[60]

Not all athletes who were featured started off as poor as, say, Malone, but the stories emphasized how hard work enabled all of them to join the upper class. Pro-golfer Johnny Miller "spent rainy afternoons driving golf balls into a tarp his father had hung in the basement," and despite a modest rookie year, had won nearly $100,000 during the previous month (the equivalent of more than $440,000 in 2010 dollars). Besides his winnings, he collected cars, possessing, "a Thunderbird, . . . a Ford station wagon and a couple of Dodges. He has a Ferrari on order."[61] Another story about Miller mentions so many figures on his winnings it could pass for a tax return. The golfer "prefers safe regular savings accounts and real estate investments (including a condominium in Hilton Head, S.C., where he once was the pro) over risky forays into oil exploration projects." The article makes the golfer come off as just a regular guy who worked hard. He and his family "live comfortably but far from expansively," the story concludes.[62]

Athletes with big endorsement deals also made *People* coverage, which like Miller's story, tended to highlight their hard work and humility despite newfound massive wealth. Olympian Mark Spitz, the son of a scrap-metal dealer, turned down dozens of movie roles and exhibited the value of thrift. "The Spitzes live more or less just like folks in a two-bedroom condominium in West Los Angeles, which they are decorating themselves." Spitz told *People* that he and his wife "think about the value of a dollar," and that "it would have been pretty simple to just go out and spend the money as fast as I made it."[63]

The Joy of Marrying Rich

Not only were athletes like Spitz extremely wealthy, but their hard work, humility, and thrift made them seem deserving—an important distinction during a time when images of people on public assistance suggested many of the poor deserved their fate as well. Single-mother-headed households rose from about 12 percent of households with children in 1970 to 18 percent in 1980 and 22 percent in 1990, and Aid for Families with Dependent Children (AFDC) caseloads rose from about 1.9 million in 1970 to 3.6 million families in 1980. Public debate began to focus on the alleged failures of these families to stay above the poverty line.[64]

As the conservative movement grew in power, so too did the concept of "family values", which emphasized the value of marriage. *People*'s coverage of celebrity unions emphasized the value of marriage as well—literally. Rather than the romantic fantasy postwar fan magazines offered, countless stories highlighted a new couple's net worth. The first line of a story about model Cristina Ferrare's marriage to auto executive John DeLorean included his six figure salary. The next paragraph includes her hourly rate as a top model.[65] "It was the perfect way to launch the perfect marriage. The bridegroom gave the bride a $24,000 beige Mercedes-Benz," a 1975 story about model Margeaux Hemingway's marriage to her manager began.[66] Zsa Zsa Gabor received a Rolls-Royce from her sixth husband as a wedding gift, an article that same year announced.[67] Singer Billy Joel and model Christie Brinkley's 1985 wedding aboard a yacht seemed to belie Joel's "working-class origins," according to anonymous critics referenced in a *People* story. Joel responded that he hadn't "sold out" and would continue to work hard as a musician.[68]

When tennis stars Chris Everett and Jimmy Connors became engaged in 1974, the magazine emphasized that their training came first, but that the engagement brought great rewards, including a diamond and sapphire engagement ring, and a combined income of $308,000 (the equivalent of nearly $1.4 million in 2010 dollars) before endorsements—information that the article included in the first paragraph.[69] Dozens of relationship stories emphasized the couples' combined earning power. In "Dollars Can't Buy You Love, but They Sure Spiff up a Relationship," *People* enumerated the combined income of several celebrity couples, with emphasis on the women who out-earned their husbands (such as Elizabeth Dole and Madonna).[70]

As the gap between men and women's wages began to shrink—women earned about 60 percent of what men did yearly in 1970, increasing to nearly 72 percent in 1990—the notion of the power couple took on new meaning.[71] Marriage was no longer just a way for women to improve their economic position, but increasingly it seemed like an avenue for celebrity men to do so as well. That is, if they were already rich and famous. Just as with non-celebrities, those already financially well-off would financially benefit most from marriage. A 2010 Pew Research Center report examines the well being of dual-earner couples over the past forty years and found that those with the highest levels of education and income tend to marry one another and stay married longer than couples with less education and lower incomes.[72] Rather than address the growing concentration of wealth that marriage between economic elites produces, however, the *People* stories suggest that marrying rich is about individual happiness rather than patterns of inequality.

Pulling Themselves up by Gilded Bootstraps

Just as some people might have had unique opportunities to marry rich, they might also have had a boost up the ladder to becoming famous in the first place. Making it big in Hollywood may seem to be the ultimate example of a meritocracy, but many people get a head start. And yet many *People* stories of success downplayed advantages someone might have started with, whether that advantage was a privileged upbringing or already being wealthy or already being famous before experiencing another round of success. Actor Richard Chamberlain became wealthy and famous playing Dr. Kildare on television for five years, and a 1975 story implies that Chamberlain rose from humble beginnings: "born on the wrong side of Wilshire" in Beverly Hills. Chamberlain's success came from his humility and hard work, according to the article. When *Dr. Kildare* ended he went to work as an apprentice in the London theater and chided the Hollywood social scene as "phony." This commitment to his craft brought success and wealth, helping to "set him up beyond his boyhood dreams of avarice." As a reward for his hard work, he lived in an "elegant Coldwater Canyon house."[73]

People profiled fellow actor Jack Lemmon in 1974, describing his work ethic as rooted in his upbringing. Despite a childhood plagued by illness, he began running to improve his endurance, became stronger, and began getting work as an actor who would appear in films with major directors for decades. Lemmon "developed a sturdy New England character. He is obsessively responsible about his work, his family, his friends, his civic duties." Although his background was likely one of privilege—he attended Andover and Harvard—the story focuses on his slow but steady progress in show business.[74]

Just as *People* emphasized hard work and humble beginnings, profiles such as these tended to minimize the opportunities that their subjects inherited. This was particularly true when covering children of celebrities. *People* often suggested that famous children's success was primarily the result of their own hard work, and stressed their independence from their parents. A 1974 story focused on recent college graduates of well-known parents, "ordinary graduates in many ways but quite special in others." Many of the graduates—including children of members of Congress, professional athletes, and journalists—insist that in college they blended in and had "normal" experiences, downplaying any advantages they might have had due to their famous and often wealthy parents. Christie Hefner's (daughter of *Playboy* founder Hugh Hefner) bodyguards, for instance, were only a precaution after Patricia Hearst's kidnapping. That many attended exclusive universities seemed a testament to their intelligence, rather than any parental influence.[75]

Lucie Arnaz, daughter of Desi Arnaz and Lucille Ball, was featured in a story called "Lucie Arnaz: Doing It Her Way" about her burgeoning acting career. Although she got her start on her mother's show, *The Lucy Show*, the article describes the then twenty-three-year-old as striking out on her own in the New York theater world. The story notes that she and brother Desi lived for a time with another child of celebrities, Liza Minnelli, implying that they struggled to make it like anyone else hoping to break into show business and needed roommates to make ends meet.[76] Oscar winner Lee Grant's daughter, Dinah Manoff, might have had some advantages getting roles (including on the television series *Soap* and the Neil Simon play and movie *You Ought to Be in Pictures*), but a 1982 story emphasizes Manoff's challenges. Her father was a blacklisted television writer who died when she was nine. She was a rule-breaker in high school, smoking and going to class barefoot. But she turned things around, taking acting classes and spending a year in college before starting to get guest roles on television. Manoff might have had advantages, but the story describes her biggest struggle as creating a distinct identity from her mother.[77]

Pam Tillis, daughter of country singer Mel Tillis, and an aspiring rock singer herself, also seems to have made it on her own in the music world without her father's help—at least that's what the 1983 feature on her suggested. "Pam started studying piano at 8, got her first guitar at 11 and began writing songs at 12 with a gospel number," and then formed a band when she went to college. She describes her appearances with her father at The Grand Ole Opry as more of a setback than an opportunity. "I hated it. It was an ego-bruiser. I just couldn't stand getting up there and having all that in me and having to go through his material." She moved to San Francisco, lived on a barge, and worked as an Avon lady before making her first album—presumably without her father's help.[78]

One *People* magazine staple represents a recurring theme embedded within both celebrity stories and the American Dream: the comeback. Despite F. Scott Fitzgerald's famous assessment that "there are no second acts in American life," celebrity tales are filled with them, often downplaying the advantages built into having already made it big once before. These comeback stories often cast the celebrity as down on their luck, as Debbie Reynolds was in a 1974 story. Painting her as a has-been, *People* describes Reynolds as "40 and Hollywood's oldest ingénue. She could not find a suitable movie role, had flunked a TV series and seemed to be stuck for the rest of her performing days in the lucrative but limited Las Vegas club circuit."[79] Typically the story ends with a footnote about the celebrity's current bankability; Reynolds' "comeback" role in the

Broadway production of *Irene* yielded an average of $146,000 a week (the equivalent of about $645,000 in 2010 dollars), thus making it the highest grossing musical at that time.[80] Sometimes the "comeback" story was an exaggerated way of describing a performer who had taken some time off. As with Reynolds, by suggesting that a celebrity had fallen on hard times, this could serve to re-emphasize the role of individual hard work as central to success and wealth.

The Dark Side of Wealth

While the virtue of wealth was clear in *People*'s coverage, there was also a dark side for those who squandered their money or were not otherwise productive contributors to society. While most of *People*'s early stories about the wealthy were celebratory, some could be read as cautionary tales. For those who did not seem morally deserving, either because they did not work hard, wasted an inheritance, or were of questionable moral virtue, coverage could be quite critical. Whether royalty, heirs to fortunes, celebrities, or business executives, those displaying a lack of effort or morality, or a surplus of greed, could serve as warnings about what can happen to those lacking the values championed in the traditional Alger stories.

While royals frequently appeared in the magazine, those who seemed to have wasted their fortunes served as warnings about what happens to wealth when it is not properly cared for. Deposed King Constantine of Greece and his wife Anne-Marie "have spent seven aimless years with no sign whatsoever of deprivation or hardship," despite their claims of poverty in exile. The story paints the couple as mooching off of other European royals since the Greek coup, and suggests that they are still incredibly wealthy. Enumerating their possessions, including dozens of cars, twenty-seven yachts, seven palaces, and other markers of wealth discourages sympathy for the now "unemployed" former king.[81]

Likewise, when a French Baron died after he refused to leave his chateau when it went into foreclosure, *People* described his family's "tendency for the bizarre."[82] In another morality tale, the magazine profiled a British Lord who allegedly killed his children's nanny and was on the run. Besides the murder, he had allegedly committed another crime: running out of money after a bitter divorce and having to borrow money from a loan shark. In case the allegations of murder were not enough to discredit this once wealthy man, he also "kept a collection of Hitler's recorded speeches," according to the story.[83]

Aside from lack of thrift, *People* coverage criticized wealthy people exhibiting greed. In 1974, financier Robert Vesco was accused of having bilked investors of $224 million (the equivalent of close to a billion dollars in 2010) when he fled the country. *People* described Vesco's private jet, valued at $3.5 million (the equivalent of $15 million in 2010 dollars), which was impounded by a court order. The Boeing 707 had its own sauna and dance floor.[84] When his associate, Bernie Cornfeld, was released from a Swiss prison on bail for fraud, the magazine described him as a "kosher leprechaun" surrounded by bikini-clad women, presumably attracted to his money. Upon his release, the article notes that Cornfeld "plopped his paunch into . . . [an] exquisitely appointed, 40-room mansion in Beverly Hills," presumably undeserving of his vast wealth and its perks.[85]

Greed combined with hedonism also leads to condemnation. A 1983 story about a member of Saudi Arabia's royal family describes how he had taken several wives and was a profligate spender, and yet he "had stiffed the Hotel Diplomat in Hollywood, Fla. for $1.4 million, and spent six hours in jail before consenting to pay the bill. Numerous other debts remain, notably a tab for more than $1 million in support payments." He also displayed a lack of taste, according to *People*:

> Even if he never heard of Thorstein Veblen's prophecy of the curse of conspicuous consumption, Mohammed was bound to fulfill it. He bought a three-acre Sunset Boulevard estate for $2.4 million in 1978, built a mosque on the property, painted the mansion a bright green, planted plastic flowers in the stone urns, and had the genitalia on the nude garden statues rendered in red . . .
>
> [He] bought fleets of automobiles and houses and other properties for $17 million, papered the town with bad checks, fought with the police, and provoked a slew of lawsuits and a diplomatic crisis, not to mention charges of enslaving and beating their servants. All this time there were monumental parties, chartered jet trips, high times on the high seas, and jewelry by the scoopful . . .[86]

His wife told *People* that she felt like a prisoner in this mansion, which was eventually "gutted in a fire set by an ex-chauffeur to hide the theft of valuable art works." Despite being awarded $3 billion in the divorce case, the story noted that she was looking to start a career of her own. Clearly the sympathetic figure in the piece—she is pictured appearing forlorn in front of the gutted estate—his wife is cast as a victim of her husband's behavior, not a participant.

By contrast, Leona Helmsley, wife of Harry Helmsley, was perhaps vilified even more than her husband when they were charged with tax evasion, allegedly underpaying the federal government by more than $4 million. A 1988 story about the Manhattan real estate moguls listed the extravagances they enjoyed, which they attempted to write off as business expenses, including: "a $130,000 indoor-outdoor stereo system for their home . . . a $45,000 silver clock Leona bought Harry for his birthday . . . a pink satin dress and jacket . . . and $500,000 worth of jade." Leona—later dubbed the "queen of mean" for allegations of cruelty to staff—was also indicted for extortion and fraud. She allegedly charged shareholders more than $83,000 (the equivalent of more than $153,000 in 2010 dollars) in monthly consulting fees. The article describes the couple as erratic—at times incredibly generous but at other times shockingly stingy, noting that when Leona's son died at the age of forty they sued his estate to recover the costs of shipping his body and even served his widow with an eviction notice.[87] The Helmsleys represented the height of greed in this and other stories; when Leona died in 2007 she left $12 million to one of her dogs and nothing to two of her deceased son's children.

The Von Bülow saga also emphasized the sadness money could cause families who suspected one another of greed. Featured in the 1990 film *Reversal of Fortune*, Claus Von Bülow had been accused of attempting to murder his wife, allegedly for the $14 million she would leave him in her will. Sunny Von Bülow was in a persistent vegetative state, and he was tried twice for allegedly injecting her with an overdose of insulin, but in the second trial he was found not guilty. Her children were divided about her husband's role in her illness; her children from a previous marriage believed he was guilty, but her daughter with Claus Von Bülow supported her father—this support allegedly leaving Von Bülow's daughter disinherited when her maternal grandmother passed away.[88]

Greed also apparently led to the demise of John and Cristina DeLorean's wealth. "John and Cristina DeLorean were a man and a woman in love—in love with each other, it seemed, but also with power and wealth," according to a 1984 story, which recounted the charges that he had intended to distribute $24 million worth of cocaine. John wasn't alone in his greed, according to the article. "Cristina is not an easy woman," said *People*, describing how she refused to part with their $5 million Fifth Avenue duplex in Manhattan when her husband wanted to use the money to try and keep his auto company afloat. While stories of rising above one's origins flourished in *People*, the magazine chided those who failed to remain humble. Cristina, the "symbol of the rise of an Italian butcher's daughter from Cleveland into the social stratosphere," apparently was too greedy to part with the duplex. And Mr. DeLorean seemed to commit another sin against the Alger myth: wanting to take shortcuts around work to become wealthy:

> There has always been a murkiness to John DeLorean's goals, his ambitions, his life. As a promising engineering student in Detroit, he was caught bilking businesses by selling advertising in a fake telephone yellow pages. No charges were pressed after he returned the money, but the incident has followed him ever since, usually invoked by those in search of his life's true motives. Did he want to succeed by using his formidable talents for great achievements, earning satisfaction and acclaim as well as the financial rewards that go with success, or did he simply want to get rich quick, at any cost?

Ultimately, DeLorean successfully argued that the FBI had entrapped him, and he was found not guilty, but filed for bankruptcy in 1999.[89] Despite his acquittal, DeLorean's story still seemed to serve as a cautionary tale about the possibility of losing it all by trying to avoid hard work.

Stories addressing wealth's dark side tended to focus on those who failed financially. Personal excesses would not yield the same negative coverage, at least not yet. At the time, those who lived lavishly did so as a reward for their talent and hard work. And while excess could certainly have been a contributing factor to many a rich and/or famous person's downfall, *People* curiously treaded lightly on this issue. After Elvis Presley's sudden death in August 1977, an interview with his girlfriend downplays his use of pills and casts his behavior—such as sleeping all day and staying up all night—as part of his eccentric personality.[90] The cover story on the first anniversary of his death largely focused on how his fortune continued to grow despite his death, with no mention of how his unfettered access to drugs likely hastened his demise.[91] If you earned it or could afford it, you deserved it.

Fantasy Meets Reality?

In stark contrast to traditional fan magazines, which lacked a clear vision of an American Dream in the 1970s, the birth of *People* meant that readers had a positive alternative to stories of celebrity unhappiness and unconventionality. By expanding the meaning of celebrity to include those who had achieved some degree of wealth and power beyond Hollywood, *People* stories echoed the political shift taking place that articulated a clear return to the American Dream of the past. Judging from its rise in circulation (from 1.4 million copies in 1974 to 3.73 in 2006), these stories resonated with a growing portion of the public. By contrast, the old fan magazine circulations dwindled to less than 100,000 per issue before they ceased publication.[92]

The affinity for stories about happy, wealthy, famous people was clear during a time when Americans seemed desperate to feel good about things again. With the energy crisis and the Vietnam war in the past, clearly the public was in the mood for some good news. *People*'s stories about the wealthiest 1 percent offered both an escape and the implication that the pathways to wealth were open to everyone willing to work hard. Even as inflation and unemployment remained high, this collective fantasy of individual wealth seemed better than nothing. This fantasy also helped convince a growing number of Americans to support more tax cuts for the wealthy and further reductions in social programs for those who appeared "unwilling" to work hard.

Time would suggest that for most Americans, this collective fantasy of striking it rich could not bear out. The gap between the wealthiest 1 percent and the rest of Americans would continue to grow. Declines in spending power would continue. But two things would continue to make the dream of massive wealth appear to be just around the corner: the expansion of consumer credit and—thanks to the internet and reality television—new opportunities to become famous.

9

SUCCESS JUST FOR BEING YOU

OPPORTUNITY IN THE INTERNET AGE

In the internet age, there are no longer only a handful of powerful gatekeepers deciding who will be in the public eye, but instead it is often individuals themselves who can take advantage of blogs, social networking tools, video sharing, and digital downloading to act as their own studio, record company, publicist, or publishing company. Celebrity represents the notion of individualism today perhaps more than ever—it has never seemed easier to be famous just for being you, and possibly get rich in the process. At the same time, the gap between the wealthiest 1 percent and the rest of Americans has widened and wages remain stagnant, even if opportunities for fame have expanded, offering the appearance of greater mobility and the chance to cash in on the new media environment. As traditional modes of entertainment confront the challenge of making money in the face of free internet content, the very mechanisms creating celebrity have forever been altered.

Delving into celebrities' personal lives has become a low-cost product as many traditional forms of media struggle for revenue. Celebrity gossip is both easy to produce and consume; coverage of bad behavior and relationship sagas also feeds modern-day morality tales, warning of the dangers of excess and infidelity, as well as attempting to mark the shifting boundaries of what constitutes acceptable behavior. Coverage of celebrities has expanded far beyond magazines, and although celebrity magazines still enjoy healthy revenues they are but a small piece of the puzzle today.

Magazines such as *People* certainly do not comprise the entire realm of celebrity culture today; the landscape is so vast it would be impossible to capture the entirety adequately. But *People* still matters, mainly because its large circulation and reputation lends an air of mainstream legitimacy to its stories in an age characterized by an abundance of information about celebrities. The magazine also relies on the cooperation of celebrities, unlike many other sources today, providing some continuity with the fan magazines of old. To that end, *People* often dwells on the more positive and triumphant aspects of celebrities' lives, and, as we will see in this chapter, still largely champions the notion of the American Dream.

Just as someone can become famous very quickly, today's rapid cycle of celebrity means one can become a has-been overnight too. Former stars provide examples of downward mobility, which is often cast as the result of personal failure, such as substance abuse, overspending or overeating, or personality problems. This book ends by considering how celebrity tales not only provide visible examples of upward mobility, but also how they seem to explain downward mobility as an individual, rather than structural, phenomenon. This chapter addresses the following questions: How do stories about reality show participants and those "famous for being famous" serve as modern day Horatio Alger stories? In what way might stories about a celebrity's private behavior reflect structural shifts in journalism and media production? And finally, how does celebrity culture provide a narrative explaining both upward and downward mobility in the United States?

Opportunity in the Internet Age

If Andy Warhol had lived to see the internet age, he might have expanded his well-known dictum to suggest that in the future everyone would be famous beyond fifteen minutes. Never before has fame seemed so available to so many or for such trivial reasons. The dream of making it big and living a luxury lifestyle—even without any traditional form of talent— seems more feasible with the advent of MySpace, YouTube, and reality television. Getting enough attention, be it positive or negative, could yield a new career as a celebrity during a time when the gap between the wealthy and everyone else has widened.

The celebrations of massive wealth that began with the resurgence of conservatism in the 1970s and 1980s never completely faded away, but the stock market crash of 1987 and the savings and loan crisis of the late 1980s and early 1990s dampened them. After stocks lost about a third of their value, and more than 700 savings and loan institutions failed—leaving taxpayers to bail them out—the morality of the wealthy was no longer as clear cut as it once had seemed. Business titans and heirs to fortunes play less of a role in *People's* celebrity coverage now. And yet entertainers' net worth and consumption habits remain central themes in the magazine. Readers can read specifics about how much a celebrity paid for her jeans or handbag, how much the Mexican resort where a celebrity couple vacationed costs per night, and what newest gadgets stars collect as gifts for presenting at awards shows. Perhaps not coincidentally, it had never been easier for Americans to buy more despite being able to afford less. That is, until the 2008 economic collapse.

And yet for most Americans, paydays remained stagnant despite the seemingly endless examples of people who become famous and lead lavish lifestyles almost instantly. Median household incomes have been relatively flat for the past ten years when adjusted for inflation.[1] Individuals' real wages, reflecting the purchasing power of the median weekly wage, have remained sluggish for thirty years, and are lower now than they were in the early 1970s.[2] In 2006, workers' wages reached their lowest share of the Gross Domestic Product (GDP) since records for this measure were first collected in 1947.[3]

This is not the result of poor effort by American workers: between 1990 and 2009 productivity grew an average of 2.4 percent each year, meaning that workers produced more goods and services per hour than the year before.[4] High school and college graduation rates continued to rise. In 1990, about 78 percent of Americans aged 25-and-over had completed high school; in 2009 nearly 87 percent had. And while about 20 percent of Americans aged 25-and-over had earned at least a bachelor's degree in 1990, nearly 30 percent had by 2009.[5]

Despite the somewhat dour economic reality for most Americans, both the Clinton administration and the newly expanded cable news business channels billed the 1990s as the largest period of economic expansion. Buoyed by an eight-year stock market surge and business reporters championing the possibilities for individual investors who could now trade stocks online, it seemed as if prosperity was here for good, especially when unemployment dipped below 4 percent in December 2000, a thirty-year low.

But a 2001 Congressional Budget Office (CBO) study reported that the top 1 percent enjoyed nearly all of the income gains of the 1990s. Between 1989 and 1997, the income of this group rose by 36 percent on average ($180,000) after taxes. By contrast, households in the middle 20 percent saw their incomes increase by $2,000, while those in the bottom 20 percent saw no income gain.[6] Individual poverty rates remained in the double digits, falling modestly between 1993 and 2000 from 15.1 percent to 11.3 percent before inching up again to 14.3 percent in 2009.[7]

There was even more of an imbalance in the economic expansion of the 2000s than there was during the 1990s; two-thirds of all income gains went to the top 1 percent. Those who earned more than 99.9 percent of Americans—the top *tenth* of 1 percent—amassed $3,455,384 in average annual income gains between 2002–2007, with the top 1 percent gaining an average of $521,127 per year during this five-year block. The bottom 90 percent of Americans' income grew by an average of $1,206 during this time, the huge difference primarily the result of tax cuts.[8] In 1995, the wealthiest 400 families paid an effective tax rate of 30 percent of their income. By 2007, their effective tax rate—after deductions and factoring in a lower rate for earnings on capital gains—was less than 17 percent.[9]

The expansion of consumer credit alleviated what could have been a recipe for economic revolt, making it easier for more people to feel like they could participate in the economic party. Maybe your earnings were stagnant, barely keeping up with inflation, but if you could juggle the credit card payments—or absorb them into a mortgage when home prices were rising—you too could participate in celebrity-style consumption. Most Americans might not have gotten wealthy during the boom years, but they could buy many of the same products as the affluent did if they were willing to accumulate debt.

Robert Manning, author of *Credit Card Nation: The Consequences of America's Addiction to Credit*, details how credit card companies began marketing to working-class consumers and college students during the 1980s. It turned out that those with lower credit scores who could rarely pay their balances in full each month were a very profitable sector. Manning notes that between 1980 and 1990, household charges grew from an average of $885 to $3,753, double the rate of growth of disposable income, the amount of money one can save or spend after all expenses are paid.[10] Extending more credit to more people was very lucrative; during the 1990s, interest charges and fees tripled to $78 billion.[11] And more and more Americans began carrying consumer debt, which increased tenfold between 1982 and 2001.[12]

Despite falling unemployment rates in the 1990s, more Americans found themselves in financial trouble. Savings rates began dropping from nearly 10 percent of disposable income in 1980 to less than 3 percent in 2000.[13] A U.S. Commerce report indicated that Americans' average savings rate dipped below zero in 2005, meaning that on average, Americans spent more money than they earned.[14] Consumer bankruptcy filings nearly doubled between 1990 and 1998 before reaching a thirty-year high in 2005, when more than two million Americans filed—nearly ten times the bankruptcy rate of 1980, despite relatively low unemployment rates.[15]

Rather than recognize a central source of the problem—that the economic boom had benefited only a small proportion of Americans and that banks created conditions for consumers to take on massive debt—politicians and the banking industry considered consumers themselves the problem. Instead of examining the economic realities most Americans faced, Congress passed the Bankruptcy Abuse Prevention and Consumer Protection Act of 2005 (BAPCPA), making it more difficult for consumers to discharge their debts in bankruptcy court.

For many Americans, the solution to deal with consumer debt was to refinance their mortgage to help them manage their debt load. Many mortgage brokers offered loans that required no proof of income, job, or assets, making it easy for many Americans to upgrade to larger homes without any money down. Believing that home prices would continue to rise, consumers could even borrow more than the home was worth in order to pay other debt or buy more stuff. In the lead-up to the so-called "mortgage meltdown" of 2007–2008, banks offered a variety of loans that seemed like a great deal, unless consumers could understand the fine print.

Contrary to popular belief, it wasn't just the first-time homebuyer who took on more debt than they could afford who expanded the housing bubble. Homeownership rates in 2000, before the housing boom began, were around 67 percent of Americans, growing only to about 69 percent in 2007.[16] Instead, homebuyers purchased increasingly larger homes. The median square footage of a newly built home grew steadily from just over 1,000 square feet midcentury to about 1,600 square feet in the mid-1980s to more than 2,277 square feet during the peak boom year of 2007.[17]

More space meant room for more things, but Americans still needed more room for storage. In 2006, the Self Storage Association reported an 81 percent growth in new storage facilities from 2000 and that nearly one in ten American families rented a storage space.[18]

In this economic environment, fame might seem a reasonable escape from limited financial opportunities. In September 2009, when national unemployment rates reached 8.6 percent, young people under 25 faced 16.7 percent unemployment; 8.4 percent for college graduates, 14.7 percent for those with high school diplomas, and a staggering 26.6 percent unemployment rate for those without a high school degree.[19] For someone with few other options, a reality show based on being a celebrity's mistress or someone who gets drunk and fights at bars could be one of their only likely means of social mobility. A changing media environment favoring cheap programming over substance means that even the most morally questionable characters might find themselves in the spotlight.

And while it may seem that this environment of instant celebrity offers many a shot at moving up economically, it has largely served to reinforce an illusion that anyone—no matter where they come from—can still make it big in America. The message seems to be that if they can do it, so can you.

The Decline of Journalism and the Quest for Cheap Content

The idea of fans enjoying their celebrity fix of studio-crafted stories once a month when their favorite movie magazine arrived in their mailbox seems quaint today. The internet provides a constant stream of celebrity gossip and updates, often created by celebrities themselves (or their assistants) through Twitter or Facebook accounts. The E! Channel has hours of celebrity news programming and a ticker with updates during their other shows, and "celebrity journalism" programs such as *Entertainment Tonight*, *Extra*, *Access Hollywood*, *Inside Edition*, *The Insider*, and *Showbiz Tonight* provide regular coverage of celebrities. Celebrity stories even permeate traditional news sources; log on to just about any commercial news outlet's website and you'll likely see items about celebrities right next to news about politics, whether you are interested or not. How did it come to this?

While it might seem as if the public just has an insatiable appetite for celebrity gossip, the reasons for this shift are more complex than simply news organizations giving the public what it wants. Put simply, mainstream news organizations are going broke and are desperate for cheap content. According to a 2010 study by the Pew Research Center's Project for Excellence in Journalism (PEJ), newspapers collectively spent $1.6 billion less on reporting and editing than they did a decade ago. Newspaper ad revenues fell 26 percent between 2008 and 2009, while television news revenues fell 22 percent during that time.[20]

These losses are not only due to the recession, but are part of a larger trend. Since 2000, newspaper advertising revenues have fallen about 50 percent, and many dailies have had to stop daily print runs—for example, Denver's *Rocky Mountain News* and the *Seattle Post-Intelligencer*, which are now only available online.[21] Other cities' newspapers are in serious financial straits, like the *Chicago Tribune*, *San Francisco Chronicle*, and the *Los Angeles Times*.[22] Cable news revenues remain healthy, with their emphasis on opinion and frequent coverage of celebrity news (especially on CNN's sister network, HLN).[23] The PEJ report notes that broadcast television revenues are harder to assess, but concludes that CBS and ABC's news divisions are not currently profitable. In 2010, ABC News closed all of its national bureaus outside of Washington, DC, and laid off half of its domestic correspondents.[24]

It's not just newspapers and television news that are suffering. News magazines are also struggling; between 2008 and 2009, ad revenues fell by more than 25 percent for the eight best-selling magazines.[25] Circulations for the big three, *Time*, *Newsweek*, and *U.S. News & World Report*, had declined only slightly between 1989 and 1999, before diving by 2007.[26]

By contrast, sales of magazines based on celebrity content are strong. While several news magazines are struggling for their very survival— in May 2010 the Washington Post Company put *Newsweek* for sale after "multiyear losses"—celebrity magazines are holding their own, even with the internet and the addition of several new magazines to the genre during the last decade.[27] *People*'s circulation has remained steady at about 3.6 million, outselling *Time* by several hundred thousand copies in 2009.[28] *US Weekly*'s circulation grew from about 1.1 million in 2000 to 1.9 million in 2009 as it cut back on lengthy, in-depth stories and focused more on gossip.[29] New celebrity-based magazines such as *In Touch* (launched in 2002) and *Life & Style* (launched in 2004) boast circulations on par with traditional news outlets *The Economist* and *The Atlantic*.[30] In 2004 *Star* magazine reinvented itself, moving from a newspaper tabloid to a glossy celebrity magazine and expanding its readership. Its 2009 circulation was higher than *U.S. News & World Report*'s.[31]

Ironically, traditional journalism's struggles are not for want of an audience—millions log onto their websites—but the internet has made people accustomed to free content and online ad revenues are a tiny fraction of traditional advertising income. Journalism has yet to figure out how to stay financially healthy in the internet age. In contrast with celebrity stories, in-depth news reporting can be costly and time consuming. Celebrity stories often cost next-to-nothing to gather and report and may attract younger readers less likely to buy a newspaper subscription.

It is not just news divisions that are strapped. Traditional television networks have seen their programming revenues decline and depend on sister cable networks' incomes (or selling syndicated programs such as *Law and Order* to cable channels) to make money. As audiences have more and more entertainment choices beyond television, in order to maintain profitability television producers have sought to cut production costs. Broadcast networks have to compete with cable for cheap, year-round content. No longer can the networks get by just running reruns and movies during the summer; they need to provide something new to stay in the game.[32]

Unscripted programming—so-called "reality" television and game shows—can save money in many ways. Filming in someone's home reduces the need to design and build elaborate sets. If a show is simply following someone's life or is about a contest, producers don't need to hire a team of writers. Most of these shows do employ people who write, dress, and design. But by hiring people to write without calling them writers, it is cheaper. Non-unionized writers do not earn as much as Writers Guild members, nor do they receive writing credits, which are crucial for getting future writing jobs and career advancement.[33] To further cut costs, networks offer participants in unscripted shows stingier rewards, according to a 2008 *Hollywood Reporter* story.[34] The proliferation of cheaply produced talent shows (*So You Think You Can Dance*, *America's Got Talent*, *Minute to Win it*) reflect the networks' financial problems. And to minimize the risk, even the cheapest of shows are often imports from other countries, where they have already enjoyed success—most famously, the British import *Pop Idol*, known as *American Idol* in the U.S.

Perhaps one of the biggest cost savings comes from the casting process: hiring "ordinary" people to participate dramatically reduces what it would cost to hire actors (and to adhere to union rules), particularly well-established actors who command higher fees and perhaps a portion of the show's profits. Instead, the myriad of so-called reality shows promise the possibility of creating new celebrities, which is compelling in a whole different way from watching a well-known star in a sitcom. Audiences may feel as if they have something at stake in shows such as these, creating what on the surface may appear to be a meritocracy. Texting for your favorite *American Idol* contestant is a form of participation, but as cultural studies scholar Graeme Turner notes in his book *Ordinary People and the Media*, this is also a form of labor. It might not feel like work, but traditionally, record companies paid talent scouts to do what the public now does for free; even audience members who participate in traditional focus groups get paid, no longer necessary when you can get millions to vote online or by text for free. This minimizes the producers' risk and also puts reality show contestants in a financially compromising position—winners and runners up do not have the chance to negotiate for a record deal or allow competing record companies to bid for their talent. Instead, winners pre-sign contracts that essentially make them employees of the show's production company. Being a reality star is big business—but mostly for the show's producers. And yet the explosion of these kinds of shows adds to the illusion that just about anyone can make it big in America today. While fame might never have been more possible, wealth does not always follow.

Reality Stars and the Illusion of Mobility

Changes in technology, stagnant wages, and the demand for cheap media content have created a perfect storm of sorts: it has never been easier for people to be famous just for being themselves, and there has never been more demand for cheap entertainment. Being famous for being famous might seem like a viable career option for many people. Have more kids than you can afford? A reality show could solve that problem. Too obnoxious to keep a job for long? Your personality could be perfect for *Big Brother* or any show where casting directors need conflict. Not afraid to take off your clothes or reveal intimate details about your sex life? A MySpace page might make you a star like Tila Tequila with your own show on MTV. An affair with a celebrity could mean a *Vanity Fair* photo shoot or *Playboy* pictorial.

Or maybe you do have traditional talent and are looking for your big break. The internet age presumably affords anyone with a camera the chance to be a star. Eighteen-year-old Michael Essany, an aspiring *Tonight Show* host, started a talk show in his living room in 2001 drawing celebrity guests like Ray Romano, Jenny McCarthy, Ed McMahon, and Alex Trebek via phone or in some cases in his Indiana living room.[35] Teen idol Justin Bieber's YouTube video apparently led to his discovery and record deal.[36] Being interesting enough for people to want to watch, if even for a little while, might seem like enough to rise from nowhere, particularly because television producers routinely air YouTube clips as a form of cheap programming.

The new media environment contributes to the notion that the Horatio Alger story is still a real possibility if your video goes viral or a reality show appearance spawns a new career. Although the possibility of becoming a reality star is relatively new, the reality genre has been around in some form nearly as long as television itself. Some scholars view *Candid Camera* (1959–1967), a hidden-camera show involving unsuspecting ordinary members of the public, as a precursor to today's ubiquitous programming.[37] Quiz shows of the 1950s are the ancestors of extended contests such as *Survivor*, *Amazing Race*, and *The Biggest Loser*.

You might be surprised to learn that PBS also played a major role in introducing cameras into people's private lives. A documentary crew followed the Loud family of Santa Barbara, California, starting in 1971 and began airing episodes of *An American Family* in 1973. Pat and Bill Loud had five children and lived what seemed to be a typical upper-middle-class lifestyle, but the program documents the family coming apart. In one episode, son Lance comes out as gay, a shocking revelation at the time when the gay liberation movement was in its infancy and the American Psychiatric Association had just removed homosexuality from its list of mental illnesses. Ten million viewers tuned in to the episode when Pat told Bill she wanted a divorce after twenty-three years of marriage.[38] The series followed Pat's move to Manhattan, as she struggled to start a new life after divorce. She was, according to a 1993 issue of *People*, "a celebrity essentially created by the media."[39] PBS continued to follow the family, airing a documentary in 2002 called "Lance Loud! A Death in an American

Family," chronicling the eldest son's death from AIDS at age fifty. Setting the tone for the documentary-style genre today, MTV's *The Real World* began airing in 1992, and shifted the format from *An American Family* by introducing greater producer manipulation—choosing a "cast," and placing the sometimes volatile young adults in situations sure to create conflict.

Just as with *People*'s coverage of celebrities in the 1980s, the implication is that the doors to fame are now wide open, as are opportunities for wealth. Today no actual talent is necessary as long as the public finds someone interesting. Reality show contestants started appearing regularly in *People* around 2000, with stories ranging from what their lives were like before and after the show, their health and weight issues, and their romantic relationships (even if they did not appear on a dating show). Reality contestants appeared alongside actors and athletes in *People*'s 2002 list of the hottest bachelors. Being on a reality show meant more than the chance to win a lot of money—it also seemed to present the chance to become a celebrity.[40] A spot on a reality show could mean making the morning and late night talk show rounds, being cast in bit parts and commercials, getting paid for personal appearances, a clothing line, fragrance, or skin care line.[41] If all else fails, being famous for being famous can bring the opportunity to attend movie premieres, get into the hottest clubs, and at least *feel* like a celebrity. And of course the likelihood of appearing on another reality show goes up the more the new celebrity gets mentioned in *People* and other celebrity news outlets.

People often emphasized reality stars' ordinary origins. A September 2000 article about Richard Hatch, the winner of the first season of *Survivor*, focused on how his hard work and effort led to newfound fame and wealth. Hatch's win by manipulation and guile shaped the strategy for the show's subsequent casts. It was not the most physically fit contestant who would win, but the participant who focused on his or her own individual success while giving lip service to supporting the group, social Darwinism at its best.

The story describes how Hatch's life improved dramatically after the show: his million dollar win meant former enemies became friends, Hatch's estranged father said he was proud of him, and authorities dropped pending child-abuse charges. Most of all, he had both wealth and fame: "life since the Aug. 23 *Survivor* finale has been a tapestry of microphones, cell phones, green rooms, photo ops and autograph scrums," according to the story, which also detailed a six-figure advance Hatch got for a book deal.

Hatch had worked hard to get there, according to the story. He joined the Army years earlier and even gained admission to West Point (though he dropped out). He later worked as a chauffeur before rising to become a corporate trainer. When the opportunity for *Survivor* arrived, Hatch was up before dawn, doing push-ups, egged on by his adopted son who encouraged him, saying, "c'mon Dad ... We need the money." Hatch won the money and apparently much more. "I've gotten countless offers. Literally. I can't count them. For a number of different arenas for television, radio, movies," he told *People*.[42]

The show's second season winner, Tina Wesson, told *People* about all the free stuff she had received since winning the million dollar prize. In contrast to Hatch, the magazine describes Wesson as sweet but cunning, and casts her as very giving and down-to-earth. She told *People* that she would not just pay off her mortgage, but a friend's too. Her husband told the magazine that they might buy a slightly larger home. "We're not looking for a mansion. Just a little more closet space," he noted, reinforcing the couple's ordinariness.[43] A story on the third season's winner, Vecepia Towery, describes her as hard-working, having served in the Air Force during Desert Storm. Her husband's nickname for her, "frugalicious," underscores that she values thrift as well.[44]

Likewise, the magazine characterized winners from *Who Wants to be a Millionaire?* as hardworking, modest, and deserving of their prizes. The 2000 article also stressed the six winners' ordinariness. One winner bought a used car and donated part of his winnings to three separate churches. "It couldn't have happened to a nicer guy," the story says of another winner, who gave his mother and brothers some of his jackpot. The story emphasized another contestant's humble beginnings after he had to go shopping at the last minute for a solid colored shirt appropriate to wear on the air. "My lifestyle hasn't changed," said the show's first winner, who bought a new house and two cars with his winnings. "I'm thrifty. I'm frugal," he assured readers. The winners' generosity, kindness, and thrift cast them as deserving of their newfound wealth, presumably more available than ever in the era of TV-based contests.[45]

A 2003 story about Evan Marriott (who starred in Fox's *Joe Millionaire*) describes him as a regular guy who lived in a messy apartment and enjoyed watching sports on TV. "Marriott has always preferred forklifts to chilled forks," the article notes, describing how he once had a bit part on a soap opera before getting a construction job to pay the bills. That he wasn't really a millionaire—the show's ruse—seemed to make him more relatable. Marriott "plans on returning to a hard-hat life," the article concludes, quoting the reality star's affirmation of his everyman lifestyle. "At the end of the day I'm just a bulldozer operator from Orange County." The article does mention that Marriott's father was a bank vice president, so he was hardly of working-class origin, but by emphasizing Marriott's manual labor the story magnifies reality show's supposed opportunities for social mobility (while downplaying what could be interpreted as generational downward mobility).[46] Other contestants from not-so-humble beginnings seemed like everyday, ordinary individuals in *People*'s coverage. Firestone tire and winery heir Andrew Firestone told the magazine that he and his family "work in the fields" regularly, so whoever he chose on his season of *The Bachelor* would have to be someone who "wouldn't be afraid to get her hands dirty."[47]

While Evan Marriott's background might not have been quite as modest as first implied, the woman he selected as the show's winner, Zora Andrich, seemed to be really struggling before she won $500,000 and jewelry on *Joe Millionaire*. Andrich had "lived in a cramped, unheated apartment above Bell's Tavern in Lambertville, N.J.," according to *People*, and was "raised in near poverty" by her astrologer single mother. Andrich told the magazine she would use part of her winnings to provide her mother with much needed dental work and to help support an aunt with cancer.[48]

A profile of Kelly Clarkson, the season one winner of *American Idol*, describes her modest upbringing. "There were always worries financially," she told the magazine. Despite her prior attempts to make it in the music industry, she had many "doors slammed in [her] face." Clarkson "worked three jobs (including comedy-club cocktail waitress) to pay for her apartment and car," and had moved from Dallas to Los Angeles to pursue her dream, "but . . . her new apartment burned down . . . [the] same day" she rented it. Despite winning the contest, getting a record deal, and filming a movie, judge Simon Cowell told the magazine, "I haven't seen any difference in her . . . there's no arrogance."[49] A profile of the first winner of *America's Top Model*, Adrianne Curry, also highlighted that she worked waiting tables before winning a modeling contract and becoming a "supermodel-in-training." Her mother had been laid off from her factory job the year before, and she was going to help her out with her winnings.[50] Her win later yielded her a spot on *The Surreal Life*, where she met husband Christopher Knight, who played Peter Brady on *The Brady Bunch*. Curry has since appeared on several other game shows and reality programs (including *My Fair Brady*, documenting her relationship with Knight). For Curry, winning a reality show spawned both her career and marriage to a former television star, and presumably entre to the world of celebrity.

Elisabeth Hasselbeck may have parlayed a 2001 appearance on *Survivor* into a host position on *The View* in 2003, but for most people, being on a reality program is not really a lucrative career path. As a 2007 *Forbes* article notes, in the long run, most people do not make much money out of the experience. With so many reality show personalities, the average reality show participant might earn $500–$3,000 for an occasional personal appearance, but even this is likely to taper off over time. Getting cast on another reality show might help, but traditional acting jobs can be harder to come by for those with reality show roots.[51] A handful make a lot of money—Jon and Kate Gosselin reportedly earned $75,000 an episode for *Jon and Kate Plus 8*, and the *Real Housewives of New York City* tried to negotiate for a six-figure salary per episode after their show became successful. The big money goes to those who are celebrities to begin with; the Osbournes allegedly earned $5 million per episode after their show became a hit. And producer/judge Simon Cowell earned an eight-figure salary for his work on *American Idol* in 2009.[52]

While Pat Loud might have become an accidental celebrity in the 1970s, today's reality show participants are anything but accidental. Ironically, the rise of reality-based fame has altered the landscape of traditional celebrities, whose private lives have become central to their "brand"—in many cases without their consent. While reality show participants may not typically change tax brackets permanently, the genre has reshaped how the public consumes information about celebrities, with an increased focus on their private lives.

The Celebrity Life as Brand

As author Neal Gabler discusses in his 1999 book, *Life, The Movie: How Entertainment Conquered Reality*, in many instances a celebrity's life has become more important, and perhaps more entertaining, than their day job. That is, if they have a job outside of being themselves. The celebrity industry that started with fan magazines and grew into the multimedia entity it has become today needs to be fed regularly, and famous peoples' lives can provide continual content, particularly with so many people willing to provide intimate details about themselves in order to get into the public eye or enhance their existing fame. Social networking sites such as Facebook and Twitter allow near constant updates about celebrities who post their random thoughts and whereabouts; even CNN sometimes posts celebrity Twitter feeds on its ticker. The value placed on privacy means that information about those in the public eye who would rather keep their private lives private can be sold at a premium, especially if it contradicts a person's public image, such as with Tiger Woods' sex scandal. As traditional-style soap operas go off the air, real-life celebrity soap operas have taken their place. These stories, what Gabler calls "lifies," are never-ending sagas of easily relatable human events about relationships, families, health, and lifestyle. And in contrast with soap operas, they provide an incredibly cheap and continual stream of content, even after a celebrity's death.

The 1998 film *The Truman Show* provides a prescient critique of the self-as-brand. Jim Carrey's character, Truman Burbank, thinks he lives an ordinary, middle-class American life as a married man working in the insurance industry. In reality, everyone in his life is a paid actor and he is the child of a corporation, unbeknownst to him, and he is horrified when he learns that nothing in his life is authentic, that it is all a commercial enterprise. The items in his house are all product placements, and anyone who threatens to tell him the truth about his life disappears and producers remove them from the set, which is Truman's whole world.

More than a decade later, this film could be interpreted as a warning about the dangers of living your life wholly in the public eye and how relationships lose true intimacy when people are motivated to be "cast" as friends or family members, not to mention the shallowness of the voyeuristic public that watches. While Truman breaks down when he discovers that his whole life is a lie, many families have *chosen* to take this path: Nick Lachey and Jessica Simpson, the *Real Housewives* families, the Osbournes, the Hogans, and the Kardashians are but a few who have made this choice. Their motivations might have been different, but it seems that allowing cameras into their homes enhanced their fame and piqued public curiosity about their private lives. By contrast, many "traditional" celebrities struggle to maintain a boundary around their personal lives, despite public interest. When information does slip out, such as when a tabloid discovered that Sandra Bullock's husband Jesse James had been unfaithful, celebrities might find their private lives under a microscope in the same fashion as their reality show counterparts—who, in contrast, invited the cameras in.

Personal information about celebrities' lives serves many purposes, but I will focus on three specifically: First, personal stories can humanize celebrities, helping us to sympathize with them while masking some of the privileges that wealth may bring. Second, details about what stars wear, the products they use, and the vacations they take highlight celebrity-style consumption, and lastly, a celebrity behaving badly can serve as a morality tale condemning those who dramatically violate the values of hard work and self-control.

Special, but Just Like Us

For people who are already famous, a reality show can offer fans a behind-the-scenes look at what it is really like to be a celebrity. It can also be an attempt to shape public opinion and create a sympathetic perspective. Actress Denise Richards got a lot of bad press after her 2006 divorce from Charlie Sheen and subsequent relationship with musician Richie Sambora. Her show, *Denise Richards: It's Complicated*, focused mostly on her family, including her children, sister, and recently widowed father. Allowing cameras into their homes not only offer celebrities a chance to redefine their image, but can reinforce the notion that the wealthy are really just like us. While their material privileges are clearly visible, other opportunities the elite may enjoy mostly remain in the shadows.

At first glance, the Osbourne family might seem to have little in common with the average American family. Ozzy Osbourne, the self-proclaimed "prince of darkness" who bit heads off of live animals during the heyday of his heavy-metal career, probably bears little resemblance to most dads on the surface. When *The Osbournes* premiered on MTV in 2002, viewers got an inside look at the family's gothic Beverly Hills mansion and lifestyle, as well as the family's love for one another, allowing the audience to relate to them on a very basic level.

A *People* story that year described the Osbournes as "equal parts *Brady Bunch* and *Addams Family*." The article compared them to other traditional television families, and invited stars of popular family sitcoms to compare the situations the Osbournes face on their show to those their fictional families faced. Henry Winkler, star of the 1970s hit *Happy Days*, commented that "watching the Osbournes you watch your own family."[53] When wife Sharon made her colon cancer diagnosis public, she told *People* how the family members struggled emotionally with the news and described the side effects of her chemotherapy in graphic detail.[54] By humanizing the Osbournes, audiences can see them primarily as family members, rather than as wealthy decadents. Even their many struggles with substance abuse (Ozzy and two of his kids have publicly acknowledged seeking treatment) help them seem more relatable since they "invited" us into their home. Revealing their human failings helped the family make millions from the show and also likely added to the commercial success of Ozzfest, an annual concert tour the family produces.

The Osbournes inspired *Hogan Knows Best*, a reality show about pro-wrestler Hulk Hogan's family, with Hulk presenting himself as Ozzy's antithesis. "This show is about our family behind closed doors, with all the love and support of the Osbournes, but without the drugs and the rehab," said Hogan in a 2005 interview before the show's debut. While the Osbourne kids cursed and seemed to have free rein tooling around Hollywood, *Hogan Knows Best* suggested that the Hogan kids had to abide by their father's strict rules—including GPS monitoring. Yes, they might have lived in a 20,000 square-foot estate, but they were apparently just like any other family with teenagers.[55] By offering viewers an inside look into the world of wrestling, *Hogan Knows Best* also highlighted how hard Hulk Hogan had to work and the toll that many years of performing took on his body.

Hogan's "father knows best" image began to unravel when son Nick was arrested and later incarcerated for reckless driving when he crashed into a tree at age 17, critically injuring his passenger. When tapes of a conversation between Hogan and his jailed son seemed to blame the passenger for his injuries, the privileges of wealth began seeping through the cracks, especially when Nick asked his father to help him get a larger cell and a reality show upon his release.[56] The Hogans' messy divorce ultimately undermined the image the show sought to create, but perhaps Hulk salvaged some of it by releasing a memoir in 2009 detailing his thoughts of suicide and the personal rejection he felt during his marriage, reinforcing his humanness and downplaying any privilege that his wealth might have brought him.[57]

Just as the Hogans probably revealed more about their marital problems than they intended when they signed on to do their show, singers Jessica Simpson and Nick Lachey's 2003 MTV show *Newlyweds* exposed their many differences, although the show used the conflict to create an *I Love Lucy*-style comedy. "We would fight almost every day, sometimes three or four times," Simpson told *People* in a story about the show's debut, perhaps making their divorce a few years later less of a surprise in retrospect. The program was meant to be a vehicle to promote their careers and boost sales of her new CD, which was released the day the show debuted. Ironically, many of the couple's conflicts were over lifestyle and spending issues—something many couples could likely relate to, and unwittingly the show became at least in part a show about consumerism. For instance, the couple went camping in Yosemite National Park during one of the episodes, and Simpson had a hard time with the sparse accommodations. "It was like cultures colliding!" said Lachey. "One item he says she couldn't live without: Her $1,700 Louis Vuitton purse, which had to go into a bear-proof bin at night."[58]

The show frequently followed Simpson on shopping trips, documenting her lavish purchases, such as buying expensive linens, a Louis Vuitton dog carrier, and spending over $1,000 on lingerie. While Lachey might not have approved of her spending, shows featuring the lifestyles of celebrities and the well-to-do often highlight their purchases, offering viewers both the chance to experience vicarious pleasures of consumption while also being able to maintain an air of judgment about celebrity spending. Lachey emphasized the value of thrift in *Newlyweds*, as other participants occasionally do in other shows, such as Bruce Jenner in *Keeping Up with the Kardashians*. But sometimes it is left to the audience to question the value of the participants' spending habits. In the *Real Housewives* series, shopping trips sometimes include an onscreen graphic revealing the price of a purchase; whether this creates a sense of admiration or scorn is up to the audience.

Ambivalence about Consumption

It's not just reality shows that reflect mixed feelings about hyper-consumption. Celebrity profiles, gossip, and even paparazzi shots can reveal our culture's ambivalence about materialism. "The beauty of being rich, of course, is that you can throw caution to the wind, leave your coupons at home," noted a 1995 *People* article, "Born to Spend," which chronicles the high-priced items stars supposedly buy. From Jerry Seinfeld's eight Porches to Whoopi Goldberg's clothes shopping spree at a trendy boutique and John Travolta's $30 million Gulfstream jet, details of celebrities' personal purchases highlight that wealth means consumption.[59] The tension between the pleasure of affording luxury items and the value of thrift plays itself out over and over through celebrities, often without their intention or cooperation. For instance, when a magazine runs a paparazzo's picture of a celebrity walking down the street and emphasizes that she is wearing a $200 t-shirt, $300 jeans, and carrying a $5,000 bag, the reader can both fantasize about having those things, learn about what constitutes the most exclusive and high-end branded merchandise, and view the celebrity as wasteful. The contradiction often stays unresolved.

A 1993 story about Madonna exemplifies this contradiction. That year, she apparently paid $4.9 million in cash for a home with an appraised value of $1.5 million, implying that in her haste to get the house she paid more than three times what it was worth. The story notes that she "grew up lower-middle-class in suburban Detroit," but would not "change her financial habits any time soon." "I do what I want," she told the magazine, which valued her wealth at $100 million at the time.[60] While there is a critical undertone to this anecdote, it also celebrates the power of Madonna and other wealthy women in show business to buy whatever they want, regardless of the price. In 1999, *People* ran an article "Ready, Set, Go Buy Something," which quotes Spice Girl Victoria Adams (soon to be Victoria Beckham) about her shopping habits. "When I see something I like, I buy it in every color, and I buy shoes in every color to match, as well as handbags. If I could, I'd go shopping every single day. I'm definitely a shopaholic." As with many others of its kind, this story goes on to detail the many purchases of other stars and how much they spent. Although the article pauses to quote a psychotherapist who warned that compulsive shopping is really about trying to fill an emotional void, the multipage story continues with its celebrity shopping list, peppered with pictures of ecstatic-looking celebrities shopping and carrying their purchases. The story ends with a quote from self-proclaimed shopaholic, actress Jennifer Tilly. "People will look back at my life and say, 'She didn't accomplish much, but she wore great clothes.'" The photo of Tilly with her new goods illustrates how happy shopping makes her.[61]

Stories detailing the expensive touches to celebrity weddings (such as Victoria Beckham's $100,000 wedding dress),[62] pricey divorces and huge settlements, new homes filled with amenities, and luxury vacations both serve to provide "inside" information on the latest developments in celebrity lives, and also provide a shopper's guide to what constitutes the height in style. Just as *The Oprah Winfrey Show*'s "Favorite Things" episodes purport to inform viewers of the best of the best, celebrity stories emphasizing consumption provide readers with details of how to have the same stuff as the rich and stylish and thus join their status communities through consumption.

Some fan magazine spreads directly link celebrities to products; while stars have appeared in ads since practically the beginning of the fan magazine, these ads often pose as regular content. A 2009 *People* story about Tom Cruise and Katie Holmes purports to debunk a rumor that the couple spent $3 million outfitting their toddler daughter, Suri. The article features the girl in several outfits, each with the price, and in many cases including the store the items came from.[63]

Fashion photos often include both the price of the designer dress a celebrity wore for an appearance (which they usually get to wear for free), and also feature a similar item readers can order from a more reasonably priced retailer. A celebrity's red carpet pose or gotcha paparazzi shot can easily turn into a de facto advertisement, with or without the star's knowledge or consent. Magazines like *US Weekly*, *Star*, and *Life & Style*, which are much more photo-based than *People*, are basically product catalogues filled with celebrity models. Celebrities' lives can easily become advertisements for a myriad of products. The more we know about them, the more we can know about their stuff. They might not care if we know—or even prefer that we didn't—but advertisers like that we do. It is therefore in advertisers' best interest to keep celebrity stories as personal as possible so they can continue to be unwitting spokespeople for consumption.

Morality Tales

Of course, stories about celebrities' private lives aren't always celebratory; in fact, with the advent of blogs and the proliferation of opinion-based television programming, celebrities' personal lives are frequent fodder for judgment. Also serving as cheap entertainment, panels of critics regularly appear on *Showbiz Tonight* and similar fare to opine about celebrity missteps. Typically, critics pile on about behavior that shows a lack of self-control, a central tenet of both the Puritan ethic and Horatio Alger stories. Substance use, promiscuous sexual behavior, and sometimes poor financial judgment can land a celebrity in the center of non-stop commentary. These attacks serve to reinforce the idea that some people are undeserving of wealth and fame, and the critics seem to cheer on their downfall by highlighting their excesses. This Greek chorus of sorts narrates any celebrity scandal and demands retribution, ranging from getting fired to going to jail or divorce by the errant party's spouse. Not only do these discussions provide forums to debate and in some cases reaffirm societal values, but they also offer an opportunity to condemn those seen as unworthy recipients of wealth.

Former child stars frequently find themselves in the crosshairs of public condemnation, leading to questions about what happens to those who get too much too soon. Britney Spears and Lindsay Lohan's very public problems with relationships, substance use, and the law have made them prime subjects for these modern-day morality tales. Their every movement documented by the dozens of paparazzi swarming around them, the celebrity soap opera industry eagerly awaits the latest twist, be it a shaved head, arrest warrant, or rehab stint. During May of 2010, when Lohan missed a court date for a DUI arrest, she came under fire for living it up at the Cannes Film Festival. "Just days before an irate judge is expected to wrap an alcohol-monitoring anklet around the troubled starlet, Lohan partied all night Thursday and into Friday at Cannes, according to reports," *People.com* reported. "Lindsay was drinking Dom Pérignon, Cristal Roederer champagne and Belvedere vodka," an employee of a local club told *E! Online*.[64] The gossip industry pounced on her apparent lack of self-control, reporting on the number of nights she was out partying and what time she went home the previous night. Lohan and other former child actors who appear to indulge in a lifestyle of excess violate the notion that material success is the result of hard work.

We tend to tolerate excess if it at least appears to be moderated by hard work. The younger the celebrity, the less they have appeared to paid their dues through work.

While many celebrities have been caught driving under the influence, young female stars who fail to exhibit enough public contrition and appear to be flouting the law are likely to come under especially intense scrutiny. Lohan and Spears' nighttime exploits yielded daily television coverage on gossip shows, which aired new video by paparazzi regularly. By contrast, actor Kiefer Sutherland, star of television show *24* and son of actor Donald Sutherland, has had numerous public displays of alcohol-fueled misbehavior. While his behavior gets coverage, the intensity and volume of coverage is much lighter despite his much longer history of illegal behavior. He was charged with driving drunk in 1989, 1993, 2004, and 2007, and was sentenced to 48 days in jail in 2007.[65] In 2009, he allegedly head-butted a fashion designer in a New York club, although charges against him were later dropped.[66] In 2010, he was allegedly kicked out of a London strip club, accused of being drunk and disorderly (and shirtless).[67] Despite more than twenty years of trouble, we might ask why he and other actors with similar histories have avoided the ongoing paparazzi scrum and chorus of judges that Lohan, Spears, and others have faced. Perhaps, like Charlie Sheen, son of actor Martin Sheen, who was arrested for domestic violence in 2009 and had previously admitted to hiring prostitutes in the 1990s and a history of drug and alcohol problems, Sutherland was the star of a hit television show. Being considered economically productive seems to reduce—although not eliminate—the amount of public derision a celebrity receives.

The lack of public pillory does not mean the absence of problematic behavior. When actor Heath Ledger died of a prescription drug overdose in 2008, it took the public by surprise, just as when actor River Phoenix died in 1993. According to a 1994 *People* story, drugs are a regular part of the Hollywood club scene:

> If [Phoenix] didn't stand out in his final weeks as someone who desperately needed help, that may be, at least in part, because he blended so perfectly with his surroundings. In the particular Hollywood subculture that Phoenix came to inhabit, the drugs can be hard and the getting easy.[68]

Female celebrity substance use tends to elicit much more intense criticism than it does for young male celebrities, despite the fact that men dramatically outnumber women arrested for drunk driving—several studies find that more than 90 percent of repeat offenders are men, who are almost three times more likely to be drunk and involved in fatal crashes than women are.[69] According to the National Survey on Drug Use and Health (NSDUH), young men (aged 18–25) are more likely to drink alcohol than their female counterparts (64 percent versus 58 percent), and men are more likely to binge drink than women.[70] Substance abuse rates for men over eighteen are nearly double the rate for women.[71] And yet in 2007, Newsweek featured young female celebrities' antics in a cover story called "Girls Gone Bad." "Paris, Britney, Lindsay & Nicole: They seem to be everywhere and they may not be wearing underwear," the story began, warning that these women might be a bad influence on young girls.[72] Much as during the 1920s, when stories of young female celebrities warned of the dangers of the "new woman," young female celebrities today do more than violate the law or lose control: they also violate expectations of femininity. While male celebrities' substance use might contribute to a marketable "bad boy" persona, female celebrities' lack of self-control casts them as immoral and unworthy of wealth and fame. And for all celebrities who seem unable to manage what fame bestows upon them, their downfall appears to be self-inflicted and just punishment for a lack of self-restraint, not to mention a plot-point in the celebrity-life-as-soap-opera industry.

Downward Mobility

Despite the growing wealth gap, stories about celebrities, reality stars, and game show winners reinforce the idea that anyone can be blessed by a spontaneous windfall. Just as with its coverage of reality show contestants, *People* profiled lottery winners in 2002, emphasizing how your life can change with one lucky break:

> Just pencil in your birthday plus your high school locker combination, plunk down a buck or maybe 50, cross your fingers and . . . next thing you know you're sipping mai tais in the Jacuzzi of your stretch Mercedes SUV. Never mind that you're 10 times more likely to be killed by a bee sting—winning a whopping lottery

jackpot is still the quickest, easiest way to realizing the American Dream.

And like reality contest winners, this story about of lottery winners emphasizes their worthiness: one winner had recently lost several family members as well as her job. One dreamed of being a figure skater before a car accident caused a severe injury. Another was a single mother-to-be working as an Army clerk. One couple had serious financial problems and never went on a honeymoon. Several winners highlight the simple pleasures the money brought: sending kids to college, opening a skating school, vacationing at a motorcycle rally. But this story also details what happens to winners who don't deal with their winnings properly. One couple admitted that they lost about $200,000 through bad investments, while another winner ended up filing for bankruptcy after several business ventures failed.[73] The message: you can get lucky in America and have a lifestyle of luxury, but don't blow it. If you do, you have no one to blame but yourself. Celebrity stories of "has-beens" also reinforce this message.

Those who achieve celebrity status and experience sudden movement up the social mobility ladder are practically guaranteed to experience downward mobility also at some point. Fame is fleeting and fickle, and someone who earns a seven-figure paycheck one year could earn just a fraction years later. Not only do celebrity tales offer an abundance of rags-to-riches stories, seemingly providing endless examples of American upward mobility, but celebrity stories of falling from the top provide ready-made explanations for downward mobility. Just as during the Great Depression, when fan magazines emphasized a former silent star's personal failures, modern-day downfalls reinforce the idea that we succeed and fail based on our own merit, masking the systemic nature of social inequality.

There are likely thousands of former television, movie, and music stars who were once household names that graced pages of celebrity magazines, who have vanished from public consciousness. Most presumably find other forms of work, whether in the entertainment industry or another field, presumably with far lower salaries. Celebrities' downward mobility becomes visible when they are involved in scandals, like those noted above, or if they take part in reality shows such as *The Surreal Life*, *Celebrity Fit Club*, or *Celebrity Rehab*, which highlight the dark side of a celebrity's fall from stardom for our viewing pleasure. These and other shows emphasize individual failure as central to downward mobility, the result of weight gain, substance abuse, or a difficult personality. The structure of the entertainment industry, as well as the industry's focus on youth and a narrow version of beauty rarely become part of the discussion about how fame ends.

Just as during the Depression, the story of the celebrity who lost a fortune due to their own excesses remains a central explanation of celebrities' downward mobility today. When *People* reported that actor Nicolas Cage owed $6.3 million in back taxes and defaulted on a $2 million loan in 2009, the story enumerated his many homes—including three that he allegedly spent a total of $33 million on two years prior—and suggested his "lavish properties and prized toys" were at least partially to blame for his financial woes. Yes, he was suing his financial manager, "but will he stop shopping?" the article asked.[74] Cage's story is part of a long tradition of hostility directed towards those who had wealth but lost it due to a lack of thrift.

Before his untimely death in 2010, former child star Gary Coleman's financial troubles were regular tabloid fodder; his 1999 bankruptcy, job as a security guard, and subsequent assault charges appeared more like a sideshow of his own making rather than a reality for former child actors struggling to support themselves as adults. Always identified as the child he no longer was, the transition for Coleman and others is often incredibly difficult.

"There is grim fascination in watching the mighty stumble," noted a 1997 *People* story about many celebrities who have had money problems. Citing their elaborate home furnishings, vast entourages, penchant for trashing rented houses, and even "costly hairpieces," bankruptcy seems to be the result of absurd levels of spending and poor personal choices, a sentiment that often extends to non-celebrities who file for bankruptcy.[75] And yet according to a 2009 study, medical expenses caused 62 percent of all personal bankruptcy filings.[76] Tales of celebrity excess help further the notion that economic problems are only the result of poor choices.

Deep in the 1997 article an entertainment lawyer notes that a new recording artist, for instance, "has to sign whatever contract is offered" and may generate millions for a record company while pocketing only a small fraction for themselves. The musical group TLC, then the most successful female group of all time, earned $92 million for their record company from the success of their number one 1995 single "Waterfalls," of which they earned about $1.2 million between the three artists, who filed for bankruptcy that same year. "There were no Mercedeses, no Rollses, no yachts," according to the group's attorney. They each owed their management company about $500,000 in "unrecouped balances"— a sum larger than their income from their hit record.[77] Yes, many celebrities fail to live within their means, just as non-celebrities might spend themselves into poverty. But the continued emphasis on out-of-control spending reinforces the notion that downward mobility is solely the individual's fault, rather than something built into the structure of the entertainment industry or the larger society. Even during times of recession, stories of celebrity excesses and subsequent financial failure suggest that people's financial struggles are of their own making.

Stardom and Social Mobility in America

The seemingly endless stories about celebrities published in print, online, and on television tell us many things about American life. These tales reflect contemporary debates about gender, relationships, consumption, and status. And as I have argued throughout this book, celebrity stories appear to provide visible and pervasive examples that anyone can rise to the top of the economic ladder. Celebrities seem to show us what it looks like to make it big in America, which changes based on economic, social, and political realities.

As a collective fantasy, we are active participants in both the American Dream and the meaning of celebrity culture. Rather than something imposed from above, the idea that through hard work or just being special and unique we too can enjoy the bounty of America is very compelling. Not only do celebrities appear to embody the possibilities our economic system holds, they can also serve as targets for criticism of the elite. As I noted in Chapter 1, the truly rich and powerful do not need to sell their private lives or endure the volatility of fame. True, executives and CEOs can and do lose their jobs and sometimes even go to prison, but typically severance packages and business connections enable them to continue to reap the benefits of their prior status for years. While we chitchat about celebrities' relationships and sex lives, log on to snarky websites highlighting a star's weight gain, bad hair day, or what they look like without makeup, the sometimes shady behavior of the true elite remains under the radar. Ponzi schemes, insider trading, embezzling, price fixing, and other criminal activities seem like boring business news compared with a surprise celebrity divorce or the sudden death of a star, which can distract public attention for weeks at a time. It is too simple to say we are manipulated by the powerful to focus on trivialities; we actively collude by paying more attention to celebrity stories. If the press made more money telling us stories about white collar criminals, I am sure we would have more websites, magazines, and television shows devoted to corporate crime.

Celebrity culture can be fun and feel like mind candy when news of serious social issues starts to feel overwhelming. And yet we should not dismiss the pervasiveness of celebrity stories in our culture as meaningless. In contrast to other industrialized nations, the American economic system enables many to live in poverty based on the possibility of achieving great wealth. In reality, rising from the lower rungs to the top is extremely difficult and highly unlikely. But celebrities, whose personal histories are often well known, serve as modern-day Horatio Alger characters who rise from obscurity to fame, and in some cases from poverty to wealth. Their experiences reaffirm the presence of the American Dream, and provide guideposts for how we too might achieve upward mobility. And when they fall from stardom, as so many inevitably do, celebrity stories provide an explanation for downward mobility, too. Celebrity culture provides an important narrative about the meaning of success, and about the meaning of America itself.

NOTES

1 The American Dream

1 Joshua Gamson, *Claims to Fame: Celebrity in Contemporary America* (Berkeley, CA University of California Press, 1994).

2 Anthony Slide, *Inside the Hollywood Fan Magazine: A History of Star Makers, Fabricators, and Gossip Mongers* (Jackson, MS: University of Mississippi Press, 2010), p. 7.

3 For more discussion see Erving Goffman, *The Presentation of Self in Everyday Life* (New York: Doubleday, 1959).

4 Daniel Dayan and Elihu Katz, *Media Events: The Live Broadcasting of History* (Cambridge, MA: Harvard University Press, 1992).

5 Francesco Alberoni, "The Powerless 'Elite': Theory and Sociological Research on the Phenomenon of the Stars," trans. Denis McQuail, in *The Celebrity Culture Reader*, Ed. P. David Marshall, (London: Routledge, 2006), pp. 108–123.

6 Ibid., p. 119.

7 For more discussion, see Stephen J. McNamee and Robert K. Miller, Jr., *The Meritocracy Myth*, 2nd edn. (Lanham, MD: Rowman & Littlefield, 2009), pp. 1–11.

8 Richard Dyer, "Stars as Images," in *The Celebrity Culture Reader*, Ed. P. David Marshall, (London: Routledge, 2006), p. 157.

9 See Paul Taylor et al., "Inside the Middle Class: Bad Times Hit the Good Life," (Washington, DC: Pew Research Center, 2008), http://pewresearch.org/pubs/793/inside-the-middle-class [accessed September 8, 2010].

10 Roland Marchand, *Advertising the American Dream: Making Way for Modernity 1920–1940* (Berkeley, CA: University of California Press, 1985).

11 Slide, Appendix 1.

12 For more discussion, see Gamson, Chapter 7.

2 Beyond Subsistence

1 See Richard Schickel, *Intimate Strangers: The Culture of Celebrity* (New York: Doubleday Books, 1985).

2 Robert D. Plotnick et al., "The Twentieth Century Record of Poverty in the United States," (Madison, WI: Institute for Research on Poverty, 1998), Figure 4, www.irp.wisc.edu/publications/dps/pdfs/dp116698.pdf [accessed September 8, 2010].

3 John K. Folger and Charles B. Nam, "Education of the American Population," U.S. Census Bureau, Current Population Reports, "Table P20–536: Years of School Completed by People 25 Years Old and Over, by Age and Sex: Selected Years 1940 to 2004," (Washington, DC: Government Printing Office, 2005), www.census.gov/ population/socdemo/education/tabA-1.pdf [accessed September 8, 2010].

4 U.S. Census Bureau, "Table 225: Social-Economic Group of Persons 14 Years Old and Over in the Experienced Labor Force in 1940 and Gainful Workers 14 Years and Over in 1930, in 1920, and in 1910, By Sex," *Statistical Abstract of the United States: 1950 (71st Edition)* (Washington, DC: Government Printing Office, 1950), p. 190, www2.census.gov/prod2/statcomp/documents/1950-01.pdf [accessed September 8, 2010].

5 America at the Millennium Project, "The Social Structure of Unemployment in the United States: 1910, Working Paper 2," (Philadelphia: University of Pennsylvania, 2001), www.sp2.upenn.edu/america2000/wp2txt.pdf [accessed September 8, 2010].

6 "Both Carry the Same Food Value," advertisement, (Quaker Oats, 1919), from *Motion Picture Classic*, March 1919, p. 65.

7 Department of Health and Human Services, Morbidity and Mortality Weekly Report, "Achievements in Public Health, 1900–1999: Healthier Mothers and Babies," (Atlanta, GA: Centers for Disease Control and Prevention, 1999), see figure 1, www.cdc.gov/mmwr/preview/mmwrhtml/mm4838a2.htm#fig1 [accessed September 8, 2010].

8 Suellen Hoy, *Chasing Dirt: The American Pursuit of Cleanliness* (New York: Oxford University Press, 1995), pp. 108–109.

9 Stanley Lebergott, *Pursuing Happiness: American Consumers in the Twentieth Century* (Princeton, NJ: Princeton University Press, 1993), p. 113.

10 Ibid., p. 125.

11 U.S. Census Bureau, "Table 110: Immigration: 1820 to 1949," *Statistical Abstract of the United States: 1950 (71st Edition)* (Washington, DC: Government Printing Office, 1950), p. 97, www2.census.gov/prod2/statcomp/documents/1950-01.pdf [accessed September 8, 2010].

12 U.S. Census Bureau, "Table 217: Farm Employment and Wage Rates: 1909 to 1949," *Statistical Abstract of the United States: 1950 (71st Edition)* (Washington, DC: Government Printing Office, 1950), p. 180, www2.census.gov/prod2/statcomp/ documents/1950-01.pdf [accessed September 8, 2010]. The percentage comes from a calculation of 12 million farm workers out of a population of 92 million.

13 U.S. Census Bureau, "Facts for Features," Press Release, (Washington, DC: U.S. Census Bureau, 2006), www.census.gov/newsroom/releases/archives/facts_for_ features_special_editions/cb06-ffse06.html [accessed September 8, 2010].

14 Robert D. Manning, *Credit Card Nation: The Consequences of America's Addiction to Credit* (New York: Basic Books, 2000), p. 106.

15 Ibid., pp. 104–105.

16 Ibid., p. 104.

17 Ibid., p. 108.

18 Ibid., p. 106. See also Michael Staten, Joint Center for Housing Studies, "The Impact of Credit Price and Term Regulations Supply," (Cambridge, MA: Harvard University, 2008), www.jchs.harvard.edu/publications/finance/understanding_consumer_credit/ papers/ucc08-8_staten.pdf [accessed September 8, 2010].

19 Robert Sklar, *Movie-Made America: A Cultural History of American Movies* (New York: Vintage, 1975), pp. 68–69.

20 Ibid., pp. 20, 23.

21 Ibid., p. 55.

22 Ibid., p. 18.

23 For more discussion, see Steven J. Ross, *Working-Class Hollywood: Silent Film and the Shaping of Class in America* (Princeton, NJ: Princeton University Press, 1998).

24 David P. Warren, "The Rumor Mill: How Fan Magazines Portrayed Hollywood 1911–1959," MA Thesis, University of Southern California, 1999, p. 42.

25 Augustus H. Fretz, "The Educational Value of Picture Plays," *Picture Play*, April 17, 1915, pp. 14–18.

26 For example, Elizabeth Richey Dessez, "Better Pictures for the Children," *Motion Picture Classic*, October 1916, p. 45.

27 H.Z. Levine, "In the Moving Picture World," *Photoplay*, March 1912, pp. 36–40.

28 Frank B. Coigne, "Camille: Adapted from Dumas' Great Novel," *Photoplay*, June 1912, p. 66.

29 Prof. Frederick Star, "The World Before Your Eyes," *Photoplay*, February 1912, pp. 9–10.

30 Ernest A. Dench, "Society Folk Who Have Responded to the Photoplay's Lure," *Motion Picture Classic*, October 1915, p. 50.

31 Ross, p. 19; see relevant footnote on p. 286

32 Ross, p. 32

33 Thekla D. Harrison, "Moving Picture Etiquette," *Motion Picture Classic*, September 1915, p. 40.

34 Sklar, p. 46.

35 *Chicago Tribune*, "Patriotism at the Movies," *Photoplay*, February 1918, p. 42.

36 Editorial, "The Fifth Estate," *Photoplay*, June 1918, p. 17.

37 Editorial, "The War-Time Sanctuary," *Photoplay*, October 1917, p. 15.

38 William A. Brady, "How the Motion Picture Saved the World," *Photoplay*, January 1919, p. 25.

39 K. Owen, "On 'Active Duty' with the Actor-Soldiers," *Photoplay*, March 1918, p. 20–21.

40 Stanley W. Todd, "Entertaining our Soldiers in Training: How Moving Pictures are Helping to Make the Boys Happy in Uncle Sam's Training-Camps," *Motion Picture*, July 1918, pp. 76–77.

41 "Fannie Ward's New Home," *Photoplay*, January 1919, p. 78. "Home Sweet Home with Geraldine Farrar," *Photoplay*, January 1919, pp. 24–27.

42 "Stories of the Studio People," *Picture Play*, April 10, 1915, pp. 31–32.

43 "Who Says the Stars Dont [*sic*] Work?" *Motion Picture Magazine*, November 1918, pp. 56–57.

44 "Gloria Swanson Tries the Simple Life," *Motion Picture Classic*, September 1918, p. 51.

45 "Charlie Chaplin Pursues the Elusive Pill in Honolulu," *Motion Picture*, March 1918, p. 44.

46 "Daily Program: The Life of a Comedy Star, Director and Author," *Motion Picture*, May 1918, p. 66.

47 U.S. Census Bureau, "Table 207: Persons Gainfully Employed in Agriculture and in Nonagricultural Pursuits; And Women in Labor Force or Gainfully Occupied:

1820–1940," *Statistical Abstract of the United States: 1950 (71st Edition)* (Washington, DC: Government Printing Office, 1950), p. 172, www2.census.gov/prod2/statcomp/documents/1950-01.pdf [accessed September 8, 2010].

48 Frances A. Ludwig, "From Stenography to Stardom," *Photoplay*, February, 1918, pp. 30–31.

49 "The Knothole Astronomer," *Photoplay*, January 1919, p. 87.

50 Harriette Underhill, "The Rise of Elsie Ferguson: From Chorus Girl to Star of Stage and Screen; but First Elsie Rose, and Rose," *Photoplay*, January 1919, p. 41.

51 Violet Mersereau, "A Busy Day with a Movie Actress," *Picture Play*, May 1, 1915, p. 2.

52 Kathlyn Williams, "The Jungle Actress," *Picture Play*, April 17, 1915, pp. 1–4.

53 Creighton Hamilton, "Girls Who Play with Death," *Picture Play*, May 1916, pp. 177–186.

54 Robert Grau, "Woman's Conquest in Filmdom," *Motion Picture Classic*, September 1915, pp. 41–44.

55 Ibid.

56 For more discussion, see Richard Schickel, *Intimate Strangers: The Culture of Celebrity in America* (Chicago: Ivan R. Dee, 1985).

57 Lloyd Robinson, "How They Have Changed," *Picture Play*, April 1916, pp. 17–24.

58 Dorothy Donnell, "Gladys Brockwell Does 'His' Bit," *Motion Picture*, February 1918, pp. 36–37.

59 Harriette Underhill, "Olive Tells Her Secrets," *Photoplay*, February 1918, pp. 43–45.

60 See Steven J. Ross, *Working-Class Hollywood: Silent Film and the Shaping of Class in America* (Princeton, NJ: Princeton University Press, 1998).

61 "Own this Oliver Typewriter," advertisement, (Oliver Typewriter, 1915), *Picture Play*, June 26, 1915, back cover.

62 "A High School Course at Home," advertisement, (American School of Correspondence, 1916), *Motion Picture Classic*, November 1916, p. 67. John K. Folger and Charles B. Nam, *Education of the American Population*, 1960 Census Monograph, (Washington DC: Government Printing Office, 1967).

63 "Men Wanted," advertisement, (Patterson Civil Service School, 1917), *Motion Picture Classic*, March 1917, p. 56.

64 "Let Us Start You in Business," advertisement, (M.P. Publishing Company, 1917), *Motion Picture Classic*, March 1917, p. 3.

65 "Be a Banker," advertisement, (American School of Banking, 1916), *Motion Picture Classic*, October 1916, p. 67. "A $250,000 Partnership if You 'Know How'," advertisement, (George H. Powell, 1917), *Motion Picture Classic*, March 1917, p. 5.

66 "Do You Need More Money," advertisement, (World's Star Knitting Company, 1919), *Photoplay*, January 1919, p. 102.

67 "Wanted: Traveling Saleswomen," advertisement, (National Salesmen's Training Association, 1919), *Photoplay*, January 1919, p. 12.

68 "We Need Women!" advertisement, (Marinello Company, 1916), *Motion Picture Classic*, October 1916, p. 2. U.S. Census Bureau, "Facts for Features."

69 "Learn Dressmaking and Millinery at Home in Spare Time," advertisement, (Woman's Institute of Domestic Arts and Sciences, Inc.), *Motion Picture Classic*, September 1916, p. 2.

70 Ross, p. 7.

71 Lebergott, p. 148. Estimates in 1987 dollars: 1910, $38; 1920, $44; 1929, $71.

72 See Joan Jacobs Brumberg, *The Body Project: An Intimate History of American Girls* (New York: Vintage Books, 1997), p. 68.

73 "It's a Well-Established Fact," advertisement, (Hinds Honey and Almond Cream, 1916), *Motion Picture Classic*, October 1916, back cover.

74 "In Winter Especially Your Skin Needs Two Creams," advertisement, (Pond's Extract Company, 1918), *Photoplay*, February 1918, p. 109.

75 "Kneel to the Prettiest," advertisement, (Frederick F. Ingraham Company, 1916), *Motion Picture Classic*, August 1916, p. 67.

76 "Wrinkles," advertisement, (Powdered Saxolite, 1916), *Motion Picture Classic*, September 1916, p. 69.

77 "Beneath the Soiled," advertisement, (Mercolized Wax, 1916), *Motion Picture Classic*, October 1916, p. 64.

78 "You Have a Beautiful Face," advertisement, (M. Trilety, Face Specialist, 1916), *Motion Picture Classic*, November 1916, p. 4.

79 Ibid.

80 "Good Taste," advertisement, (Bellin's Wonderstoen Company, 1916), *Motion Picture Classic*, October 1916, p. 68.

81 "X-Bazin," advertisement, (Hall and Ruckel, 1916), *Motion Picture Classic*, September 1916, p. 63.

3 Prosperity and Wealth Arrive

1 Gary Cross, *An All-Consuming Century: Why Commercialism Won in Modern America* (New York: Columbia University Press, 2002), p. 18.

2 U.S. Census Bureau, "Table 225: Social-Economic Group of Persons 14 Years Old and Over in the Experienced Labor Force in 1940 and Gainful Workers 14 Years Old and Over in 1930, in 1920, and in 1910, by Sex," *Statistical Abstract of the United States: 1950 (71st Edition)* (Washington, DC: Government Printing Office, 1950), p. 190, www2.census.gov/prod2/statcomp/documents/1950-01.pdf [accessed September 8, 2010].

3 Cross, p. 17.

4 U.S. Census Bureau, "Table 208: Gainful Workers 14 Years Old and Over, 1900 to 1930, and Total Labor Force, 1940, by Age and Sex," *Statistical Abstract of the United States: 1950 (71st Edition)* (Washington, DC: Government Printing Office, 1950), p. 173.

5 Economic History Association, "Hours of Work in U.S. History," EH.net, http://eh.net/encyclopedia/article/whaples.work.hours.us [accessed September 13, 2010].

6 Stockcharts.com, "Dow Jones Industrial Average (1920–1940 Daily)," http://stockcharts.com/charts/historical/djia19201940.html [accessed September 8, 2010].

7 Martha Olney, *Buy Now Pay Later: Advertising, Credit, and Consumer Durables in the 1920s* (Chapel Hill, NC: University of North Carolina Press, 1991), pp. 6, 86, 169.

8 Ibid., p. 49.

9 "Struggling Along on $50,000 a Year," *Motion Picture Classic*, February 1928, p. 55. Conversion rates are based on the Bureau of Labor Statistics Consumer Price Index calculator, http://data.bls.gov/cgi-bin/cpicalc.pl [accessed September 8, 2010]. All further conversions to 2010 dollars are based on this CPI calculator.

10 "The First Complete Account of How Your Screen Favorites Live," *Screenland*, February 1924, pp. 36–37.

11 Ibid., p. 37.

12 "Hollywood's Four Hundred Club," *Photoplay*, February 1926, pp. 38–39.

13 Ruth Waterbury, "Why Women Like Sophisticated Men," *Photoplay*, May 1926, pp. 32–33.

14 "Some Freak Insurance Policies," *Photoplay*, November 1925, pp. 40–41.

15 "The Little Ol' Pay Check, NOW!" *Photoplay*, February 1920, pp. 34–36.

16 "How Did He Ever Get the Money to Buy a Car," advertisement, (Ford Motor Company, 1925), *Photoplay*, June 1925, p. 87.

17 Olney, p. 95.

18 See, for example, Charles R. Hearn, *The American Dream in the Great Depression* (Westport, CT: Greenwood Press, 1977), p. 24.

19 "Don't Pay Me a Cent if I Can't Give You a Magnetic Personality," advertisement, (Ralston University Press, 1928), *Motion Picture Classic*, February 1928, p. 73.

20 "Afraid of My Own Voice," advertisement, (North American Institute, 1927), *Picture Play Magazine*, February 1927, p. 3.

21 See Robert Sklar, *Movie-Made America: A Cultural History of American Movies* (New York: Vintage, 1975), p. 78.

22 Frederick James Smith, "What is Immorality in Pictures?" *Photoplay*, August 1926, pp. 28–29.

23 Percy Stickney, "If Christ Went to the Movies," *Photoplay*, July 1920, p. 29. Editorial, "The Censor Bird," *Photoplay*, July 1926, p. 47. Karl Kitchen, "The Morals of the Movies," *Photoplay*, July 1920, p. 46.

24 Leonard Hall, "Exposing the Hollywood Orgy," *Photoplay*, November 1929, p. 96.

25 Kitchen, p. 46.

26 James R. Quirk, "Moral Housecleaning in Hollywood," *Photoplay*, March 1922, p. 52.

27 Kitchen, p. 46.

28 Lyn Gorman and David McLean, *Media and Society in the Twentieth Century: A Historical Introduction* (Malden, MA: Blackwell Publishing, 2003), p. 38.

29 U.S. Bureau of the Census, "Table 122: Universities, Colleges, and Professional Schools: Continental United States," *Statistical Abstract of the United States, 1930 (52nd Edition)* (Washington, DC: Government Printing Office, 1930), p. 110, www2.census.gov/prod2/statcomp/documents/1930-04.pdf [accessed September 8, 2010].

30 "Now for the Women," advertisement, (College Humor, 1928), *Motion Picture Classic*, November 1928, p. 10.

31 "The Great Romances of the World are Yours for the Asking," advertisement, (The McClure Book Company, 1916), *Motion Picture Classic*, December 1916, p. 5; "The Most Remarkable Love Story Ever Written," advertisement, (The McClure Book Company, 1916), *Motion Picture Classic*, February 1916, p. 61.

32 Ivan St. Johns, "It isn't Sex—It's Good Pictures' Says Elinor Glyn," *Photoplay*, March 1926, p. 58.

33 Carolyn Van Wyck, "Girls' Problems: Friendly Advice from Carolyn Van Wyck," *Photoplay*, March 1926, p. 96.

34 Dorothy Spensley, "Languishing Romances," *Photoplay*, September 1925, pp. 28–29.

35 U.S. Census Bureau, "Table 98: Marriages and Divorces: Number and Ratio of Divorces to Marriages, Continental United States," *Statistical Abstract of the United States, 1930 (52nd Edition)* (Washington: DC: Government Printing Office, 1930), p. 97, www2.census.gov/prod2/statcomp/documents/1930-03.pdf.

36 See Beth Bailey, *From Front Porch to Back Seat: Courtship in Twentieth-Century America* (Baltimore, MD: The Johns Hopkins University Press, 1989).

37 Stephanie Coontz, *Marriage, a History: From Obedience to Intimacy, or How Love Conquered Marriage* (New York: Viking, 2005).

38 Katherine Albert, "Excess Baggage," *Photoplay*, August 1929, pp. 40–41.

39 Ruth Waterburg, "Why Women Like Sophisticated Men," *Photoplay*, May 1926, pp. 32–33. Spensley, pp. 28–29.

40 Katherine Albert, "How Bachelors Manage their Homes," *Photoplay*, November 1929, p. 50.

41 For a discussion of anxiety as an advertising technique, see Roland Marchand, *Advertising the American Dream: Making Way for Modernity 1920–1940* (Berkeley, CA: University of California Press, 1985).

42 Rudolph Valentino, "Woman and Love," *Photoplay*, March 1922, p. 41.

43 Adela St. Johns, "Confessions of a Modern Woman," *Photoplay*, February 1922, p. 20.

44 Ralph Sutter, "Where *Men* are Men," *Motion Picture Classic*, May 1927, p. 88.

45 "The Man I Pity Most," advertisement, (Earle Liederman, 1929), *Photoplay*, October 1929, p. 14.

46 "Don't Commit a Crime Against the Woman You Love," advertisement, (Lionel Strongfort Physical and Health Specialist, 1922), *Picture Play*, June 1922, p. 109.

47 "Could She Love Him Were He Bald," advertisement, (Allied Merke Institutes, Incorporated, 1925), *Photoplay*, January 1925, p. 11.

48 "How I was Shamed into Popularity!" advertisement, (Arthur Murray, 1925), *Photoplay*, November 1925, p. 141.

49 "The Seven Ages of a Gold-Digger," *Motion Picture Classic*, December 1927, p. 54.

50 Charleston Gray, "Oh, it is, is it?" *Photoplay*, December 1929, p. 43.

51 Marquis Busby, "What Every Lover Should Know," *Motion Picture Classic*, June 1929, p. 28.

52 "Me and the Boy Friend," advertisement, (Photoplay Magazine, 1929), *Photoplay*, October 1929, p. 111.

53 "The Most Daring Book Ever Written!" advertisement, (The Authors' Press, 1925), *Motion Picture*, February 1925, p. 89. "The Naked Truth About this Passion Called Love!" advertisement, (The Authors' Press, 1925), *Motion Picture*, July 1925, p. 9.

54 "What Made Him Propose?" advertisement, (The Psychology Press, 1925), *Photoplay*, June 1925, p. 12.

55 "Often a Bridesmaid but Never a Bride," advertisement, (Lambert Pharmacal Company, 1925), *Photoplay*, July 1925, p. 91.

56 "Society Never Winks at this Weakness," advertisement, (Ruth Miller, 1925), *Motion Picture*, April 1925, p. 103.

57 "Beauty's Truthful Suitor," advertisement, (The Proctor and Gamble Company, 1926), *Photoplay*, January 1926, p. 26.

58 "Which Girl Would You Marry?" advertisement, (The Association of American Soap and Glycerine Producers, Incorporated, 1928), *Motion Picture*, February 1928, p. 83.

59 U.S. Department of Labor, "Earnings Differences Between Men and Women," *Facts on Working Women* (Washington, DC: Government Printing Office, 1993), http://permanent.access.gpo.gov/lps49666/wagegap2.htm [accessed September 8, 2010].

60 See Cross, pp. 71, 87.

61 Hillel Schwartz, *Never Satisfied: A Cultural History of Diets, Fantasies and Fat* (New York: The Free Press, 1986), p. 140.

62 Glenn Chaffin, "She Rolls her own Fat Away," *Photoplay*, June 1925, p. 78.

63 For more discussion on fasting for suffrage, see Schwartz, p. 123, and Joan Jacobs Brumberg, *Fasting Girls: The History of Anorexia Nervosa* (New York: Vintage Books, 2000). For a discussion of shifts in advertisers' perceptions of women, see Michael Schudson, *Advertising: The Uneasy Persuasion and its Dubious Impact on American Society* (New York: Basic Books, 1984), pp. 185–197.

64 "Wholesale Murder and Suicide," *Photoplay*, July 1926, pp. 30–33; "Wholesale Murder and Suicide," *Photoplay*, August 1926, p. 36.

65 See Joan Jacobs Brumberg, *The Body Project: An Intimate History of American Girls* (New York: Random House, 1997), introduction.

66 See Brumberg, *Fasting Girls*, Chapter 2.

67 Katherine Albert, "The Passing of the Extra Girl," *Photoplay*, August 1929, pp. 30–31.

68 Sklar, p. 154.

69 See data from Thomas Piketty and Emmanuel Saez, cited in David Cay Johnston, "Income Gap is Widening, Data Shows [*sic*]," *New York Times*, March 29, 2007, www.nytimes.com/2007/03/29/business/29tax.html?ex=1332820800&en=fb472e7246 6c34c8&ei=5088&partner=rssnyt&emc=rss [accessed September 8, 2010].

4 Pull Yourself up by Your Bootstraps

1 Robert VanGiezen and Albert E. Schwenk, "Compensation from before World War I through the Great Depression," *Compensation and Working Conditions*, (Washington, DC: Bureau of Labor Statistics, 2001), www.bls.gov/opub/cwc/cm20030124ar03p1. htm [accessed September 8, 2010].

2 Robert D. Plotnick et al., "The Twentieth Century Record of Poverty in the United States," (Madison, WI: Institute for Research on Poverty, 1998), pp. 10, 22, figure 4, www.irp.wisc.edu/publications/dps/pdfs/dp116698.pdf [accessed September 8, 2010].

3 See Robert Sklar, *Movie-Made America: A Cultural History of American Movies* (New York: Vintage, 1975), p. 162.

4 Michelle Pautz, "The Decline in Average Weekly Cinema Attendance: 1930–2000," *Issues in Political Economy* 11 (2002), http://org.elon.edu/ipe/pautz2.pdf [accessed September 8, 2010].

5 Charles R. Hearn, *The American Dream in the Great Depression* (Westport, CT: Greenwood Press, 1977), pp. 58, 75.

6 Ibid., p. 193.

7 "The Audience Talks Back," *Photoplay*, March 1933, p. 6.

8 Ibid.

9 Ibid.

10 "That 4 O'clock Let Down? Not for Shirley!" *Photoplay*, October 1936, p. 8.

11 Carl Vonnell, "How Movie Babies are Guarded," *Photoplay*, May 1932, pp. 28–29.

12 See Paula S. Fass, *Kidnapped: Child Abduction in America* (New York: Oxford University Press, 1997).

13 Robert VanGiezen and Albert E. Schwenk, "Compensation from before World War I through the Great Depression," (Washington, DC: U.S. Bureau of Labor Statistics, 2003), www.bls.gov/opub/cwc/cm20030124ar03p1.htm [accessed 8 September, 2010].

14 Dick Pine, "It's the Sporting Thing to do," *Motion Picture*, October 1937, pp. 56–57.

15 Kirtley Baskette, "Everybody's Stooging Now," *Photoplay*, February 1934, pp. 52–53.

16 "The Talk of Hollywood," *Motion Picture*, March 1937, p. 52.

17 "The Talk of Hollywood," p. 53.

18 Sklar, p. 233.

19 "The Talk of Hollywood," p. 54.

20 Ibid., p. 55.

21 U.S. Census Bureau, "Table 1: Family Wage or Salary Income in 1939," *Sixteenth Census of the United States—1940* (Washington, DC: Government Printing Office, 1940), p. 7, www2.census.gov/prod2/decennial/documents/41272167ch7.pdf [accessed 8 September 2010]. U.S. Census Bureau, "Table 354: Consumer Incomes—Distribution of Families and Single Individuals and of Aggregate Income Received, by Income Level: 135–1936," *Statistical Abstract of the United States 1940 (62nd Edition)* (Washington, DC: Government Printing Office, 1940), p. 316, www2.census.gov/prod2/statcomp/documents/1940-05.pdf [accessed September 8, 2010].

22 "The Crossroads of a Nation," advertisement, (Blackstone Management, 1932), *Photoplay*, September 1932, p. 121.

23 "Red Chapped Hands," advertisement, (Lehn and Fink, Incorporated, 1933), *Photoplay*, March 1933, p. 13.

24 "Ends Poor Complexion," advertisement, (The Noxema Chemical Company, 1934), *Photoplay*, February 1934, p. 113.

25 "Does the Smart Business Woman Wear Tinted Nails or Natural?" advertisement, (Northam Warren, 1932), *Photoplay*, May 1932, p. 83.

26 "'I Like the Mildness and Flavor of Camels'," advertisement, (R.J. Reynolds Tobacco Company, 1934), *Photoplay*, February 1934, p. 85.

27 "Stars Who Have Vanished," *Motion Picture*, August 1932, p. 28.

28 Hugh Walpole, "Nobody is Safe in Hollywood," *Photoplay*, June 1936, p. 58.

29 "The New Styles are a Tribute to American Beauty," advertisement, (Kellogg Company, 1931), *Photoplay*, January 1931, p. 90. "Scrap Old Ideas about Dieting," advertisement, (Life Savers, Incorporated, 1931), *Photoplay*, March 1933, p. 26. "We Stay Slim . . . or we Lose Our Contracts," advertisement, (Borden, 1933), *Photoplay*, March 1933, p. 97.

30 Tom Kent, "Ex-Millionaire," *Photoplay*, January 1931, p. 35.

31 Ibid., p. 35.

32 Mildred Mastin, "The Star-Maker Whose Dreams Turned to Dust," *Photoplay*, May 1934, p. 50.

33 Ibid., p. 51.

34 Julie Lang Hunt, "They Aren't All Actresses in Hollywood," *Photoplay*, September 1936, pp. 50–51.

35 Ibid., p. 50.

36 "All the Newest Gossip of the Hollywood Stars and Studios," *Motion Picture*, April 1930, p. 39.

37 Illustrations, *Photoplay*, September 1932, p. 41.

38 "Though it Costs Only Half as Much I Like it Twice as Well," advertisement, (Colgate, 1932), *Photoplay*, September 1932, p. 81.

39 "Have You a Boy Friend Who Needs a Job?" advertisement, (Opportunity Magazine, 1932), *Photoplay*, May 1932, p. 128.

40 "Up to $32.00 In a Week," advertisement, (Wilknit Hosiery Company, 1937), *Motion Picture*, October 1937, p. 99.

41 U.S. Census Bureau, "Table 208: Gainful Workers 14 Years and Over, 1900 to 1930, and Total Labor Force, 1940, by Age and Sex," *Statistical Abstract of the United States 1950 (69th Edition)* (Washington, DC: Government Printing Office, 1950), p. 173. By including teen girls in these figures, who were increasingly less likely to be in the paid labor force, the statistics keep these numbers artificially low.

42 U.S. Census Bureau, "Table 207: Persons Gainfully Occupied in Agricultural and Nonagricultural Pursuits; and Women in Labor Force or Gainfully Occupied: 1820 to 1940," *Statistical Abstract of the United States 1950 (69th Edition)* (Washington, DC: Government Printing Office, 1950), p. 172.

43 Helen Louise Walker, "Hollywood is a Woman's Town," *Photoplay*, September 1932, p. 32.

44 Betty Ames, "The Women who Made them Famous," *Motion Picture*, August 1932, p. 52.

45 Douglas Fairbanks, Jr., "Why I Quit Hollywood," *Photoplay*, February 1934, p. 54.

46 Adela Rogers St. John, "Pursuit of the Hollywood He-Man," *Photoplay*, June 1936, p. 14.

47 Nancy Prior, "Is the Devil a Woman?" *Motion Picture Classic*, July 1930, p. 30.

48 Gladys Hall, "Are Women the Home Wreckers of Hollywood," *Motion Picture*, August 1932, p. 44.

49 Ruth Rankin, "A Private Wife for Me," *Photoplay*, March 1933, p. 53.

50 Reginald Taviner, "I'll Take an Actress," *Photoplay*, March 1933, p. 52.

51 George Stevens, "Why Madge Evans Has Never Married," *Photoplay*, July 1936, p. 36.

52 "Cupid Strikes," *Modern Screen*, March 1940, p. 58.

53 Kirtley Baskette, "No Time for Love," *Modern Screen*, April 1940, pp. 42–43.

54 "Shopping for Mates," *Modern Screen*, February 1940, pp. 40–41.

55 James Reid, "Why Cary Grant is Hard to Get," *Modern Screen*, March 1940, pp. 36–37.

56 Hilary Lynn, "Which Movie Star Dominates You?" *Photoplay*, March 1933, p. 30.

57 For males 15-and-older, the divorce rate jumped from 0.6 percent of the population to 1.1 percent; for females 15-and-over the percentage grew from 0.8 to 1.3. U.S. Census Bureau, "Table 37: Marital Condition of Persons 15 Years of Age and Over," *Statistical Abstract of the United States 1935 (57th Edition)* (Washington, DC: Government Printing Office, 1935), p. 46, www2.census.gov/prod2/statcomp/documents/1935-02.pdf [accessed September 8, 2010].

58 U.S. Census Bureau, Vital Statistics, "Table 107: Marriages, Divorces, and Annulments: 1887–1941," *Statistical Abstract of the United States 1942 (64th Edition)* (Washington, DC: Government Printing Office, 1942–1943), p. 120, www2.census.gov/prod2/statcomp/documents/1942-03.pdf [accessed September 8, 2010].

59 Tomas Cvrcek, "When Harry Left Sally: A New Estimate of Marital Disruption in the U.S., 1860–1948," *Demographic Research* 21 (2008): 19, http://paa2009.princeton.edu/download.aspx?submissionId=90793.

60 Ruth Biery, "Folks—That's Romance!" *Photoplay*, September 1932, p. 51.

61 Raymond Hackett, "Lessons in Love," *Motion Picture Classic*, April 1930, pp. 36–37.

62 Sara Hamilton, "Is it True You are Not Getting a Divorce?" *Photoplay*, July 1933, p. 34.

63 Ruth Biery, "As Mary Faces Forty," *Photoplay*, May 1931, p. 67.

64 Sara Hamilton, "Freedom is Glorifying Ginger," *Photoplay*, September 1936, p. 22.

65 For more discussion of this tactic during the Depression, see Roland Marchand, *Advertising the American Dream: Making Way for Modernity 1920–1940* (Berkeley, CA: University of California Press, 1985).

66 "Lady in Danger," advertisement, (Cashmere Bouquet Soap, 1937), *Screenland*, October 1937, p. 67.

67 "Daintiness is IMPORTANT," advertisement, (Lux Toilet Soap, 1938), *Screenland*, February 1938, p. 99.

68 "Ends Poor Complexion," advertisement, (The Noxema Chemical Company, 1934), *Photoplay*, February 1934, p. 113.

69 "Does Your Mirror Tell You," advertisement, (Ipana, 1938), *Screenland*, April 1938, p. 3.

70 "You Never Know How Much You've Loved," advertisement, (Bristol-Myers, 1940), *Modern Screen*, April 1940, p. 3.

71 "Bad Breath Keeps Romance Away!" advertisement, (Colgate, 1940), *Modern Screen*, April 1940, p. 85; "Bad Breath Almost Broke up Our Home!" advertisement, (Colgate, 1940), *Modern Screen*, May 1940, p. 85.

72 "There's a 'Soul Mate'," advertisement, (Woodbury's Facial Soap, 1940), *Modern Screen*, March 1940, p. 77. "Do You Want to Be Somebody's Dream Girl?" advertisement, (Palmolive, 1940), *Modern Screen*, April 1940, p. 91.

73 "Putting Him in a Mood for Matrimony," advertisement, (Pond's, 1941), *Motion Picture*, May 1941, p. 51.

74 "Get Your Man," advertisement, (Wrigley, 1941), *Modern Screen*, October 1941, p. 69. "How to Keep Your Man Happy," advertisement, (Scotch, 1941), *Modern Screen*, November 1941, p. 61.

75 "Detained at the Office Again!" advertisement, (Lehn and Fink, Incorporated, 1929), *Photoplay*, December 1929, p. 119.

76 "Who is to Blame?" advertisement, (The Authors' Press, 1923), *Photoplay*, September 1923, p. 17.

77 "Molds by Flexees," advertisement, (Artistic Foundations, Incorporated, 1936), *Photoplay*, October 1936, p. 107.

78 Dorothy Calhoun, "Taking the Die out of Diet," *Motion Picture*, July 1930, pp. 28–30.

79 "Short Cuts to Curves," *Photoplay*, September 1936, p. 72.

80 "Don't Be Skinny," advertisement, (Ironized Yeast Company, 1934), *Motion Picture*, February 1934, p. 83; "The Fellows Never Looked at Her," advertisement, (Ironized Yeast Company, 1937), *Motion Picture*, March 1937, p. 85; "No Skinny Woman has an Ounce of Sex Appeal," advertisement, (Ironized Yeast Company, 1939), *Screenland*, March 1939, p. 95.

81 Although none mentioned the economic downturn, the Ironized Yeast ads occasionally featured the National Recovery Administration (NRA) logo, the federal government's promise that the product was offered at a fair price—and a tacit endorsement. Whether Ironized Yeast actually improved anyone's health is questionable. But once people began buying bread directly from grocers, a yeast surplus led manufacturers to try and improve sales any way they could. For more discussion of marketing yeast, see Roland Marchand, *Advertising the American Dream*.

82 "The New Styles," p. 90.

83 Although this quote is widely attributed to President Herbert Hoover, it was instead part of a Republican Party campaign ad in the October 30, 1928, edition of the *New York World*.

84 *Gone with the Wind*, 1939, Metro Goldwyn Mayer.

85 See Sklar, Chapter 10.

5 We're all in this Together

1 Frank Newport, David W. Moore, and Lydia Saad, "The Most Important Events of the Century from the Viewpoint of the People," Gallup Incorporated, December 6, 1999, www.gallup.com/poll/3427/Most-Important-Events-Century-From-Viewpoint-People.aspx [accessed September 8, 2010]. See also Gordon Lightbody, *The Second World War* (New York: Routledge, 2004), p. 34.

2 Robert VanGiezen and Albert E. Schwenk, "Compensation from before World War I through the Great Depression," *Compensation and Working Conditions*, (Washington, DC: Bureau of Labor Statistics), 2001, www.bls.gov/opub/cwc/cm20030124ar03p1. htm [accessed September 8, 2010].

3 "He-Men on Horseback," *Modern Screen*, July 1940, pp. 38–39. "Off to the Races," *Modern Screen*, September 1940, pp. 30–31.

4 "Off to the Races," p. 30.

5 Hedda Hopper, "Who'$ Who in Hollywood $ociety," *Photoplay*, February 1941, p. 57. U.S. Census Bureau, Housing Census, "Historical Census of Housing Tables Home Values," (Washington, DC: Housing and Household Economic Statistics Division, 2004), www.census.gov/hhes/www/housing/census/historic/values.html [accessed September 8, 2010].

6 Hedda Hopper, "Who'$ Who in Hollywood $ociety," *Photoplay*, February 1941, p. 57.

7 Elsa Maxwell, "Hollywood's Most Successful Human Beings," *Photoplay*, February 1944, p. 28.

8 Kay Bryan, "If You Want to Get There," *Photoplay*, November 1940, pp. 16–17.

9 Helen Hoover, "You Could do it Too!" *Photoplay*, February 1941, p. 22.

10 Helen Louise Walker, "Act of Providence," *Photoplay*, February 1941, p. 29.

11 John R. Franchey, "Life of Lynn," *Photoplay*, February 1941, pp. 32–33.

12 Ernest V. Heyn, "To the Navy!" *Photoplay*, November 1941, p. 25.

13 Ruth Waterbury, "Close ups and Long Shots," *Photoplay*, September 1940, p. 13.

14 Irving Wallace, "Conscription Hits Hollywood," *Modern Screen*, April 1941, p. 24.

15 Ben Maddox, "Is Hollywood Getting Sensible?" *Modern Screen*, September 1940, p. 36.

16 Ruth Waterbury, "Close ups and Long Shots," *Photoplay*, September 1940, p. 13.

17 Walter Winchell, "Hollywood Joins the Navy," *Photoplay*, November 1941, pp. 26–27.

18 David W. Moore, "Support for War on Terrorism Rivals Support for WWII," *Gallup News Service*, October 3, 2001, www.gallup.com/poll/4954/Support-War-Terrorism-Rivals-Support-WWII.aspx [accessed September 8, 2010].

19 "Keep 'Em Flying," advertisement, (The American Motion Picture Industry, 1942), *Modern Screen*, June 1942, p. 17.

20 "What the American Way Means to Me," *Motion Picture*, May 1942, p. 34.

21 Adam John Yacenda, "Hollywood on the March," *Motion Picture*, March 1941, p. 30.

22 Mrs. Ray Milland, "A Pint for Life," *Photoplay*, January 1944, p. 57.

23 "We Salute Hollywood at War," *Modern Screen*, February 1943, p. 48.

24 Hedda Hopper, "Hedda Hopper's Hollywood," *Motion Picture*, June 1943, p. 25.

25 Farley Earle Granger, "I Go to War," *Photoplay*, July 1944, p. 30.

26 "Photoplay's Command Performance!" *Photoplay*, May 1944, pp. 52–53.

27 "Greyhound Does Double Duty," advertisement, (Greyhound, 1942), *Modern Screen*, April 1942, p. 85.

28 "Young America Loves Lollipop and Butterscotch," advertisement, (Northam Warren, 1941), *Modern Screen*, September 1941, p. 77

29 "We Didn't Tell it to the Marines," advertisement, (Beech-Nut Gum, 1941), *Motion Picture*, March 1941, p. 67.

30 Franklin D. Roosevelt, "An Act to Amend the Emergency Price Control Act of 1942, to Aid in Preventing Inflation, and for Other Purposes," Executive Order 9250, October 3, 1942, www.ibiblio.org/pha/policy/1942/421003a.html [accessed September 8, 2010]. "Inflation: New Deal Paradox,' *Time*, November 9, 1942, www.time.com/time/magazine/article/0,9171,884600,00.html [accessed September 8, 2010]. U.S. Census Bureau, "Table 301: Income Payments to Individuals, by States: 1929–1944," *Statistical Abstracts of the United States 1946 (67th Edition)* (Washington, DC: Government Printing Office, 1946), p. 272, www2.census.gov/prod2/statcomp/documents/1946-04.pdf [accessed September 8, 2010].

31 Paul Studenski and Herman Edward Krooss, *Financial History of the United States* (Frederick, MD: Beard Books, 1952), p. 446.

32 Jack O'Donnell, "That Ceiling Situation," *Motion Picture*, March 1943, pp. 32–33.

33 U.S. Census Bureau, "Table 301: Income Payments to Individuals, by States: 1929–1944," p. 272. Bureau of Labor Statistics, Household Data Annual Averages, "Employment Status of the Civilian Noninstitutional Population, 1940 to Date," (Washington, DC: Bureau of Labor Statistics), 2010, p. 190, www.bls.gov/cps/cpsaat1.pdf [accessed September 8, 2010].

34 Employee Benefit Research Institute, "EBRI Databook on Employee Benefits," Washington, DC: EBRI.org, 2010, ch. 9, p. 4, www.ebri.org/pdf/publications/books/databook/DB.Chapter%2009.pdf [accessed September 8, 2010].

35 "Seven Things You Should Do," advertisement, (War Advertising Council, 1943), *Motion Picture*, December 1943, p. 94.

36 "Make Your Dollars Fighting Dollars," advertisement, (U.S. Defense Bonds, 1942), *Motion Picture*, June 1942, p. 2.

37 "How to Prevent Inflation in One Easy Lesson," advertisement, (War Advertising Council, 1944), *Motion Picture*, October 1944, p. 142.

38 "Perhaps I'm One War Older than You Are!" advertisement, (War Advertising Council, 1944), *Motion Picture*, December 1944, p. 138.

39 "Don't Waste Pepsodent," advertisement, (Pepsodent, 1943), *Motion Picture*, January 1943, p. 18.

40 "Bulletin from Washington," *Motion Picture*, July 1943, pp. 17–18.

41 "Bulletin from Washington," *Motion Picture*, October 1943, pp. 23–24.

42 Catherine Roberts, "Fashion Multiplication 2+2=6," *Motion Picture*, November 1944, p. 53.

43 "Bulletin from Washington," *Motion Picture*, November 1943, pp. 21–22.

44 "Fabrics are Getting Scarce!" advertisement, (Nonspi, 1942), *Modern Screen*, July 1942, p. 97.

45 "Gotta Watch the Figure!" advertisement, (Kleenex, 1942), *Modern Screen*, November 1942, p. 76.

46 "Fighting Food Waste," *Motion Picture*, October 1943, p. 59. Also see Joan Jacobs Brumberg, *Fasting Girls: The History of Anorexia Nervosa* (New York: Vintage Books, 2000), p. 246.

47 "Bulletin from Washington," *Motion Picture*, November 1943, pp. 21–22.

48 "Straw Men," advertisement, (National Nutritional Defense, 1941), *Photoplay*, November 1941, p. 13.

49 "Your Government Says U.S. Needs Us Strong," advertisement, (Office of Defense and Welfare Services, 1942), *Modern Screen*, September 1942, p. 62.

50 "Rich in Dextrose," advertisement, (Baby Ruth, 1942), *Modern Screen*, April 1942, p. 71.

51 "The Doctor Oughta Know about This," advertisement, (Corn Products Refining Company, 1943), *Modern Screen*, April 1943, p. 44.

52 Marjorie Deen, ". . . On the Homefront," *Modern Screen*, October 1942, p. 64.

53 Robert VanGiezen and Albert E. Schwenk, "Compensation from before World War I through the Great Depression," *Compensation and Working Conditions*, (Washington, DC: Bureau of Labor Statistics, 2001), www.bls.gov/opub/cwc/cm20030124ar03p1.htm [accessed September 8, 2010].

54 "The Free Education and the Monthly Allowance are Wonderful . . .," advertisement, (U.S. Cadet Nurse Corps, 1944), *Photoplay*, April 1944, p. 63.

55 "Of Course . . . You May Marry!" advertisement, (Beech-Nut Gum, 1944), *Motion Picture*, August 1944, p. 25.

56 "After Hours," advertisement, (Bristol-Myers, 1944), *Motion Picture*, October 1944, p. 3.

57 "She'll Do a Man-Sized Job Tomorrow!" advertisement, (Beautyrest, 1944), *Motion Picture*, December 1944, p. 65.

58 "Who's a War Worker?" advertisement, (Modess Sanitary Napkins, 1942), *Motion Picture*, December 1942, p. 3.

59 "All Clear," advertisement, (Ligget and Myers Tobacco Company, 1942), *Motion Picture*, December 1942, back cover.

60 "Women in the War," advertisement, (R.J. Reynolds Tobacco Company, 1943), *Motion Picture*, January 1943, back cover.

61 Ibid.

62 "America's Smart Flying Women," advertisement, (Northam Warren, 1943), *Motion Picture*, September 1943, p. 63.

63 "We are Still the Weaker Sex," advertisement, (Tangee, 1944), *Photoplay*, October 1944, inside cover.

64 "When is a Tampon Right for You?" advertisement, (Modess Tampon, 1942), *Modern Screen*, July 1942, p. 74.

65 "Get Young Ideas," advertisement, (Tampax Incorporated, 1942), *Motion Picture*, June 1942, p. 12.

66 Catherine Roberts, "Entirely Suitable," *Motion Picture*, October 1942, pp. 42–43.

67 Catherine Roberts, "Calling All Girls," *Motion Picture*, March 1944, p. 56.

68 Dora Albert, "Who Said Women Aren't Men's Equals?" *Photoplay*, October 1942, p. 38.

69 Helen Louise Walker, "Don't Be a Doormat!" *Photoplay*, November 1942, p. 42.

70 "Pick Your Movie Job," *Motion Picture*, June 1942, pp. 26–27.

71 Ibid.

72 James Richardson, "Matrimony in Movieland," *Modern Screen*, February 1941, pp. 46–47.

73 James Carson, "Annie Meets the Boys," *Modern Screen*, July 1940, pp. 30–31.

74 Margaret Lindsay, "Doing Anything Tonight?" *Photoplay*, January 1941, pp. 30–31.

75 U.S. Census Bureau, Vital Statistics, "Table 99: Marriages, Divorces, and Annulments: 1887–1944," *Statistical Abstracts of the United States 1944–1945 (66th Edition)* (Washington, DC: Government Printing Office), p. 95, www2.census.gov/prod2/stat comp/documents/1944-02.pdf [accessed September 8, 2010].

76 U.S. Census Bureau, "Table 99: Marriages and Divorce Estimates: 1867–1946," *Statistical Abstract of the United States 1948 (69th Edition)* (Washington, DC: Government Printing Office, 1946), p. 89, www2.census.gov/prod2/statcomp/documents/ 1948-02.pdf [accessed September 8, 2010].

77 U.S. Census Bureau, Vital Statistics, "Table 101: Marriages, Divorces, and Annulments: 1887–1945," *Statistical Abstract of the United States 1947 (68th Edition)* (Washington, DC: Government Printing Office, 1947), p. 90, www2.census.gov/ prod2/statcomp/documents/1947-02.pdf [accessed September 8, 2010].

78 Kathryn Grayson, "Are American Women Good Wartime Wives?" *Photoplay*, March 1944, p. 29.

79 Bette Davis, "Code for American Girls," *Photoplay*, September 1940, pp. 17, 82.

80 Bette Davis, "Draft Bride," *Photoplay*, January 1941, p. 27.

81 Ann Sothern, "What Kind of Woman Will Your Man Come Home to?" *Photoplay*, November 1944, p. 44. Mary Astor, "Will He Want to Come Home?" *Photoplay*, May 1945, p. 59.

82 Denise Caine, "Figure-Atively Speaking," *Motion Picture*, March 1941, p. 16.

83 "'Wives Should Never—' 'Husbands Should Never—'," *Photoplay*, August 1944, pp. 58–59.

84 See data from Thomas Piketty and Emmanuel Saez, cited in David Cay Johnston, "Income Gap is Widening, Data Shows [*sic*]," *New York Times*, March 29, 2007, www.nytimes.com/2007/03/29/business/29tax.html?ex=1332820800&en=fb472e7246 6c34c8&ei=5088&partner=rssnyt&emc=rss [accessed September 8, 2010].

6 Suburban Utopia

1 See, for example, Ira Katznelson, *When Affirmative Action was White: An Untold History of Racial Inequality in Twentieth Century America* (New York: W.W. Norton and Company), 2005.

2 Bureau of Labor Statistics, "Labor Force Statistics from the Current Population Survey," (Washington, DC: U.S. Department of Labor, 1948–1975), http://data. bls.gov/PDQ/servlet/SurveyOutputServlet?data_tool=latest_numbers&series_id=LNS 14000000 [accessed September 8, 2010]. User-generated data.

3 See data from Thomas Piketty and Emmanuel Saez, cited in David Cay Johnston, "Income Gap is Widening, Data Shows [*sic*]," *New York Times*, March 29, 2007, www.nytimes.com/2007/03/29/business/29tax.html?ex=1332820800&en=fb472e7246 6c34c8&ei=5088&partner=rssnyt&emc=rss [accessed September 8, 2010].

4 Marshall B. Reinsdorf, "Alternative Measures of Personal Saving," *Survey of Current Business* 87 (Washington, DC: Bureau of Economic Analysis, 2007), p. 7, www.bea. gov/scb/pdf/2007/02%20February/0207_saving.pdf [accessed September 8, 2010]. See chart 1.

5 "Hollywood Tour," *Photoplay*, July 1947, pp. 44–45.

6 Fredda Dudley, "So You're Going to Hollywood," *Photoplay*, July 1948, pp. 40–45.

7 Elsa Maxwell, "Palm Springs Spree," *Photoplay*, June 1947, pp. 44–45.

8 Jerry Asher, "Dangerous Dan," *Photoplay*, January 1948, pp. 64–65.

9 "Hollywood's New Rendezvous," *Photoplay*, October 1948, pp. 40–41.

10 Sara Hamilton, "Home is the Sailor," *Photoplay*, December 1948, pp. 59–60.

11 "Sand Spree," *Photoplay*, June 1947, pp. 50–53.

12 Bob Wagner, "Today—I'm Living it Up," *Photoplay*, November 1954, p. 44.

13 Marie McDonald, "I Learned About Men," *Photoplay*, January 1946, p. 40.

14 Kenneth Tobey, "My Pal Peck," *Photoplay*, April 1947, p. 38.

15 Eve Arden and Kirk Douglas, "You Don't Have to be Beautiful," *Motion Picture*, May 1948, p. 48.

16 "Caught!" *Photoplay*, November 1957, pp. 58–59.

17 Hedda Hopper, "The Ten Great Myths of Hollywood," *Modern Screen*, January 1949, pp. 28–29.

18 Internal Revenue Service, "Table A, U.S. Individual Income Tax: Personal Exemptions and Lowest and Highest Bracket Tax Rates, and Tax Base for Regular Tax, Tax Years 1913–2003," *Statistics of Income Bulletin*, 2004, http://findarticles.com/p/articles/mi_m2893/is_2_24/ai_n9508935/ [accessed September 8, 2010]. See also "Top U.S. Marginal Income Tax Rates," Truthandpolitics.org, www.truthandpolitics.org/top-rates.php [accessed September 8, 2010].

19 Sheilah Graham, "Flat on their Bank Accounts," *Photoplay*, April 1952, pp. 60–61.

20 Sheilah Graham, "Where Does the Money Go?" *Photoplay*, February 1950, p. 38.

21 Alan MacDonald, "Tony's Wife," *Motion Picture*, March 1953, p. 36.

22 Fred D. Brown, "Women are a Nuisance," *Motion Picture*, September 1953, p. 48.

23 Helen Hover, "Glamour on a Shoestring," *Motion Picture*, April 1953, pp. 34–35.

24 Peer Oppenheimer, "That Cracker-Jack-of-All-Trades, Calhoun," *Photoplay*, February 1955, pp. 42–43.

25 Reba and Bonnie Churchill, "Murph and His Money," *Motion Picture*, September 1953, p. 36.

26 Katherine Albert, "Hollywood's Young Unmarrieds," *Photoplay*, June 1951, p. 44.

27 "Hollywood's Young Bachelors," *Modern Screen*, December 1955, pp. 40–43.

28 George S. Masnick, "Home Ownership Trends and Racial Inequality in the United States in the Twentieth Century," (Cambridge, MA: Joint Center for Housing Studies, Harvard University), 2001, www.jchs.harvard.edu/publications/homeownership/masnick_w01-4.pdf [accessed September 8, 2010].

29 Guy Madison, "Bachelors, Ltd.," *Photoplay*, March 1947, p. 38.

30 "Let's Visit with Vera Ralston," *Motion Picture*, January 1948, pp. 25–30.

31 Marva Peterson, "Abra-ca-Debra," *Modern Screen*, October 1954, pp. 50–51.

32 "How Can I Have a Hollywood Dream House," *Photoplay*, September 1958, pp. 62–73.

33 For more discussion, see Lizbeth Cohen, *A Consumer's Republic: The Politics of Mass Consumption in Postwar America* (New York: Vintage, 2003).

34 "Jack Lemmon: He Doesn't Look Like a Comic or Live Like a Star," *Photoplay*, January 1955, p. 56.

35 Maxine Block, "A Girl on the Go Go Go," *Motion Picture*, December 1953, p. 35.

36 Don Allen, "Country Gal," *Motion Picture*, June 1953, p. 36.

37 "Photoplay Photo Day," *Photoplay*, January 1948, p. 49.

38 Marva Peterson, "Lanza Lives Big," *Modern Screen*, November 1953, pp. 46–48.

39 Martha Wolfenstein, "The Emergence of Fun Morality," *Journal of Social Issues* 7 (1951): 15–25.

40 Andre de Toth, "Marriage is Such Fun," *Photoplay*, August 1948, p. 58.

41 "Hands that Work Look Lovelier in 24 Hours," advertisement, (Noxzema, 1952), *Motion Picture*, March 1952, p. 65.

42 U.S. Census Bureau, Current Population Survey, Table MS-2, *Estimated Median Age at First Marriage, by Sex, 1890 to the Present* (Washington, DC: Government Printing Office, 2009), www.census.gov/population/socdemo/hh-fam/ms2.xls [accessed September 8, 2010].

43 Kay Proctor, "Love is Young," *Photoplay*, April 1948, p. 52.

44 Shirley Temple Agar, "Ten Rules for a Happy Honeymoon," *Photoplay*, June 1947, p. 34.

45 Shirley Temple, "Shirley Temple's Ten Commandments for Teen-Age Marriages," *Motion Picture*, August 1946, pp. 26–27.

46 "Should You Go to College?" *Motion Picture*, December 1946, pp. 44–45.

47 Claudette Colbert, "What Should I Do?" *Photoplay*, May 1947, p. 70.

48 Claudette Colbert, "What Should I Do?" *Photoplay*, October 1947, p. 66.

49 M. D. Bramlett and W. D. Mosher, "Cohabitation, Marriage, Divorce, and Remarriage in the United States," National Center for Health Statistics, *Vital Health Statistics* 23, no. 22 (2002), www.cdc.gov/nchs/data/series/sr_23/sr23_022.pdf [accessed September 8, 2010].

50 Ted Wilson, "Are Odds Against Teen-Age Brides?" *Modern Screen*, September 1949, pp. 56–57.

51 Shirley Emerson, "Teen-age Tragedy," *Motion Picture*, August 1953, p. 26.

52 Elsa Maxwell, "This You Must Understand," *Photoplay*, February 1950, pp. 34–35.

53 Ida Zeitlin, "Liz: Spoiled Brat or Mixed-Up Teenager," *Photoplay*, May 1951, pp. 40–41.

54 "We Applaud Mrs. Robert Taylor," *Photoplay*, November 1957, p. 60.

55 Hedda Hopper, "Hollywood's Forgotten Wives," *Modern Screen*, November 1949, pp. 40–41.

56 Viola Moore, "They Mind Their Husbands' Business," *Movieland*, June 1951, pp. 60–61.

57 Sheilah Graham, "Wives Make the Best Husbands!" *Photoplay*, November 1952, pp. 56–57.

58 Barbara Berch Jamison, "Hollywood's Biggest Headaches," *Motion Picture*, September 1953, pp. 30–31.

59 Betty Grable, "Rules for Wives," *Photoplay*, April 1948, p. 51.

60 Luella O. Parsons, "The Strange Case of Hedy Lamarr," *Photoplay*, September 1947, p. 37.

61 Sheilah Graham, "Till Work Do Us Part," *Photoplay*, September 1947, pp. 38–39.

62 Elsa Maxwell, "Hollywood's Marriage Morals," *Photoplay*, September 1948, pp. 42–43.

63 "Verdict on Jane," *Photoplay*, November 1953, p. 47.

64 Sheilah Graham, "Trouble on Cloud 9," *Photoplay*, August 1954, p. 43.

65 Shirley Emerson, "Ann Blyth's Wedding," *Motion Picture*, July 1953, pp. 50–51.

66 Ruth Waterbury, "The Family Ann Married," *Photoplay*, November 1953, pp. 48–49.

67 Luella Parsons, "Luella Parsons' Good News," *Modern Screen*, January 1955, pp. 10–13.

68 Ida Zeitlin, "Three Loves has Susan," *Photoplay*, November 1952, pp. 42–43.

69 Brady E. Hamilton, Joyce A. Martin, and Stephanie J. Ventura, "Births: Preliminary Data for 2006," *National Vital Statistics Reports* 56, no. 7 (Hyattsville, MD: National Center for Health Statistics, 2007), p. 8, www.cdc.gov/nchs/data/nvsr/nvsr57/nvsr57_12.pdf [accessed September 8, 2010].

70 Mary Bailey, "Bring Back Your Beauty after Baby's Born," *Motion Picture*, March 1946, p. 56.

71 Sheilah Graham, "Babies, Babies, Babies," *Photoplay*, July 1946, pp. 62–63.

72 See, for example, Susan Peters, "My Hollywood Friends Give a Baby Shower," *Photoplay*, August 1946, pp. 30–31.

73 Diane Scott, "Betty and Buttercup," *Photoplay*, March 1947, p. 61.

74 Faith Baldwin, "A Christmas Prayer," *Photoplay*, December 1947, p. 44.

75 Ruth Waterbury, "How They'll Spend Christmas Morning," *Photoplay*, December 1952, pp. 46–47.

76 Luella O. Parsons, "Temple Lullaby," *Photoplay*, August 1948, pp. 34–35.

77 Fredda Dudley, ". . . Room for One More," *Photoplay*, November 1952, p. 39.

78 Caryl Posner, "Why Bing and Kathy *Need* this Baby So Much," *Photoplay*, September 1958, p. 51.

79 Elsa Maxwell, "Liza, Liza Smile at Me," *Photoplay*, May 1947, pp. 40–43.

80 Ruth Rowland, "I Wish Elizabeth and Eddie all the Happiness . . .," *Photoplay*, August 1959, pp. 27–29.

81 Joan Crawford, "I'm an Adopted Mother," *Photoplay*, February 1948, p. 40.

82 Hymie Fink, "I Was There," *Photoplay*, July 1948, pp. 6–7.

83 Wynn Roberts, "The Littlest Ladd," *Photoplay*, August 1947, pp. 50–53.

84 Helen Gould, "Deep in the Heart of Hollywood," *Photoplay*, August 1953, pp. 64–65.

85 "Photoplay's Photolife of Glenn Ford," *Photoplay*, October 1946, pp. 52–53.

86 Diane Scott, "The Man from Rising Sun," *Photoplay*, November 1946, pp. 68–69.

87 Cameron Shipp, "Even Stevens," *Photoplay*, April 1947, pp. 66–67.

88 Jerry Asher, "Beachcomber De Luxe," *Photoplay*, October 1946, pp. 64–65.

89 Dick Haymes, "Us," *Photoplay*, June 1947, pp. 54–57.

90 Daniel Stern, "Just Where Do I Belong?" *Modern Screen*, November 1957, pp. 38–40.

91 Shirley Temple, "For My Baby," *Photoplay*, March 1948, pp. 44–45.

92 Marc Norman, *What Happens Next: A History of American Screenwriting* (New York: Harmony Books, 2007), p. 236.

93 Morton Thompson, "Exposing Hollywood's Red Menace," *Photoplay*, March 1940, pp. 19, 78.

94 Sylvia Kahn, "Good News," *Modern Screen*, November 1940, p. 48.

95 Sally Reid, "Is Melvin Douglas a Communist?" *Photoplay*, September 1940, pp. 23, 88.

96 Larry Ceplar and Steven Englund, *The Inquisition in Hollywood: Politics in the Film Community, 1930–1960* (Urbana and Chicago, IL: University of Illinois Press, 2003), pp. 137, 139.

97 Adele Whitley Fletcher, "Proceed at Your Own Risk," *Photoplay*, November 1940, p. 20.

98 Lyn Gorman and David McLean, *Media and Society in the Twentieth Century: A Historical Introduction* (Malden, MA: Blackwell Publishing, 2003), p. 113.

99 James M. Cain, "Is Hollywood Red?" *Photoplay*, August 1947, p. 31.

100 Larry Parks, "I Believe," *Photoplay*, February 1948, pp. 45, 99.

101 For more discussion, see Neal Gabler, *An Empire of Their Own: How the Jews Invented Hollywood* (New York: Crown Publishers, 1988).

102 Ceplar and Englund, p. 373.

103 Humphrey Bogart, "I'm No Communist," *Photoplay*, March 1948, pp. 52–53, 86.

104 Ceplar and Englund, p. 289.

105 Ray Manning, "Rock Hudson's Love Affair with the USA," *Photoplay*, January 1955, p. 41.

106 Norman, p. 326.

107 Gorman and McLean, pp. 151–153.

108 See Joshua Gamson, *Claims to Fame: Celebrity in Contemporary America* (Berkeley, CA: University of California Press, 1994).

7 Is That All There Is?

1 Micki McGee, *Self-Help, Inc.: Makeover Culture in American Life* (New York: Oxford University Press, 2005), p. 52.

2 See Henry E. Scott, *Shocking True Story: The Rise and Fall of* Confidential, *America's Most Scandalous Scandal Magazine* (New York: Pantheon, 2010).

3 Michelle Pautz, "The Decline in Average Weekly Cinema Attendance: 1930–2000," *Issues in Political Economy* 11 (2000): http://org.elon.edu/ipe/pautz2.pdf [accessed September 8, 2010].

4 Robert Sklar, *Movie-Made America: A Cultural History of American Movies* (New York: Vintage, 1975).

5 Ellis Cashmore, *Celebrity/Culture* (London: Routledge, 2006), pp. 19–20.

6 "David Cassidy Needs Lots of Love!" *Movieland and TV Time*, August 1972, pp. 20–21.

7 "Why Daddy is His Biggest Problem!" *Photoplay*, October 1963, pp. 29–31.

8 Bethel Every, "The Hidden Life of Jackie Kennedy," *Modern Screen*, January 1963, pp. 36–37.

9 "In the News," *Movieland and TV Time*, October 1972, p. 31.

10 "The Saddest Day in the World for Ari," *Movieland and TV Time*, May 1973, pp. 6–7.

11 Luella Parsons, "Sad News," *Modern Screen*, January 1963, p. 16.

12 "Mrs. Peter Sellers' Death Watch," *Photoplay*, July 1964, p. 46.

13 "Connie Stevens: What Gives?" *Photoplay*, January 1961, p. 45.

14 "Suicide," *Photoplay*, December 1960, p. 71.

15 Richard Aimes, "Why Liz Can't Help Cure Burton of his Thanatophobia," *Movieland and TV Time*, September 1972, pp. 23–24.

16 "Liz in Physical Agony," *Photoplay*, May 1964, p. 41.

17 "The Stories Behind the Year's Hottest Headlines," *Modern Screen*, January 1963, p. 46.

18 "Scoop: Marilyn Monroe's Mother Escapes Mental Hospital," *Photoplay*, October 1963, pp. 42–43.

19 John Howard, "He Died Alone!" *Movieland and TV Time*, August 1972, pp. 37–38.

20 "What's Up Lately?" *Movieland and TV Time*, September 1972, p. 38.

21 U.S. Census Bureau, "Table 4: Poverty Status of Families, by Type of Family, Presence of Related Children, Race, and Hispanic Origin: 1959 to 2008," (Washington, DC: Government Printing Office, 2009), www.census.gov/hhes/www/poverty/data/historical/hstpov4.xls [accessed September 8, 2010].

22 For more discussion of black Hollywood during the twentieth century, see Donald Bogle, *Bright Boulevards, Bold Dreams: The Story of Black Hollywood* (New York: Ballantine Books, 2005).

23 Herbert Howe, "A Jungle Lorelei," *Photoplay*, July 1929, pp. 36–37.

24 Henry A. Phillips, "Drums in the Jungle," *Photoplay*, February 1934, pp. 78–80.

25 "Yeah Man Friday," *Modern Screen*, November 1941, p. 39.

26 Henry A. Phillips, "Drums in the Jungle," *Photoplay*, February 1934, pp. 78–80.

27 "Debbie Talks Sense about the Racial Crisis," *Photoplay*, May 1964, pp. 58–59.

28 "How Two Negro Showmen Fight for Integration," *Photoplay*, October 1963, pp. 58–59, 99.

29 "Chubby's Mother Tells," *Photoplay*, July 1964, p. 68.

30 "'Why is Mommy White?'" *Photoplay*, April 1964, p. 33.

31 "What's Up Lately!" *Movieland and TV Time*, February 1970, p. 36.

32 Patricia Johnson, "Raquel Welch," *Movieland and TV Time*, December 1968, pp. 34–35.

33 Robert St. Cloud, "Poitier's European Tour with his Five Girls!" *Movieland and TV Time*, December 1968, pp. 9–10, 76.

34 Fredda Dudley Balling, "All about Baby," *Photoplay*, July 1971, pp. 54–55.

35 May Mann, "May Mann's Hollywood," *Movieland and TV Time*, August 1972, p. 9. May Mann, "May Mann's Hollywood," *Movieland and TV Time*, September 1972, p. 9

36 "Peggy Lipton Tells About the Joy and Pain of Having a Black Baby," *Modern Screen*, February 1974, pp. 48–49, 82.

37 "Peggy Lipton Marries," *Movieland and TV Time*, January 1975, pp. 19, 70. Emphasis in original.

38 Census data from Roland G. Freyer, Jr., "Guess Who's Been Coming to Dinner? Trends in Interracial Marriage over the Twentieth Century," *Journal of Economic Perspectives* 21 (2) (2007): 71–90.

39 Joseph Carroll, "Most American Approve of Interracial Marriages," *Gallup News Service*, August 16, 2007, www.gallup.com/poll/28417/most-americans-approve-interracial-marriages.aspx [accessed September 8, 2010].

40 "Important 'Secrets' Revealed," advertisement, (Allied Publications Incorporated, 1963), *Modern Screen*, January 1963, p. 2.

41 Matt Fessier, "Teen Marriages are Ridiculous," *Photoplay*, May 1964, p. 57.

42 Helen Weller, "How to Be Married," *Modern Screen*, January 1963, pp. 44–45.

43 U.S. Census Bureau, "Table HS-11, Marital Status of the Population by Sex: 1900 to 2002," (Washington, DC: Government Printing Office, 2003), www.census.gov/population/www/socdemo/hh-fam.html [accessed September 8, 2010].

44 U.S. Department of Health and Human Services, Underlying Population Trends, "Divorces and Divorce Rates, 1940–1997," (Washington, DC: Government Printing Office, 2000), www.acf.hhs.gov/programs/cse/pubs/reports/projections/ch04.html [accessed September 8, 2010].

45 "As Queen, Soraya Must Produce a Male Heir to the Throne," *Modern Screen*, April 1961, p. 44.

46 Hy Gardner, "Extra: An Exclusive Interview with Eddie Fisher," *Modern Screen*, August 1962, pp. 34–35.

47 Rod Taylor, "Our Marriage Wasn't Made in Heaven—But It's Getting There," *Photoplay*, June 1964, pp. 42–43.

48 Burton Allen, "Shirley and Jack Together Again!" *Movieland and TV Time*, October 1972, pp. 19, 52, 54.

49 "Cher Hospitalized After Furious Fight with Sonny!" *Modern Screen*, February 1974, pp. 40–41.

50 K.V. Burroughs, "Elizabeth Montgomery Divorcing?" *Movieland and TV Time*, September 1972, p. 19.

51 "Fifth on the Rocks," *Modern Screen*, January 1963, p. 47.

52 Arthur Gregory, "Why Elvis and Priscilla Live in Separate Houses!" *Movieland and TV Time*, October 1972, pp. 20–21.

53 "How I Loved and Lost Elvis," *Modern Screen*, October 1973, pp. 48–49, 65.

54 Bureau of Labor Statistics, "Labor Force Statistics from the Current Population Survey," (Washington, DC: U.S. Department of Labor, 1948–1975), http://data.bls.gov/PDQ/servlet/SurveyOutputServlet?data_tool=latest_numbers&series_id=LNS14000000 [accessed September 8, 2010]. User-generated data.

55 U.S. Census Bureau, "Table HS—25: Money Income of Families—Median Income in Current and Constant (2001) Dollars," (Washington, DC: Government Printing Office, 2002), www.census.gov/prod/2002pubs/tp63rv.pdf [accessed September 8, 2010]. U.S. National Center for Education Statistics, "Table HS-21, Education Summary—High School Graduates, and College Enrollment and Degrees: 1900 to 2001," *120 Years of Education, A Statistical Portrait* (Washington, DC: Digest of Education Statistics, annual), http://nces.ed.gov/programs/digest/ [accessed September 8, 2010].

56 "Wedding Bells for Debbie!" *Movieland and TV Time*, December 1968, pp. 42–43.

57 Victoria Cole, "Victoria Cole's Hollywood Go-Round," *Movieland and TV Time*, December 1968, p. 44.

58 "What's Up Lately!" *Movieland and TV Time*, February 1970, p. 32.

59 Tony Bowen, "Denise Nicholas Talks about her Surprise Wedding!" *Movieland and TV Time*, May 1973, pp. 42–43, 76.

60 Dorothy Manners, "Two Royal Weddings," *Modern Screen*, February 1974, p. 10.

61 "Married Love is Better than Ever!" *Modern Screen*, October 1973, p. 22.

62 Howard N. Fullerton, Jr., "Labor Force Participation: 75 Years of Change, 1950–98 and 1998–2025," *Monthly Labor Review*, December 1999, pp. 3–12, www.bls.gov/opub/mlr/1999/12/art1full.pdf [accessed September 8, 2010].

63 Richard Frey and D'Vera Cohn, "New Economics of Marriage: The Rise of Wives," (Washington, DC: Pew Research Center, 2010), http://pewresearch.org/pubs/1466/economics-marriage-rise-of-wives [accessed September 8, 2010].

64 Public Broadcasting Service, "Timeline: The Pill," (Washington, DC: PBS Online, 2002), www.pbs.org/wgbh/amex/pill/timeline/timeline2.html [accessed September 8, 2010].

65 Brady E. Hamilton, Joyce A. Martin, and Stephanie J. Ventura, "Births: Preliminary Data for 2007," *National Vital Statistics Reports* 57, no. 12 (March 18, 2009), p. 1, www.cdc.gov/nchs/data/nvsr/nvsr57/nvsr57_12.pdf [accessed September 8, 2010].

66 "Why Connie is Praying for Liz!" *Movieland and TV Time*, December 1968, pp. 22–23.

67 "The Whispers about Princess Grace and Her Husband," *Photoplay*, December 1960, p. 21.

68 "Divorce," *Photoplay*, December 1960, p. 70.

69 "What's Up Lately!" *Movieland and TV Time*, September 1972, p. 31.

70 Hedda Hopper, "Under Hedda's Hat," *Photoplay*, April 1964, p. 23.

71 "To Marry Soon!" *Movieland and TV Time*, October 1972, p. 34.

72 "Not this One!" *Movieland and TV Time*, October 1972, p. 38.

73 "Susan's in Love!" *Movieland and TV Time*, October 1972, p. 33.

74 "Barbra Streisand's Love Hang-Ups," *Modern Screen*, February 1974, pp. 38–39, 84.

75 "Dean and Cathy," *Modern Screen's Hollywood Yearbook*, 1974, p. 25.

76 Dick Strout, "Connie Stevens Talks about Men, Sex, Marriage," *Modern Screen*, January 1963, pp. 18–19, 54–58.

77 Brenda Marshall, "Two Boy Friends are Better than One!" *Movieland and TV Time*, December 1968, pp. 12, 50.

78 "Twelve Careers Where Today's Woman Takes a Back Seat to No One," advertisement, (International Correspondence Schools, 1973), *Movieland and TV Time*, May 1973, p. 11.

79 "Girls Get Your Man!" advertisement, (Larch, 1970), *Movieland and TV Time*, February 1970, p. 68.

80 K.V. Burroughs, "Two Marriages that Didn't Fail!" *Movieland and TV Time*, August 1972, p. 25.

81 "Natalie and Bob Wagner Remarry!" *Movieland and TV Time*, October, 1972, p. 30.

82 "Jackie Bisset: Modern Enough to Have a Live-In Lover," *Modern Screen*, February 1971, p. 38.

83 Sid Arthur, "Jackie Bisset's Double Trouble," *Modern Screen*, February 1974, pp. 33, 35–36, 88–89.

84 "Stefanie Powers: I Wanted to be a Mother before I Became a Bride," *Photoplay*, June 1964, p. 66.

85 Victoria Cole, "Victoria Cole's Hollywood Go-Round," *Movieland and TV Time*, October 1972, p. 56.

86 Victoria Cole, "Victoria Cole's Hollywood Go-Round," *Movieland and TV Time*, February 1970, p. 16.

87 "What's Up Lately!" *Movieland and TV Time*, February 1970, p. 33.

88 Victoria Cole, "Victoria Cole's Hollywood Go-Round," *Movieland and TV Time*, February 1970, pp. 16–17.

89 "What's Up Lately!" *Movieland and TV Time*, September 1972, p. 31.

90 "Did You Know?" *Movieland and TV Time*, August 1972, p. 32.

91 Karen G. Jackovich, "Barbara Hershey Drops her Hippie Past and a Name, Seagull, and Her Career Finds Wings," *People*, May 28, 1979, p. 119–120.

92 May Mann, "I am Barbara Seagull," *Movieland and TV Time*, September 1972, pp. 28–30.

93 "Patty Duke has Baby All Alone," *Modern Screen*, February 1971, p. 46.

94 "Marilyn Bares All!" *Modern Screen*, August 1962, p. 8.

95 Dr. W. Tenenoff Reich, "Now Liz Poses Nude!" *Photoplay*, April 1963, pp. 36–38.

96 "The Horst Buchholz Tragedy," *Photoplay*, December 1961, pp. 42–43.

97 "How Long Can Burton Hold Liz—and His Liquor, Too?" *Photoplay*, April 1964, pp. 52–54.

98 "Liz and Burton Break Up . . .," *Modern Screen*, October 1973, pp. 44–45.

99 "19-Year-Old Girl: Stop Saying Those Hateful Things about Richard & Me," *Photoplay*, July 1974, p. 17.

100 Amanda Murrah Matetsky, "An Open Marriage for Liz and Dick," *Photoplay*, December 1975, p. 19.

101 John Merrill, "The Inside Story of David Carradine's Arrest!" *Movieland and TV Time*, January 1975, pp. 46–47.

102 John J. Miller, "Jack Nicholson Tells What It's Like to Get Stoned on Pot, Cocaine and LSD," *Photoplay*, November 1975, p. 47.

103 "Jane Fonda Arrested for Assault and Drug Smuggling!" *Modern Screen*, February 1971, pp. 48–49.

104 May Mann, "May Mann's Hollywood," *Movieland and TV Time*, August 1972, p. 8.

105 Cited in William L. Lunch and Peter W. Sperlich, "American Public Opinion and the War in Vietnam," *Political Research Quarterly* 32 (1) (1979): 21–44.

106 "Valerie Perrine Confesses," *Photoplay*, January 1977, p. 41.

107 Anthony Slide (Ed.), *International Film, Radio, and Television Journals* (Westport, CT: Greenwood Press, 1985), p. 335.

108 Kirk Terry, "Kathy Lennon's Faith!" *Movieland and TV Time*, August 1972, pp. 6–7, 60, 62, 64.

109 "Why Connie is Praying for Liz!" *Movieland and TV Time*, December 1968, pp. 22–23.

110 Duane Valentry, "She Prays a Lot!" *Movieland and TV Time*, January 1975, pp. 4, 49.

111 Duane Valentry, "I Owe You, God!" *Movieland and TV Time*, September 1972, pp. 40–41.

112 Marilyn T. Ross, "The Most Conventional Unconventional Lady in Town," *Movieland and TV Time*, October 1970, pp. 26–27, 58.

113 "In the News," *Movieland and TV Time*, October 1972, p. 36.

8   Massive Wealth as Moral Reward

1 Anthony Slide, *Inside the Hollywood Fan Magazine: A History of Star Makers, Fabricators, and Gossip Mongers* (Jackson, MS: University of Mississippi Press, 2010), p. 221.

2 Speech delivered from the White House on July 15, 1979.

3 Speech delivered from New York City on November 13, 1979.

4 U.S. Census Bureau, "Table HS-11, Marital Status of the Population by Sex: 1900 to 2002," (Washington, DC: Government Printing Office, 2003), www.census.gov/population/www/socdemo/hh-fam.html [accessed September 8, 2010]. The percentages for men are slightly lower.

5 Calculation based on rate of $143.91 in 1972 ($751.15 in 2010 dollars) and $273.09 ($617.43 in 2010 dollars). See Bureau of Labor Statistics, "Table B-2, Average Hours and Earnings of Production and Nonsupervisory Employees on Private Nonfarm Payrolls by Major Industry Sector, 1964 to Date," (Washington, DC: Government Printing Office, 2010), http://ftp.bls.gov/pub/suppl/empsit.ceseeb2.txt [accessed September 8, 2010].

6 U.S. Census Bureau, "Table HS—25: Money Income of Families—Median Income in Current and Constant (2001) Dollars, by Race and Type of Family: 1947 to 2001," (Washington, DC: Government Printing Office, 2002), www.census.gov/prod/2002pubs/tp63rv.pdf [accessed September 8, 2010]. U.S. Census Bureau, "Table HS—22, Educational Attainment by Sex: 1910 to 2002," (Washington, DC: Government Printing Office, 2003), www.census.gov/population/socdemo/education/tabA-1.pdf [accessed September 8, 2010].

7 Bureau of Labor Statistics, "Civilian Labor Force Participation Rates by Sex, 1950 to 2005 and Projected 2010 to 2050," (Washington, DC: Government Printing Office, 2007), www.bls.gov/opub/ted/2007/jan/wk2/art03.txt [accessed September 8, 2010].

8 U.S. Census Bureau, Current Population Survey, "Table 4: Poverty Status of Families, by Type of Family, Presence of Related Children, Race, and Hispanic Origin: 1959 to 2008," (Washington, DC: Government Printing Office, 2009).

9 See data from Thomas Piketty and Emmanuel Saez, cited in David Cay Johnston, "Income Gap is Widening, Data Shows [sic]," New York Times, March 29, 2007, www.nytimes.com/2007/03/29/business/29tax.html?ex=1332820800&en=fb472e7246 6c34c8&ei=5088&partner=rssnyt&emc=rss [accessed September 8, 2010].

10 Internal Revenue Service, "Table A, U.S. Individual Income Tax: Personal Exemptions and Lowest and Highest Bracket Tax Rates, and Tax Base for Regular Tax, Tax Years 1913–2003," Statistics of Income Bulletin, 2004, http://findarticles.com/p/articles/mi_m2893/is_2_24/ai_n9508935/ [accessed September 8, 2010]. See also "Top U.S. Marginal Income Tax Rates," Truthandpolitics.org, www.truthandpolitics.org/top-rates.php [accessed September 8, 2010].

11 See Henry E. Scott, Shocking True Story: The Rise and Fall of Confidential, America's Most Scandalous Scandal Magazine (New York: Pantheon, 2010), p. 40.

12 Slide, p. 218.

13 Slide, p. 211.

14 Jeanette Walls, Dish: How Gossip Became the News and the News Became Just Another Show (New York: Perennial, 2000), p. 117.

15 Ibid., p. 130.

16 See Joshua Gamson, Claims to Fame: Celebrity in Contemporary America (Berkeley, CA: University of California Press, 1994), p. 43. Safire quote from Walls, p. 121.

17 Walls, p. 131.

18 Ibid., p. 129.

19 Sheilah Graham, "Seven Parties in a Single Day," People, March 4, 1974, p. 9. It's a fair assessment to say that the People piece did not go over well. Author Jeannette Walls writes that editors were shocked to see that Graham could barely write. "She was almost illiterate," the editor working with Graham told Walls. And Graham later sued People for what she claimed was a typo: a statement in the piece where Graham said she had been a call girl. Graham later claimed that the "I" should have been a "J," referring to the anonymous author of The Sensuous Woman (see Walls, pp. 122–124).

20 "The 'Beautiful People' at Play," People, March 18, 1974, p. 26.

21 "Just Henry and Nancy and the Diplomatic Pouch," People, April 15, 1974, p. 10.

22 "Henry's Big Night—without Nancy," People, July 8, 1974, p. 16.

23 "Rocky and Happy and Henry and Nancy," People, January 13, 1975, p. 8.

24 "World's Richest Man," *People*, March 18, 1974, pp. 24–29.

25 Christopher P. Andersen, "The Barron of Las Vegas Is a Buttoned-Down Hilton Cashing In on Gambling Rooms," *People*, September 8, 1975, p. 68.

26 Michael Ryan, "Too Darn Rich," *People*, December 7, 1987, p. 55.

27 Mary Anne Cravens, "The Murrays' Ball Is Never Over," *People*, August 5, 1974, p. 50.

28 "Peeking at Some Corporate Paychecks," *People*, April 15, 1974, p. 56.

29 "James Lee: Rich Winner in the Waiting Game," *People*, July 22, 1974, p. 22.

30 "Christina Onassis at 24," *People*, March 3, 1975, p. 66.

31 "A Bold, New Christina Onassis Takes Over Ari's Empire," *People*, June 23, 1975, p. 8.

32 "A Surprise Bridegroom Joins Hands and Fortunes with Christina Onassis," *People*, August 4, 1975, p. 6.

33 Michelle Green, Cathy Nolan, and Mirka Gondicas, "Born in Fortune's Uneasy Shadow," *People*, February 6, 1989, pp. 70–74.

34 "An Arab King Under the Eye of Allah," *People*, March 18, 1974, p. 14.

35 "The Duchess Dispatches an Uninvited Visitor for Tea," *People*, October 21, 1974, p. 12.

36 "Just the Royal Folks Next Door," *People*, March 18, 1974, p. 10.

37 R.T. Kahn, "Duchess of Windsor Always Puts on a Great Show," *People*, August 12, 1974, p. 6.

38 "Gstaad: Where Celebs Can Ski and See—Each Other," *People*, January 20, 1975, p. 14.

39 "Billie Blair: Hot Model 'On the Wild'," *People*, March 18, 1974, p. 56.

40 Ron Scott, "The Roller Life for Mike and Judi is Hell on Wheels," *People*, March 18, 1974, p. 56.

41 Jim Watters, "Valerie Perrine of Lenny, the Sex Goddess of the 70s," *People*, December 2, 1974, p. 22.

42 Barbara Wilkins, "Susan Blakely: At Last, A Model Who Can Act," *People*, February 17, 1975, p. 64.

43 Lee Wohlfert, "Ex-Groupie Cherry Vanilla Puts the Bad Old Days to Rhyme," *People*, March 3, 1975, p. 34.

44 John E. Frook, "By Making Stars Out of Cars, a Junkman Turned Movie Mogul Has Already Grossed $10 Million," *People*, September 22, 1975, p. 62.

45 James F. Jerome, "Wrestling Champ Sammartino, a Big Man at the Bank," *People*, July 1, 1974, p. 19.

46 John Stark, "Kids for Sale," *People*, November 12, 1984, pp. 116–118.

47 David Harrop, "A Fab Fortune," *People*, November 14, 1983, pp. 142–144.

48 David Harrop and Ned Geeslin, "Who Makes What $," *People*, March 25, 1985, pp. 96–98.

49 Jill Krementz, "Star Bucks," *People*, March 10, 1986, pp. 33–36.

50 "Here Comes '87," *People*, January 5, 1987, pp. 44–45.

51 Mary Vespa, "Arresting Face," *People*, August 19, 1974, p. 17.

52 "Barry, the Big Daddy of Love Unlimited, Is 'White On'," *People*, February 17, 1975, p. 24.

53 Robert Windeler, "The Silver Fox Strikes Gold," *People*, May 6, 1974, p. 38.

54 Kent Demaret, "Country Crooner, Actor and Now—Father," *People*, March 29, 1982, pp. 44–46.

55 Mark Goodman, "Elton Tones Up and Down," *People*, August 18, 1975, pp. 54–58.

56 Rudolph Chelminski, "Yves St. Laurent: 'I Sell Happiness, Not $1,500 Dresses'," *People*, September 9, 1974, p. 40.

57 Shirley Clurman, "King of Clothes," *People*, January 18, 1982, pp. 98–99.

58 Ron Scott, "Mrs. Malone's Only Son Moses Becomes an Instant Millionaire," *People*, September 16, 1974, p. 62.

59 "Harness Racing's Herve Filion IS the World's Winningest Athlete," *People*, November 25, 1974, p. 58.

60 Jane Rieker, "The Fullback Branches Out," *People*, July 22, 1974, pp. 4–5.

61 Ron Scott, "Johnny Miller," *People*, April 1, 1974, p. 38.

62 Ron Scott, "Johnny Miller Has to Work to Spend $700,000," *People*, November 4, 1974, p. 58.

63 Bill Bruns, "The Shark Gets Soft," *People*, July 8, 1974, p. 48.

64 U.S. Census Bureau, Current Population Survey, "Table CH-1: Living Arrangements of Children Under 18 Years Old: 1960 to Present," (Washington, DC: Government Printing Office, 2009), www.census.gov/population/www/socdemo/hh-fam.html [accessed September 8, 2010]. U.S. Department of Health and Human Services, "Table TANF 1, Trends in AFDC/TANF Caseloads, 1962–2001," *Indicators of Welfare Dependence: Annual Report to Congress, 2003*, (Washington, DC, Government Printing Office, 2003), www.aspe.hhs.gov/HSP/indicators03/apa.htm#ttanf1 [accessed September 8, 2010].

65 Julie Greenwalt, "The Deloreans: Swinger Tycoon Gets Domesticated Model," *People*, July 29, 1974, p. 50.

66 "Honeymooners Errol Wetson and Margaux Hemingway Have a Vintage Season," People, September 29, 1975, p. 24.

67 Richard Warren Lewis, "Jack Ryan and Zsa Zsa: A Millionaire Inventor and His Hungarian Barbie Doll," *People*, July 14, 1975, p. 60.

68 Steve Dougherty, Mary Vespa, Lee Wohlfert-Wihlborg, "A Dreamboat Wedding," *People*, April 8, 1985, pp. 54–56.

69 Bina Bernard, "Chris and Jim: Love On and Off the Court," *People*, April 1, 1974, p. 53.

70 Jill Krementz, "Dollars Can't Buy You Love, but They Sure Spiff up a Relationship," *People*, March 10, 1986, p. 36.

71 See Table 1, Institute for Women's Policy Research, "The Gender Wage Gap: 2009," (Washington, DC: IWPR, 2010), www.iwpr.org/pdf/C350.pdf [accessed September 8, 2010].

72 Richard Frey and D'Vera Cohn, "New Economics of Marriage: The Rise of Wives," (Washington, DC: Pew Research Center, 2010), http://pewresearch.org/pubs/1466/economics-marriage-rise-of-wives [accessed September 8, 2010].

73 Barbara Wilkins, "Old Young Dr. Kildare Becomes Hollywood's Prime Period Piece," *People*, January 13, 1975, p. 60.

74 Brad Darrach, "Smilin' Jack Lemmon," *People*, June 17, 1974, p. 36.

75 "What Generation Gap? These Grads Feel Great About Their Famous Parents," *People*, June 3, 1974, p. 4.

76 China Altman, "Lucie Arnaz, Doing It Her Way," *People*, May 20, 1974, p. 60.

77 Richard K. Rein, "She's Lee Grant's Daughter, but Dinah Manoff Figures She Ought to Be in Pictures Too," *People*, April 26, 1982, p. 113.

78 David Sheff, "Pam Tillis Kicks Up Her Heels to a Real Punk Beat That Daddy Mel Finds, Um, a Little Fowl," *People*, November 14, 1983, p. 99.

79 Jim Watters, "Unsinkable Debbie Reynolds: At 42 She Salvages Her Career," *People*, November 25, 1974, p. 54.

80 "The Quiet Beatle Revs Up for a Crash Comeback," *People*, November 25, 1974, p. 26.

81 "Exiled and Unemployed, King Constantine Has a Royal Fortune Tied Up in Greece," *People*, January 5, 1975, p. 12.

82 "A Baron Dies Tragically Defending the Family Chateau," *People*, February 3, 1975, p. 10.

83 "A Dead Nanny, a Wounded Wife—and Lord Lucan Vanishes," *People*, July 14, 1975, p. 6.

84 "Dancing Was Allowed on Vesco's Fugitive Jet," *People*, June 3, 1974, p. 10.

85 "Bernie Cornfeld, Living Well Is His Revenge," *People*, June 10, 1974, p. 8.

86 William McWherter, "Tales From an Arabian Nightmare," *People*, May 2, 1983, p. 95.

87 Joyce Wadler et al., "For the Love of Money," *People*, May 2, 1988, pp. 91–92.

88 Michael Ryan, "The Death of Her Family," *People*, June 17, 1985, pp. 106–107.

89 Michael Ryan, "DeLorean's Days of Reckoning," *People*, April 16, 1984, pp. 96–101.

90 Judy Kessler, "The King's Legend," *People*, September 5, 1977, pp. 26–29.

91 Judy Kessler and Laura Nelson, "One Year Later," *People*, August 21, 1978, pp. 20–25.

92 Slide, pp. 219, 225.

9 Success Just for Being You

1 U.S. Census Bureau, Current Population Survey 2008, "Table 674: Money Income of Households—Percent Distribution by Income Level, Race, and Hispanic Origin, in Constant (2007) Dollars," (Washington, DC: Government Printing Office, 2008), www.census.gov/compendia/statab/2010/tables/10s0674.xls [accessed September 8, 2010].

2 Bureau of Labor Statistics, "Table B-2, Average Hours and Earnings of Production and Nonsupervisory Employees on Private Nonfarm Payrolls by Major Industry Sector, 1964 to date," (Washington, DC: Government Printing Office, 2010), http://ftp.bls.gov/pub/suppl/empsit.ceseeb2.txt [accessed September 8, 2010].

3 Steven Greenhouse and David Leonhardt, "Real Wages Fail to Match a Rise in Productivity," *New York Times*, August 28, 2006, www.nytimes.com/imagepages/2006/08/28/business/28wages_chart.html [accessed September 8, 2010].

4 Bureau of Labor Statistics, "Major Sector Productivity and Costs Index," (Washington, DC: U.S. Department of Labor, 1990–2009), http://data.bls.gov/PDQ/servlet/SurveyOutputServlet?data_tool=latest_numbers&series_id=PRS85006092 [accessed September 8, 2010]. User-generated data.

5 U.S. Census Bureau, "Table HS-22: Educational Attainment by Sex: 1910 to 2002," (Washington, DC: Government Printing Office, 2003), www.census.gov/population/socdemo/education/tabA-1.pdf [accessed September 8, 2010]. U.S. Census Bureau, Current Population Survey, 2009, "Table 2: Educational Attainment of the Population 25 Years and Over, by Selected Characteristics: 2009," (Washington, DC: Government Printing Office, 2010), www.census.gov/population/socdemo/education/cps2009/Table1-01.xls [accessed September 8, 2010].

6 Isaac Shapiro, Robert Greenstein, and Wendell Primus, "Pathbreaking CBO Study Shows Dramatic Increases in Income Disparities in 1980s and 1990s: An Analysis of the CBO Data," (Washington, DC: Center on Budget and Policy Priorities, 2001), www.cbpp.org/cms/index.cfm?fa=view&id=1926 [accessed September 8, 2010].

7 U.S. Census Bureau, "Table B-1: Poverty Status of People by Family Relationship, Race, and Hispanic Origin: 1959 to 2008," *Income, Poverty, and Health Insurance Coverage in the United States: 2008* (Washington, DC: Government Printing Office, 2009), p. 44, www.census.gov/prod/2009pubs/p60-236.pdf [accessed September 8, 2010]. U.S. Census Bureau, "Table 4: People and Families in Poverty by Selected Characteristics: 2008 and 2009," *Income, Poverty, and Health Insurance Coverage in the United States: 2009* (Washington, DC: 2010), www.census.gov/hhes/www/poverty/data/incpovhlth/2009/table4.pdf [accessed September 8, 2010].

8 Avi Feller and Chad Stone, "Top 1 Percent of Americans Reaped Two-Thirds of Income Gains in Last Economic Expansion," (Washington, DC: Center on Budget and Policy Priorities, 2009), www.cbpp.org/cms/index.cfm?fa=view&id=2908 [accessed September 8, 2010].

9 Avi Feller and Chuck Marr, "Tax Rate for Richest 400 Taxpayers Plummeted in Recent Decades, Even as Their Pre-Tax Incomes Skyrocketed," (Washington, DC: Center on Budget and Policy Priorities, 2010), www.cbpp.org/cms/index.cfm?fa=view&id=3090 [accessed September 8, 2010].

10 Robert D. Manning, *Credit Card Nation: The Consequences of America's Addiction to Credit* (New York: Basic Books, 2000), p. 11.

11 Ibid., p. 12.

12 Ibid., p. 130.

13 Data from National Income and Product Accounts of the United States (NIPA), found in Employee Benefit Research Institute, "Personal Savings," *EBRI Databook on Employee Benefits*, (Washington, DC: EBRI.org, 2010), www.ebri.org/pdf/publications/books/databook/DB.Chapter%2009.pdf [accessed September 8, 2010].

14 "U.S. Savings Rate Hits Lowest Level Since 1933," *Associated Press*, January 30, 2006, www.msnbc.msn.com/id/11098797/ [accessed September 8, 2010].

15 Manning, p. 128. See also American Bankruptcy Institute, "Total Number of Bankruptcy Filings 1980–2009, Selected States," (Alexandria: VA: ABI.org, 2010), www.abiworld.org/bkstats/historical.html [accessed September 8, 2010].

16 U.S. Census Bureau, Housing Vacancies and Ownership, "Table 14: Homeownership Rates for the US and Regions: 1965 to Present," (Washington, DC: Government Printing Office, 2009), www.census.gov/hhes/www/housing/hvs/historic/files/histtab14.xls [accessed September 8, 2010].

17 U.S. Census Bureau, "Median and Average Square Feet of Floor Area in New Single-Family Houses Completed by Location," (Washington, DC: Government Printing Office, 2010), www.census.gov/const/C25Ann/sftotalmedavgsqft.pdf [accessed September 8, 2010]. Median home size has fallen slightly since 2007.

18 "Self Storage Association: 81 Percent Growth in Number of U.S. Facilities Since 2000," *Business Wire*, August 31, 2007, www.allbusiness.com/construction/building-renovation/5268603-1.html [accessed September 8, 2010].

19 "The Jobless Rate for People Like You," *New York Times*, November 6, 2009, www.nytimes.com/interactive/2009/11/06/business/economy/unemployment-lines.html [accessed September 8, 2010].

20 Project for Excellence in Journalism, *State of the Newsmedia 2010* (Washington, DC: Pew Research Center, 2010), www.stateofthemedia.org/2010/press_page.php [accessed September 8, 2010].

21 Project for Excellence in Journalism, "Newspapers," *State of the Newsmedia 2010* (Washington, DC: Pew Research Center, 2010), www.stateofthemedia.org/2010/ newspapers_economics.php [accessed September 8, 2010].

22 See also John Nichols and Robert W. McChesney, "The Death and Life of Great American Newspapers," *The Nation*, April 6, 2009, www.thenation.com/article/ death-and-life-great-american-newspapers [accessed September 8, 2010].

23 Project for Excellence in Journalism, "Cable News Profitability by Channel," *State of the Newsmedia 2010* (Washington, DC: Pew Research Center, 2010), www.state ofthemedia.org/2010/chartland.php?id=1219&ct=line&dir=&sort=&c1=1&c2=1&c3= 1&c4=0&c5=0&c6=0&c7=0&c8=0&c9=0&c10=0&d3=0&dd3=1 [accessed September 8, 2010].

24 Matea Gold, "ABC News to Cut Half its Domestic Correspondents, Close Bricks-and-Mortar Bureaus," *Los Angeles Times*, February 26, 2010, http://latimesblogs. latimes.com/entertainmentnewsbuzz/2010/02/abc-news-to-cut-half-its-domestic-correspondents-shut-down-all-bureaus-except-washington.html [accessed September 8, 2010].

25 Project for Excellence in Journalism, "Magazines," *State of the Newsmedia 2010* (Washington, DC: Pew Research Center, 2010), www.stateofthemedia.org/2010/ magazines_economics.php [accessed September 8, 2010]. Includes *Time*, *Newsweek*, *U.S. News & World Report*, *The Atlantic*, *The New Yorker*, *The Economist*, and *The Week*.

26 Project for Excellence in Journalism, "Circulations for Magazines Over Time: 1988–2009," *State of the Newsmedia 2010* (Washington, DC: Pew Research Center, 2010), www.stateofthemedia.org/2010/chartland.php?chartland.php?chartland.php? chartland.php?chartland.php?chartland.php?chartland.php?msg=1&id=1196&ct=line &dir=&sort=&c1=1&c2=1&c3=1&c4=1&c5=1&c6=1&c7=1&c8=0&c9=0&c10=0&d 3=0&dd3=1 [accessed September 8, 2010].

27 "Washington Post Co. to Sell Newsweek," *Newsweek*, May 5, 2010, www.newsweek. com/2010/05/05/washington-post-co-to-sell-newsweek.html [accessed September 8, 2010].

28 *People*'s reported circulation in 2009 was 3.6 million, compared with 3.3 million for *Time*. For *People* data, see www.people.com/people/static/mediakit/pdfs/ demographics/circulation/abc_statement.pdf [accessed September 8, 2010]. For *Time* data see Project for Excellence in Journalism, "Magazines," www.stateofthemedia.org/ 2010/magazines_audience.php [accessed September 8, 2010].

29 *US Weekly*'s 2000 data from Ruth McFarland, Bacon's Information Company, cited in Jake Halpern, *Fame Junkies: The Hidden Truth Behind America's Favorite Addiction* (New York: Houghton Mifflin, 2007), p. 217. *US Weekly*'s 2009 circulation data from their website, www.srds.com/mediakits/us_weekly/circulation.html [accessed September 8, 2010].

30 *In Style*'s 2009 circulation was about 800,000, according to its website, www. instyle.com/instyle/static/advertising/mediakit/instyle/mmr.html [accessed September 8, 2010], while *The Economist*'s was 813,240 that year according to Project for Excellence in Journalism, "Magazines," www.stateofthemedia.org/2010/magazines_

audience.php [accessed September 8, 2010]. *Life & Style*'s 2009 circulation was about 450,000, according to its website, www.bauerpublishing.com/LNS/LNS_mk/LNS_mk.html [accessed September 8, 2010], while *The Atlantic*'s was 471,548 according to the Project for Excellence in Journalism, "Magazines," www.stateofthemedia.org/2010/magazines_audience.php [accessed September 8, 2010].

31 *Star*'s circulation was about 1.5 million in 2009 (based on its claim of 7.32 readers per copy and nearly eleven million readers), according to its website, www.american mediainc.com/mediakits/star/kit_readers.htm [accessed September 8, 2010]. *U.S. News & World Report*'s 2009 circulation was about 1.2 million according to The Project for Excellence in Journalism, "Magazines," www.stateofthemedia.org/2010/magazines_audience.php [accessed September 8, 2010].

32 David Kronke, "It's Time to Get Serious," *Los Angeles Times*, June 6, 2010, p. D23.

33 Writers Guild of America, West, "Reality and Game Show Writers," (Los Angeles: Writers Guild of America, West, 2010), www.wga.org/content/default.aspx?id=2630 [accessed September 8, 2010].

34 James Hibberd, "Nets Look to Cut Reality Costs," *The Hollywood Reporter*, May 28, 2008, www.hollywoodreporter.com/hr/content_display/television/news/e3ied2fbcd4 ab528373629e6a40262ed1ce [accessed September 8, 2010].

35 "Fresh Prince of Talk," *People*, April 2, 2001, p. 72.

36 Jessica Herndon, "Five Things to Know About Justin Bieber," *People.com*, January 8, 2010, www.people.com/people/article/0,,20335294,00.html [accessed September 8, 2010].

37 See, for example, Anna McCarthy, "Stanley Milgram, Allen Funt, and Me," in Susan Murray and Laurie Ouellette (Eds.), *Reality TV: Remaking Television Culture* (New York: New York University Press, 2004).

38 Sally Moore, "A Rare Reunion for TV's Own Family, the Louds," *People*, March 4, 1974, p. 58.

39 Craig Horowitz, "Reality Check," *People*, March 22, 1993, p. 61.

40 "The Bachelors," *People*, June 23, 2002, p. 64.

41 Jenna Goudreau, "Reality TV Stars Turned Entrepreneurs," *Forbes*, April 13, 2010, www.forbes.com/2010/04/13/reality-tv-celebrity-fame-forbes-woman-entrepreneurs-business.html [accessed September 8, 2010].

42 Michael A. Lipton, "Celebrity Tsunami!" *People*, September 11, 2000, p. 87.

43 Tom Gliatto, "Nice Going," *People*, May 21, 2001, p. 184.

44 Tom Gliatto, "Vee for Victory," *People*, June 3, 2002, p. 93.

45 "Millionaire Makeovers!" *People*, September 11, 2000, p. 47.

46 "Hunk or Skunk?" *People*, January 20, 2003, p. 64.

47 "Wine and Roses," *People*, March 17, 2003, p. 122.

48 "The Morning After," *People*, March 3, 2003, pp. 80–82.

49 Jason Lynch, "From Idol to Star?" *People*, April 28, 2003, pp. 71–72.

50 "Runway Success," *People*, July 21, 2003, p. 74.

51 Lacey Rose, "Reality Stars' Second Acts," *Forbes*, March 15, 2007, www.forbes.com/2007/03/15/reality-survivor-apprentice-tech-media-cx_lr_0314reality.html [accessed September 8, 2010].

52 Jessica Goldberg, "What Do Reality TV Stars Make, Anyway?" *CNN.com*, November 5, 2009, www.cnn.com/2009/LIVING/11/04/reality.stars.paycheck/index.html [accessed September 8, 2010].

53 "Ozzy's World," *People*, April 29, 2002, p. 58.

54 Tom Gliatto, "Daze of their Lives," *People*, December 9, 2002, pp. 66–71.

55 Chris Strauss and Kristin Harmel, "The Incredible Hulks," *People*, July 25, 2005, pp. 95–96.

56 Mike Fleeman, "Hulk Hogan's Son Sues Sheriff over Jailhouse Tapes," *People.com*, June 3, 2008, www.people.com/people/article/0,,20204193,00.html [accessed September 8, 2010].

57 "Hulk Hogan Considered Suicide When Wife Sought Divorce," *People.com*, October 27, 2009, www.people.com/people/article/0,,20315585,00.html [accessed September 8, 2010].

58 Stephen M. Silverman, "Simpson, Lachey Flirt with Reality TV," *People.com*, August 18, 2003, www.people.com/people/article/0,,626643,00.html [accessed September 8, 2010].

59 Carolyn Ramsay et al., "Born to Spend," *People*, March 20, 1995, pp. 100–104.

60 Shelley Levitt, "Success Becomes Her," *People*, August 30, 1993, pp. 64–68.

61 Karen S. Schneider, "Ready, Set, Go Buy Something," *People*, June 21, 1999, pp. 106–112.

62 Joanna Blonska, "How Posh?" *People*, July 19, 1999, p. 58.

63 Michelle Tauber et al., "Tom and Katie: The Real Story," *People*, December 7, 2009, pp. 76–81.

64 "Lindsay Lohan Parties Away Her Legal Woes," *People.com*, May 21, 2010, www.people.com/people/article/0,,20387226,00.html [accessed September 8, 2010].

65 Ken Lee, "Kiefer Sutherland Busted for DUI in Hollywood," *People.com*, September 25, 2007, www.people.com/people/article/0,,20058518,00.html [accessed September 8, 2010]. Ken Lee, "Kiefer Sutherland's 'Sorry'," *People.com*, October 9, 2007, www.people.com/people/article/0,,20151447,00.html [accessed September 8, 2010].

66 Associated Press, "Kiefer Sutherland Headbutt Assault Charge Dropped," *Huffington Post*, July 22, 2009, www.huffingtonpost.com/2009/07/22/kiefer-sutherland-headbut_0_n_242534.html [accessed September 8, 2010].

67 "Drunk Shirtless Kiefer Sutherland Kicked out of London Strip Club," April 6, 2010, *Huffington Post*, www.huffingtonpost.com/2010/04/16/drunk-shirtless-kiefer-su_n_540135.html [accessed September 8, 2010].

68 Susan Schindehette, "High Life," *People*, January 17, 1994, p. 56.

69 See Ralph K. Jones and John H. Lacey, "State of Knowledge of Alcohol-Impaired Driving: Research on Repeat DWI Offenders," (U.S. Department of Transportation, National Highway Traffic Safety Administration, February 2000), www.nhtsa. dot.gov/people/injury/research/pub/dwioffend.pdf [accessed September 8, 2010]. Also see NHTSA, "Traffic Safety Facts, 2005, Table 6," (U.S. Department of Transportation, National Highway Traffic Safety Administration, 2006), www-nrd.nhtsa. dot.gov/Pubs/810616.pdf [accessed September 8, 2010].

70 National Survey on Drug Use and Health, "Alcohol Use," *2008 National Survey on Drug Use and Health* (Rockville, MD: Substance Abuse and Mental Health Services Administration, 2009), www.oas.samhsa.gov/nsduh/2k8nsduh/2k8Results.cfm#3.1.2 [accessed September 8, 2010]. National Survey on Drug Use and Health, "Figure 3.7 Current, Binge, and Heavy Alcohol Use among Persons Aged 12 to 20, by Gender:

2008," *2008 National Survey on Drug Use and Health* (Rockville, MD: Substance Abuse and Mental Health Services Administration, 2009), www.oas.samhsa.gov/nsduh/2k8nsduh/2k8Results.cfm#Fig3-7 [accessed September 8, 2010].

71 National Survey on Drug Use and Health, "Figure 7.6 Substance Dependence or Abuse in the Past Year, by Age and Gender: 2008," *2008 National Survey on Drug Use and Health* (Rockville, MD: Substance Abuse and Mental Health Services Administration, 2009), www.oas.samhsa.gov/nsduh/2k8nsduh/2k8Results.cfm#Fig7-6 [accessed September 8, 2010].

72 Kathleen Deveny, "Girls Gone Bad," *Newsweek*, February 12, 2007, p. 40.

73 Pam Lambert, "After the Jack Pot," *People*, June 10, 2002, pp. 82–86.

74 "Nicolas Cage Losing His Treasures," *People*, December 7, 2009, pp. 162–163.

75 George Kalogerakis, "Red Alert!" *People*, February 24, 1997, pp. 100–104.

76 Catherine Arnst, "Study Links Medical Costs and Personal Bankruptcy," *Bloomberg Businessweek*, June 4, 2009, www.businessweek.com/bwdaily/dnflash/content/jun2009/db2009064_666715.htm [accessed September 8, 2010].

77 Kalogerakis, p. 108.

SELECTED BIBLIOGRAPHY

Austin, Thomas, and Barker, Martin. *Contemporary Hollywood Stardom.* New York: Oxford University Press, 2003.

Bogle, Donald. *Bright Boulevards, Bold Dreams: The Story of Black Hollywood.* New York: Ballantine Books, 2005.

Braudy, Leo. *The Frenzy of Renown: Fame and Its History.* New York: Vintage, 1986 [1997].

Cashmore, Ellis. *Celebrity/Culture.* London: Routledge, 2006.

Ceplar, Larry and Englund, Steven. *The Inquisition in Hollywood: Politics in the Film Community, 1930–1960.* Urbana and Chicago, IL: University of Illinois Press, 2003.

Cohen, Lizbeth. *A Consumer's Republic: The Politics of Mass Consumption in Postwar America.* New York: Vintage, 2003.

Cowen, Tyler. *What Price Fame?* Cambridge, MA: Harvard University Press, 2000.

Cross, Gary. *An All-Consuming Century: Why Commercialism Won in Modern America.* New York: Columbia University Press, 2002.

Cullen, Jim. *The American Dream: A Short History of an Idea that Shaped a Nation.* New York: Oxford University Press, 2003.

DeCordova, Richard. *Picture Personalities: The Emergence of the Star System in America.* Urbana and Chicago, IL: University of Illinois Press, 2001.

Dyer, Richard. *Heavenly Bodies: Film Stars and Society.* New York: Routledge, 2004.

"The Faustian Bargain," *The Economist,* September 6, 1997, pp. 21–23.

Fowles, Job. *Starstruck: Celebrity Performers and the American Public.* Washington, DC: Smithsonian Institute Press, 1992.

Gabler, Neal. *Life the Movie: How Entertainment Conquered Reality.* New York: Alfred A. Knopf, 1999.

Gamson, Joshua. *Claims to Fame: Celebrity in Contemporary America.* Berkeley, CA: University of California Press, 1994.

Giles, David. *Illusions of Immortality: A Psychology of Fame and Celebrity.* New York: St. Martin's Press, 2000.

Gorman, Lyn and McLean, David. *Media and Society in the Twentieth Century: A Historical Introduction.* Malden, MA: Blackwell Publishing, 2003.

Halpern, Jake. *Fame Junkies: The Hidden Truth Behind America's Favorite Addiction.* New York: Houghton Mifflin, 2007.

Hearn, Charles R. *The American Dream in the Great Depression.* Westport, CT: Greenwood Press, 1977.

Holmes, Su and Redmond, Sean, Eds. *Framing Celebrity: New Directions in Celebrity Culture*. New York: Routledge, 2006.

Lears, Jackson. *Fables of Abundance: A Cultural History of Advertising in America*. New York: Basic Books, 1994.

Lebergott, Stanley. *Pursuing Happiness: American Consumers in the Twentieth Century*. Princeton, NJ: Princeton University Press, 1993.

Manning, Robert D. *Credit Card Nation: The Consequences of America's Addiction to Credit*. New York: Basic Books, 2000.

Marchand, Roland. *Advertising the American Dream: Making Way for Modernity 1920–1940*. Berkeley, CA: University of California Press, 1985.

Marshall, P. David. *Celebrity and Power: Fame in Contemporary Culture*. Minneapolis, MN: University of Minnesota Press, 1997.

Marshall, P. David, Ed. *The Celebrity Culture Reader*. London: Routledge, 2006.

McNamee, Stephen J. and Miller, Jr., Robert K. *The Meritocracy Myth*, 2nd edn. Lanham, MD: Rowman & Littlefield, 2009.

Murray, Susan and Ouellette, Laurie, Eds. *Reality TV: Remaking Television Culture*. New York: New York University Press, 2004.

Nayar, Pramod K. *Seeing Stars: Spectacle, Society and Celebrity Culture*. London: Sage, 2009.

O'Conner, Jane Catherine. *The Cultural Significance of the Child Star*. New York: Routledge, 2007.

Olney, Martha. *Buy Now Pay Later: Advertising, Credit, and Consumer Durables in the 1920s*. Chapel Hill, NC: University of North Carolina Press, 1991.

Orth, Maureen. *The Importance of Being Famous: Behind the Scenes of the Celebrity–Industrial Complex*. New York: Henry Holt, 2004.

Pinsky, Drew and Young, S. Mark. *The Mirror Effect: How Celebrity Narcissism is Seducing America*. New York: Harper, 2009.

Rojek, Chris. *Celebrity*. London: Reaktion Books, 2001.

Ross, Steven J. *Working-Class Hollywood: Silent Film and the Shaping of Class in America*. Princeton, NJ: Princeton University Press, 1998.

Samuelson, Robert J. *The Good Life and its Discontents: The American Dream in the Age of Entitlement 1945–1995*. New York: Vintage Books 1995, 1997.

Schickel, Richard. *Intimate Strangers: The Culture of Celebrity in America*. Chicago, IL: Ivan R. Dee, [2000], c1985.

Scott, Henry E. *Shocking True Story: The Rise and Fall of* Confidential, *America's Most Scandalous Scandal Magazine*. New York: Pantheon, 2010.

Sklar, Robert. *Movie-Made America: A Cultural History of American Movies*. New York: Vintage, 1975.

Slide, Anthony, Ed. *International Film, Radio, and Television Journals*. Westport, CT: Greenwood Press, 1985.

——. *Inside the Hollywood Fan Magazine: A History of Star Makers, Fabricators, and Gossip Mongers*. Jackson, MS: University of Mississippi Press, 2010.

Sternheimer, Karen. "Hollywood Doesn't Threaten Family Values." *Contexts 8*, no. 4 (2008): 44–48.

Turner, Graeme. *Understanding Celebrity*. London: Sage, 2004.

——. *Ordinary People and the Media: The Demotic Turn*. London: Sage, 2010.

Walls, Jeanette. *Dish: How Gossip Became the News and the News Became Just Another Show*. New York: Perennial, 2000.

Warren, David P. "The Rumor Mill: How Fan Magazines Portrayed Hollywood 1911–1959," MA Thesis, University of Southern California, 1999.

INDEX